STONELEIGH ABBEY

The House, Its Owners, Its Lands

STONELEIGH ABBEY

The House, Its Owners, Its Lands

Edited by

ROBERT BEARMAN

STONELEIGH ABBEY LIMITED
in association with
THE SHAKESPEARE BIRTHPLACE TRUST

First published
in the United Kingdom in 2004 by

Stoneleigh Abbey Limited, Stoneleigh, Warwickshire
www.stoneleighabbey.org
in association with
The Shakespeare Birthplace Trust

ISBN: 0 90420 105 8

Design: MarketPro, Ross-on-Wye

Printed: Print Plus, Hereford

COVER IMAGE
West Wing, Stoneleigh Abbey
© MarketPro, 2003

CONTENTS

PREFACE

This volume presents in edited and (in some cases) expanded form the papers which were given at a three-day conference held, in the summer of 1999, at Stoneleigh Abbey. For many years this was the ancestral home of the Leigh family but it began life, as some of its surviving fabric still bears witness, as a mid twelfth-century Cistercian foundation. Following the Dissolution, it was acquired by Thomas Leigh and converted into a family residence, but incorporating much of the medieval fabric. A dramatic modification was made in the early eighteenth century with the construction of the massive west wing in an entirely different style. Nineteenth-century alterations were more modest, more apparent from within the house than without. This was also the period, however, when the landscape setting of the house underwent the greatest change.

The Leigh family, though elevated to the peerage in the early seventeenth century, produced no figures of national importance: only one, Chandos Lord Leigh, has managed to secure a modest foothold in the *Dictionary of National Biography*. Yet their story is not without interest, punctuated as it is with stories of marital discord, manic building and nineteenth-century philanthropy. It also has two contrasting periods. The first ends in 1806 on the failure of the line descended from Thomas's younger son, who, though elevated to the peerage, made little or no impression on national affairs. The estates than passed to the descendants of Thomas's eldest son, who had settled at Adlestrop in Gloucestershire. Their story, in this earlier period, is outside the scope of this study, but they were clearly a gifted and talented family (one was the mother of Jane Austen) and their accession to the family estates ushered in a golden period in the Leigh story.

The family papers, a huge collection housed for many years at the Shakespeare Birthplace Trust Records Office, and ranging in date from c. 1150 to almost the present day, have provided many historians with a rich resource, be it for the study of mediaeval monasticism, the architectural evolution of one of the grandest of Midlands country seats, or the lives of individual members of the family.

At the conference the papers were presented in a roughly chronological sequence but for publication it seemed more appropriate to adopt a thematic approach. The first four chapters therefore trace the evolution of the Abbey buildings from their origin to the end of the nineteenth century. One deals specifically with the architecture of the Gatehouse, whilst the others examine, firstly, the layout of the original monastic buildings and their post-Reformation conversion into a residence for the Leigh family, secondly the grand rebuilding of the west wing in the eighteenth century, and, thirdly, subsequent nineteenth-century alterations.

The next three chapters are studies where personalities dominate: the first is a general overview of the Leigh family, and the third a study of two of its best documented representatives, the poet, Chandos Lord Leigh, and his son, William Henry. Between these two is a full account of Jane Austen's connection with Stoneleigh and its influence on her writing.

The final three chapters deal with the management of the medieval monastic estates, the origins of the deer park at Stoneleigh, and the more recent transformation of the landscape adjacent to the Abbey attributable to Humfrey Repton and his successors.

We acknowledge with thanks a generous grant from the Marc Fitch Fund towards the cost of this publication and I must also express my gratitude to the contributors for their tolerance and good humour while this volume has been for rather too long in preparation; also to thank Shahab Seyfollahi for his support in seeing it through to publication, to Mairi Macdonald for compiling the index, and to Jeannette Kerr of MarketPro for her cheerful patience in the final stages.

Robert Bearman
Shakespeare Birthplace Trust

FOREWORD

by

ANTHONY BIRD O.B.E.

I am delighted that the Shakespeare Birthplace Trust agreed to take on the editorial work to produce this book, capturing in print the interesting papers presented at the weekend conference at Stoneleigh Abbey in September 1999. All of us at Stoneleigh Abbey Limited were particularly interested in the presentations of the distinguished contributors and it was fascinating to hear so much in such a short time about the history of this very important Warwickshire house and its estate.

The foresight and interest of our benefactors who provided the money to Stoneleigh Abbey to carry out its preservation have, I believe, been justified by the fact that we now have an impeccably preserved collection of buildings dating from 1154 through the centuries to the 1800's. Those benefactors were the Heritage Lottery Fund, English Heritage, the European Regional Development Fund and Warwick District Council who provided us with enabling development funds. We thank them all sincerely.

The programme of repair and restoration at the Abbey was a massive undertaking. During the course of the works, over 1,000 tonnes of newly quarried cream Grinshill stone was used in the repairs to the exterior of the Baroque West Wing alone. At the height of the works up to forty-five stonemasons were employed on site at any one time, often working seven days a week. All of the work identified as being required and more was achieved, all within budget. It was not an easy task and it presented some very difficult situations. However, with a dedicated and determined team, we achieved our objectives. Many contractors, subcontractors and small specialist companies were involved, each making a valuable contribution to the overall achievement – too many to list here. It was particularly pleasing to see so many young craftsmen and women amongst our highly skilled artisans. In addition to those repairs which were initially identified, we were also able to complete further works including the recreation of Repton's lake and removing 50,000 tonnes of spoil without the need for extra funding.

Stoneleigh Abbey is once again open for the public to enjoy. The Abbey is alive once more as it was centuries ago with people living in the residential areas and visitors viewing the impressive state rooms and strolling through the riverside gardens. The stables have been restored and the riding school is now an impressive banqueting hall, playing host to such events as weddings, conferences and craft fairs. Our work carries on: there are still many challenges to take on in the parkland to reinstate the walks and vistas plus much work on the river, the weirs, the bridges and garden structures and features.

The editing of this book has been expertly carried out by Robert Bearman, of the Shakespeare Birthplace Trust, and I must also thank the ten contributors for the considerable work involved in converting the papers they gave at the conference into publishable form.

Anthony Bird, O.B.E.
Chairman, Stoneleigh Abbey Limited

LIST OF CONTRIBUTORS

Dr Richard K. Morris is an architectural historian specialising in the mediaeval and Tudor periods. He has carried out research into the architectural fabric of other monastic sites, including the Cistercian abbeys at Tintern, Croxden and Hulton. He is an Associate Fellow of the University of Warwick, and was until recently a Reader in the History of Art Department there.

Dr Rochelle Ramey obtained a DPhil in Archaeology from the University of York, with a thesis focussing on monastic visitors' buildings. She is currently Senior Project Manager for the Historic Buildings Section of Field Archaeology Specialists, based in York.

Andor Gomme is Emeritus Professor of English Literature & Architectural History at Keele University. His recent publications include *Smith of Warwick* and the full score of a performing version of Bach's *St. Mark Passion*. He is currently struggling to finish, jointly with Alison Maguire, a book on the Compact House.

Dr Geoffrey Tyack, FSA, is Fellow of Kellogg College, Oxford, and Director of the Stanford University Centre in Oxford. His publications include *Warwickshire Country Houses* (1994) and the *Blue Guide to the Country Houses of England* (1994). He is currently revising the country house entries for the Berkshire volume of Nikolaus Pevsner's *Buildings of England* series.

Mairi Macdonald, well-known as a lecturer on family and local history topics, is Deputy Head of Archives and Local Studies at the Shakespeare Birthplace Trust and has played a leading part in the cataloguing of the Leigh papers deposited there.

Gaye King has published several articles based on her extensive research into the relationship between the Austen family and the Leighs of Adlestrop, including her discovery of documentary evidence in the Leigh family archives to confirm Jane Austen's visit to Stoneleigh.

Norma Hampson has worked extensively on the Leigh family archives, particularly those for the nineteenth century. This includes an MA dissertation on William Henry Leigh, and she has also published several articles in local history journals.

Dr Andrew Watkins, now Head of History at Coleshill School, has published extensively on the society and economy of Forest of Arden in the fifteenth century, based on his wide-ranging research for a doctoral thesis.

George Demidowicz is Conservation Officer for Coventry City Council. As well as having a research interest in buildings history, he has written extensively on urban and rural historic landscapes, and industrial archaeology. He is keen to fuse the disciplines of archaeology and history.

Hazel Fryer is a landscape historian and consultant with a particular interest in Humphry Repton.

PART ONE

BUILDINGS

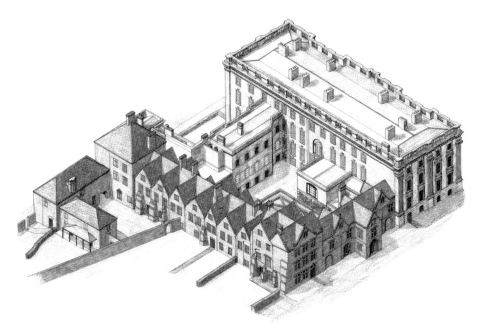

FIGURE 1
Stoneleigh Abbey: isometric perspective from the north-east
(late 1990s, © Frank Knight International)

CHAPTER ONE

From Monastery to Country House:

AN ARCHITECTURAL HISTORY OF
STONELEIGH ABBEY, 1156–*c.* 1660

Richard K. Morris

Stoneleigh Abbey is best known as an eighteenth-century country house, but its classical west wing conceals important evidence for its monastic origins and its conversion to a residence at the Reformation (Fig. 1). Only the detached gatehouse to the north of the house explicitly reminds the modern visitor of the medieval past. For Stoneleigh belongs to that fascinating group of country houses created from monastic properties, of which Longleat and Woburn are more famous examples.[1] However, Stoneleigh preserves much more extensive remains in its standing fabric to demonstrate the process, and this has been complemented by recent archaeological fieldwork. The architecture of the Cistercian abbey at Stoneleigh has never received the attention it deserves and therefore the first purpose of this chapter is to assess the evidence for its church and claustral buildings, and to set them in the context of Cistercian building as a whole.[2] The second aim is to teaze out from the fabric and surviving documents such slender clues as exist to reconstruct the main forms of the pre-eighteenth-century house of the Leigh family at Stoneleigh.

The community of Cistercian monks moved to the royal manor of Stoneleigh in 1155, settling initially on a site at Cryfield[3] but transferring almost immediately to the present location. The few documentary dates relevant to its architecture are well known and mainly derived from the Abbey's 'Leger Book' and William Dugdale's writings.[4] The first stone of the church was laid in 1156: there was a major fire in 1241 and work on the refectory in 1258-61; substantial refitting was carried out in the time of Abbot Hockele, 1308-49; and the monastery was dissolved in 1536. Medieval building fabric survives *in situ* for parts of the church, the east range of claustral buildings and the gatehouse to the north-west.[5] For understanding the layout of the monastery within the present courtyard house, we may begin with Guy Silk's isometric view, produced in the 1950s, identifying surviving features and reconstructing others (Fig. 2). He was guided by

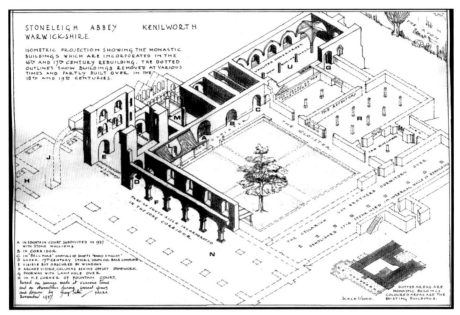

FIGURE 2

Stoneleigh Abbey: isometric projection from the north-west, showing monastic buildings incorporated in the later house (drawing, Guy Silk, 1957, in SBTRO).

The letters relate to references in the text. Silk's letters A to G have been retained.

the relative uniformity of Cistercian monastic plans,[6] but in fact no firm evidence exists for the actual form of the south and west ranges at Stoneleigh.

All the evidence in the east and north ranges points to the construction of a church and claustral buildings in the second half of the twelfth century. Thus the monks of Stoneleigh were potentially in competition with other significant contemporary works in the locality, such as the Benedictine cathedral priory at Coventry (where work resumed on the nave at this time), the Augustinian priory at Kenilworth (the patron of nearby Stoneleigh parish church) and the Cistercian abbey of Combe to the north (founded in 1150). One can only guess at King Henry II's motives in supporting the Cistercian foundation at Stoneleigh, but clearly the high status of building works in the Coventry area after the 'anarchy' of Stephen's reign helps explain the quality of the stonework at the abbey.

The church appears to have been of Cistercian Bernardine plan,[7] with two chapels on each transept and a chancel projecting further east (Fig. 2J). The only survival of the eastern parts above ground is the shell of the south transept, now disguised as three floors of accommodation at the north-east corner of the present house (Fig. 3, left). Medieval fabric rises in places as high as the present second floor, as witnessed by the twelfth-century buttresses at the southern angles of the transept (Figs 4,12) and the ghost of the former eastern crossing arch on the otherwise plain area of masonry at the east end of the north elevation. One can still perceive the outline of a prominent cone-shaped corbel supporting the southern springing of the arch (Fig. 5A).[8] In addition, field archaeology has recently detected the footings of the north-east crossing pier (Appendix, 1.1). We know from fourteenth-century documentary evidence (cited below) that these arches supported a crossing tower, a characteristic developing in most English Cistercian churches during the second half of the twelfth century.[9]

In the east wall some voussoir stones from the entrance arches to the two former eastern chapels of the south transept are visible on the exterior (Fig. 7A), and internally have also been noted behind panelling in the first-floor room during the recent archaeological watching brief.[10] No evidence is known to corroborate Guy Silk's reconstruction of the chapels as stepped in plan (Fig. 2H). Indeed, they are as likely to have been all of equal size, on the model of the excavated east end at Cistercian Bordesley Abbey, Worcestershire, with which Stoneleigh had a special relationship in its early years.[11] Four superb late Romanesque capitals, which may well have come from the entrance arches of the two south transept chapels, have been re used in the nineteenth-century neo-Norman porch in the south-east corner of the former transept (Figs 6.1, 6.2).[12] The capitals are carved from both pink and grey sandstone, implying more than one local quarry source for the building work, and are notable for the relatively rich repertoire of ornament employed in a Cistercian context. The models for carved detail in this first phase lie apparently as much in the general Romanesque style of southern England, such as the trefoil capital (Fig. 6.1) known to have been used at Cluniac Reading Abbey and Benedictine St Albans.[13]

FIGURE 3
Stoneleigh Abbey: north-east corner block and north range, north elevation (© R.K. Morris, 2001)

FIGURE 4
Stoneleigh Abbey: north-east corner block,
south face, weathering for former roof
(© R.K. Morris, 1999)

FIGURE 5
Stoneleigh Abbey: north-east corner block, north side,
scar of former east crossing arch (© R.K. Morris, 2001)

No firm evidence survives in the fabric for attempting a reconstruction of the upper parts of the transept, because the exterior masonry is so disturbed by later patching and rebuilding, presumably in the second half of the sixteenth century. Judging from comparable Cistercian churches, where the main forms of the transept east elevation survive from the twelfth century (for example, Kirkstall, Roche and Dundrennan),[14] the clerestory windows at Stoneleigh would have been at about the level of the second-floor windows of the house; an area which appears to have been substantially refaced and rebuilt after the Dissolution (Fig. 7E). One survival of the medieval design is the slight projection of the wall-face above ground-floor level, where originally it overhung the chapel vaults. This is now supported on several lengths of medieval stringcourse of various designs, probably re-used (Fig. 7B). In this projecting wall area, there would almost certainly have been a central pilaster buttress (running approximately just to the left of the central drainpipe) and intermittent stone corbels for the apex of the chapel roof (above the level of the top of the cross-mullioned window, Fig. 7D). Both features have been removed without leaving obvious traces, which is also the case for any vault scars around the chapel arches below. The vertical breaks visible in the first floor masonry to the left and right of the main window (Fig. 7C) might suggest the former existence of a middle stage (triforium), and may be the reason why Silk reconstructed the transept with a three-storey elevation internally (Fig. 2K). However, the bottoms of these features are too high up to be triforium openings, and the irregularities of their edges are more likely to be the result of patching and the introduction of new features than the survival of medieval ones.[15] Three-storey elevations were a novelty in English Cistercian churches in the 1170s,[16] and on balance a simple two-storey design like that at Buildwas Abbey is more likely at Stoneleigh (Fig. 8).[17]

Turning to the nave of the church, much of the south wall and arcade of its south aisle survive in the walls of the nineteenth-century long gallery (Fig. 2F, Plan 1A). The shafted jambs of the entrance arch from the south transept into the aisle still exist at the east end of the gallery (now part of the hall to East Wing House No.1), and retain *in situ* good examples of simple and embellished multi-scallop capitals typical of the third quarter of the twelfth century (Figs 6.3, 6.4). More multi-scallop capitals with embellishment appear in the former monks' processional door into the south aisle, an outstanding survival *in situ* in the north-east corner of the courtyard (Fig. 9). The outer order of the arch is carved with elegant directional chevrons and the two inner orders with keel mouldings typical of Cistercian-style architecture in northern England.[18] The arch is another instance in the twelfth-century work of employing both grey and pink sandstone, here almost in an alternating pattern, though probably covered by limewash and not intended to be seen. In the elaboration of its abstract carving, this door contrasts with plainer Cistercian processional doors which survive, as at Furness, and has overtones of more ostentatious examples in the houses of less austere reformed orders, such as the approximately contemporary processional door at Augustinian Lilleshall, Shropshire.[19] The overall effect of the

FIGURE 6.1, 6.2
Stoneleigh Abbey: medieval capitals reused in the east porch
(© R.K. Morris, 1978)

FIGURE 6.3, 6.4
Stoneleigh Abbey: medieval capitals, arch from the former south transept to the nave aisle
(© H. Sunley, 1998)

FIGURE 7
Stoneleigh Abbey: north-east corner block, east elevation (© R.K. Morris, 2001).
The letters relate to references in the text.

Stoneleigh door and of the ornate carved capitals assigned to the eastern chapels contrasts with the relative plainness of the capitals at the opening into the south transept, and presumably reflects the different liturgical significance of their respective locations.

Remains of the nave south arcade are visible in the exterior of the north wall of the gallery which, together with the recent discovery of the foundations of a cross-wall in the area of the church's west end, permit us to reconstruct some aspects of the nave. In the wall both to the east and west of the nineteenth-century porch one can see parts of the arcade arches, encased in later blocking masonry; not to be confused with the classical arches below (Figs 3, 10, 11). The size of the voussoir stones indicates that they must constitute the outer orders of the arches, rather than internal hoodmoulds cut back, even though the omission of the latter is unusual.[20] The voussoirs east of the porch belong to the first and second bays of the nave, and they extend sufficiently in the second bay to show that the arcades in the eastern part of the nave were round-arched, or virtually so (Fig. 11A). The pier from which they spring, the first pier from the east ('pier 1'), is no longer visible, but its position is sufficiently accurately pinpointed to calculate the east/west span of the first bay at just over 5 metres, centre to centre (Fig. 34, A-P1). The distance between pier 1 and the next visible pier location is about 14.5 metres, which must indicate that there were three bays in-between, albeit of slightly reduced size (Fig. 34, P1-P4). On this basis we can be certain that the voussoirs west of the porch represent the fourth and fifth bays of the nave, and spring from pier 4 (Fig. 10C).

Silk reconstructed a nave of eight bays, a common type for the Cistercians (Fig. 2N). However, if the recently excavated footings represent the terminal west wall of the church (Appendix, 1.3), then there would not be enough space to fit in four more bays of the same size beyond pier 4. A total of seven bays seems much more likely, though the calculations do not fit as neatly one would like (Fig. 34, P4-B, C). The nave was probably constructed in two phases, with two different bay sizes. The evidence is supplied by the voussoir stones in the fourth bay, which are longer than those of the first and second bays, and which delineate an arch which is slightly higher and more pointed than that in the second bay (cf. Figs 10A,11A respectively). Also, the springing of the arcades above pier 4 is handled more neatly, with the voussoirs of both arches directly adjacent to each other, whereas above pier 1 they are separated by a fillet of masonry. This separation may be observed in more exaggerated form in the nave arcades at Buildwas, but clearly the piers at Stoneleigh were not as bulky (Fig. 8). These differences prove that a change in construction occurred between bay 2 and bay 4, and it is assumed here that this happened in bay 3; with bays 1 and 2 each about 5 metres in span, and bays 3 to 7 each about 4.75 metres, which satisfies the measurements taken on site (Fig. 34).[21] Thus it would appear that priority was given to completing the monks' church, which probably included the first two bays of the nave, and that the remaining arcades in the lay brothers' part belong to a subsequent campaign.

FIGURE 8
Buildwas Abbey, Shropshire: ruins of church interior, looking east
(© R.K. Morris, 1980s)

FIGURE 9
Stoneleigh Abbey: north range,
south side, former processional
door to nave south aisle
(© R.K. Morris, 1999)

FIGURE 10
Stoneleigh Abbey: north range, north wall, west of porch (© R.K. Morris, 1978).
The letters relate to references in the text.

FIGURE 11
Stoneleigh Abbey: north range,
north wall, east of porch, detail
(© R.K. Morris, 2001).
The letters relate to references
in the text.

The remains of two blocked windows visible in south wall of the gallery are very unlikely to represent undisturbed twelfth-century aisle windows (Fig. 29A). One would normally expect such windows to be aligned with the centres of each bay, but here the easternmost one is located almost opposite pier 1, and the western one is off-centre in bay 3 (Fig. 34, D and E). Also the windows extend too low to accommodate a lean-to roof for the north cloister walk, in comparison with the apex of the processional door in bay 1 (Fig. 12).[22] So their position, and probably their fabric too, belongs with the post-Dissolution house.

Overall, if one wishes to envisage how the church looked on completion in the later twelfth century, the approximately contemporary church which survives at Buildwas provides numerous general points of comparison (c.1150-90, Fig. 8), though Stoneleigh was probably rather less ponderous in form, especially with regard to its piers. Like Buildwas, probably relatively few architectural changes were made to the church in the later middle ages, but Stoneleigh was not quite so much a backwater. The only information available to us is the account, in the Leger Book, of the modernisation works during the abbacy of Robert of Hockele (1308-49), which included a new east window in the chancel.[23] The updating of older churches, through the replacement of lancets with large fashionable bar-tracery windows, was occurring all over the area at this time, as testified, for example, by archaeological evidence at Kenilworth Priory and Coventry Cathedral Priory. We must assume the same process at Stoneleigh and, though the precise style of its window cannot be known,[24] the general effect can be imagined by comparison with the ruins at Lilleshall Priory, where a twelfth-century chancel received a new window, c.1330 (Fig. 13). The account of Hockele's works is also valuable in implying that Stoneleigh had a crossing tower, for he is credited with commissioning a new vault (ceiling) or perhaps a rood screen beneath the bell-tower.[25]

The east range of monastic buildings survives in remarkably complete form at ground floor level, despite later domestic partition (Fig. 2). The main rooms are the chapter house and the long southern undercroft, between which are various spaces punctuated by an interesting series of twelfth-century doors (Fig. 2A-C). The functions of such spaces are never easy to identify without additional evidence, and almost any combination of the usual Cistercian room names could fit here.[26] A possible designation is that the room between the church and chapter house was the sacristy, for it has no obvious link to the cloister (Plan 1G): the room to the south of the chapter house was an inner parlour (Plan 1J):[27] the narrow room immediately to the south was intended for the day stairs to the dormitory (Plan 1K); and the adjacent passage to the south was the slype (Plan 1L).[28] The narrow room is located where the day stairs descending from the dormitory were frequently found in Cistercian plans, as may still be seen at Byland Abbey, Yorkshire.[29] However, in its present form it is completely tunnel-vaulted and leads nowhere, suggesting that it was made redundant (perhaps adapted to a parlour) when the stair was moved to a different position. There are parallels for this happening at several major Cistercian sites,

FIGURE 12
Stoneleigh Abbey: courtyard, north and east sides (© R.K. Morris, 2001).
The letters relate to references in the text.

FIGURE 13
Lilleshall Priory, Shropshire: ruins of chancel, from south-east (© R.K. Morris, 1980s)

FIGURE 14
Stoneleigh Abbey: east
range, west side, former
chapter house door
(© H. Sunley, 1998)

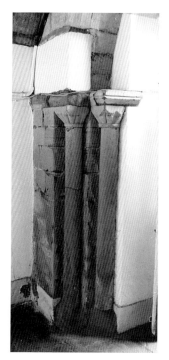

FIGURE 15
Stoneleigh Abbey: east range, former door to
parlour, detail (© H. Sunley, 1998)

FIGURE 16
Stoneleigh Abbey: east range, former slype west
door (© R.K. Morris, 2002)

such as Kirkstall and Rievaulx, when the south range was remodelled with the refectory set perpendicular to the cloister, thus creating space for the day stairs within the south range adjoining the warming room. This is how Silk reconstructed the claustral plan for Stoneleigh (Fig. 2R), and such remodellings were generally characteristic of Cistercian monasteries planned before c.1170.[30] When this change occurred at Stoneleigh may only be surmised, as the medieval south range has disappeared without trace. Various circumstances in the thirteenth century could be associated: the fire of 1241, the documented work on the refectory in 1258-61, and the probable remodelling of the east range occasioned by rebuilding the chapter house (see further below). However, it could equally well have occurred in the course of construction during the later twelfth century, for one of the slype doorways implies that work was continuing at this date in the area directly adjoining the south range.

The slype has a round-arched door of two plain orders at its east end, perhaps leading to the infirmary or the monks' graveyard (Fig. 18B), and is entered by a similar but more elaborate door from the cloister site (Figs 2C, 16). The outer order of the latter is carried on detached sandstone shafts with moulded bases and capitals carved with broadleaf foliage (Figs 17.3, 17.4). The way the leaves curl at the tips is reminiscent of the influence of French Gothic crocket capitals in English works of c.1180-90,[31] and may denote a second phase of work in the monastic buildings; though it is a trait of this period that a wide range of capital types may co-exist in one work, such as the west bays of Worcester Cathedral nave, c.1175-85.[32] Certainly these capitals are different to any others surviving in the twelfth-century fabric, such as the multi-scallop capitals of the parlour entrance (Fig. 15), which generally resemble those of the south transept opening to the nave aisle (Figs 6.3, 6.4). The finest display is reserved for the chapter house entrance, with ten capitals supporting an arch of five orders (Fig.14). Surprisingly, its jamb shafts are coursed masonry like those of the processional door to the church, and in contrast to the more refined detached shafts of the parlour and slype doors. The capitals on the north jamb are all carved with waterleaf foliage so characteristic of Cistercian work in northern England, c.1150-90 (Fig. 17.2),[33] whilst the capitals of the south jamb are a more individual design of scallop capital with a sprig of foliage at each angle (Fig. 17.1). A similar mixing of capital designs in this period may be observed in the west doors of the Cistercian church at Byland.

Amongst the claustral buildings, the former chapter house holds the greatest interest for architectural historians because of the unusualness in this Cistercian context of its tall central columnar pier (Fig.19). In fact, three main issues need to be addressed with regard to the medieval form of the Stoneleigh chapter house – its height, its length and its system of vaulting. Did it rise to the full height of the east range? Did it extend eastwards beyond the width of the range? Has the central pier been inserted later? The answers to all three questions are probably affirmative.

FIGURE 17.1, 17.2
Stoneleigh Abbey: capitals of former
chapter house door
(© 15.1, R.K. Morris 2001;
15.2, H. Sunley, 1998)

FIGURE 17.3, 17.4
Stoneleigh Abbey: capitals of former
slype west door
(© R.K. Morris, 2001)

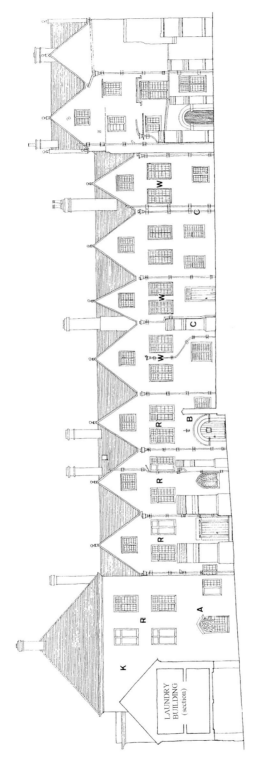

FIGURE 18

Stoneleigh Abbey: east range, east elevation (© R. Melville & Partners, 1993).
The letters relate to references in the text.

FIGURE 19
Stoneleigh Abbey: east range, former chapter house, interior looking south-west (© R.K. Morris, 2000)

A standard Cistercian chapter house consisted of three rib-vaulted aisles of equal height, separated by two rows of short piers, as illustrated in the famous fifteenth-century manuscript illumination of St Bernard preaching and as may still be seen in numerous surviving examples such as Fontenay in France and Buildwas.[34] The vaults were always contained within the ground floor of the range, so that the monks' dormitory could pass above on the first floor and link directly to the transept, where night stairs would descend into the church. However, at Stoneleigh the single pier rises to the full height of the ground floor, so that if it carried any vaulting it would have interrupted the first-floor accommodation. Consequently the dormitory would have been located entirely to the south of the chapter house. That this occurred is implied by the long southern extent of the east range (Fig. 2U), and by the fact that the thick walls of the chapter house still appear to rise through two floors of the present house (cf. Plans 1H and 2H).[35] The one general parallel for this arrangement in Cistercian monasteries is Abbot Aelred's rebuilding of the east range in the 1150s at Rievaulx, Yorkshire, with a full-height chapter house of a design unique in Cistercian architecture.[36]

Cistercian chapter houses frequently extended beyond the eastern line of the east range and this was probably the case at Stoneleigh. Looking at the east elevation of the house, at the two bays which now fill the chapter house space, on the left side is a buttress, largely modern, and on the right are vertical scars indicating a former projection (Figs 18C, 26). These features almost certainly mark the former eastern continuations of the side walls, truncated probably at the Dissolution, and the space in between walled-up as we see it now. It is not known how far the chapter room continued to the east, though recent field archaeology has located the foundations of a wall about 13 metres east (Appendix, 2.1). It is just possible that this represents its east wall, but if so the Stoneleigh chapter house was unusually long by Cistercian standards, comparable with exceptional examples such as those at Fountains and Kirkstall Abbeys.[37] So the extent of the chapter room remains a matter of conjecture.

If the extant pier at Stoneleigh is original and the chapter room was longer, then there would have been two or more piers (as in Fig. 2M) and parallels could be drawn with chapter houses with a row of central piers running east-west, as occasionally adopted by the Cistercians.[38] However, these are invariably vaulted at ground-floor level where they run under the dormitory and thus have shorter piers, in contrast to the arrangement at Stoneleigh. It would be exciting for Cistercian scholarship to argue that Stoneleigh represents an unusual and experimental design allied to the development in the early thirteenth century of Cistercian chapter houses with a single tall pier, as at Dore Abbey, Herefordshire, and Margam Abbey, Glamorgan; but these are polygonal structures built east of the east range.[39] Another possibility is that the Stoneleigh pier carried a flat wooden ceiling, as now, but unvaulted chapter houses are without precedent in the Cistercian order. Moreover, the recent removal of the modern floor directly around the pier revealed that it has no moulded base, as one would have expected. Instead, it sat directly on a slab roughly square in plan.[40] This strongly suggests that the pier is not *in situ* and opens the door to other avenues of interpretation.

The most logical solution is that Stoneleigh had a full-height rectangular chapter house vaulted in stone in a single span, not unlike Benedictine examples such as that surviving at Gloucester Cathedral. Such single-span stone vaults as are known in Cistercian examples tend to be of thirteenth-century date, as at Cleeve Abbey, Somerset, and at Kirkstall.[41] There would be no difficulty in vaulting the Stoneleigh room in one span which, at rather less than 9 metres across, is similar to Kirkstall and less than Gloucester. However, it is open to question whether this was the disposition of the first chapter house or whether it resulted from a change of plan; and, if the latter, whether the change occurred during construction in the twelfth century or in the thirteenth century.

In favour of a change of plan is the survival of part of a diagonal weathering high up on the south wall of the transept, at a point where a continuous north-to-south gabled roof over the east range at first-floor level would have adjoined the transept (Fig. 4A).[42] The north-south roof is virtually certain to have been that of the dormitory, in which case it seems that originally the dormitory came right up to the transept (or was intended to do so) with the chapter house as a ground-floor room only. In favour of the change of plan happening in the twelfth century, probably during construction, is the fact that the main entrance of this period in a late Romanesque style has been retained (Fig. 14). Had the chapter house experienced a grand rebuilding in a Gothic style in the next century, it is likely that this important door would have been updated as well. Conversely, in favour of placing the change in the thirteenth century is the record of a major fire in the monastery in 1241 and evidence for remodelling in the east range at about this date, in the undercroft (see below). Also, the parallels for surviving single-span stone vaults in Cistercian chapter houses are from the thirteenth century, as cited above – with one major exception, Aelred's mid-twelfth-century chapter house at Rievaulx, albeit a quite singular building with its martyrium associations connected with the community's veneration of their founding abbot, William.[43] Although the high vault at Rievaulx is thought to have been a wooden barrel vault,[44] precedents of the same date outside the Cistercian order prove the existence of single-span stone-vaulted chapter houses in this period, as at Gloucester and Durham.

Overall the weight of available evidence implies that Stoneleigh was planned with an east range of a conventional mid-twelfth-century Cistercian type, with a ground-floor chapter house. Subsequently, probably during construction in the second half of the twelfth century, the chapter house was redesigned into a full height structure and the dormitory moved to the south of it. To erect such a chapter house in a Cistercian monastery, whether in the twelfth or thirteenth century, appears to represent a bold, symbolic act on the part of the monastery – perhaps a riposte to a rival monastic institution in the region – which warrants further research.[45] We assume that the chapter house survived in this form down to the Dissolution, at which time its vault was demolished when the roofs and parts of the top floor of the east range were removed (see further below). The fact that the vaulting apparently did not survive the Dissolution provides some corroboration for reconstructing it as a high vault of single span, and thus more vulnerable to demolition in such circumstances. Indeed, with regard to vulnerability, the possibility that it was a wooden vault, like that reconstructed for Rievaulx, should not be discounted. When the shell of the east range was made habitable again with new joists and floors in the 1560s, the present pier was introduced because spanning this space with beams rather than a stone vault required an intermediate support. The pier is a medieval one, presumably re-used from a feature elsewhere in the ruins, quite possibly from the nave arcades where work in about the same period was converting the south arcade into the north gallery.[46]

This completes our survey of the twelfth-century church and monastic buildings. All the original details remaining confirm that a church and monastery in stone was under construction very shortly after the monks moved to Stoneleigh, in the 1160s and 1170s. Slightly later phases of work may be represented in the west bays of the nave and perhaps at the south end of the east range. Before turning to consider later medieval additions, it is worth adding that the gatehouse also incorporates twelfth-century stonework in the entrance facade and gate passage at least to the top of its ground floor, and possibly higher.[47] The two orders of the entrance arch are carved with angle rolls (Fig. 20) whilst the arch at the exit of the passage has three plain stepped orders (Fig. 35). Angle rolls have numerous precedents in Cistercian arch profiles of the second half of the twelfth century,[48] and at Stoneleigh there seems no reason to doubt that the plain stepped arch and the heavy buttresses flanking both front and rear facades date from the same period. Curiously this phase of work appears not to have been noticed in any previous publications,[49] and its identification provides a rare example of an early Cistercian gatehouse.[50] It survives because of its incorporation into the documented fourteenth-century work of Abbot Hockele, who clearly did not rebuild the gatehouse from scratch.

With the gatehouse, the most complete survival of monastic architecture at Stoneleigh is the vaulted undercroft at the southern end of the east range (Fig. 2U, Plan 1U). The splendid impression of its visual unity is entirely due to a reconstruction which introduced the present rib-vaulting, springing from conical corbels on the walls and a central row of four octagonal piers (Fig. 22). This undocumented work is usually ascribed to the early fourteenth century,[51] but it is more likely to date to the second quarter of the thirteenth century on the basis of its stylistic details. Two of the four piers are carried on bases with the typical water-holding profile of Early English Gothic, which was slipping out of fashion after the mid-thirteenth century.[52] Moreover, the conical corbels, half-octagonal in plan, and the overall polygonal aesthetic of the ribs and piers, are paralleled in Cistercian undercrofts of this period, for example in the east ranges at Furness, Lancashire (c.1220), and Croxden, Staffordshire (c.1250). The northernmost pier is larger than the others and lacks any detail capable of providing a date, but it may be surmised that it is a later replacement for structural reasons, probably of fourteenth-century date (Fig. 22, foreground).

FIGURE 20
Stoneleigh Abbey: gatehouse, north entrance
(© R.K. Morris, 1999)

FIGURE 21
Stoneleigh Abbey: east range, east side,
Gothic window (© R.K. Morris, 1978)

FIGURE 22
Stoneleigh Abbey: east range, south undercroft, interior from north (© R.K. Morris, 2001)

However, parts of the outer shell of the undercroft belong to the original stone monastic buildings. The undercroft was entered from the slype by a simple round-headed door (Plan 1P), and a small blocked Romanesque window survives *in situ* in the third bay of the west wall, indicating that the twelfth-century range came at least this far south. Rebuilding in the thirteenth century might have been precipitated by a structural collapse: the range descends towards the river valley at this point, and the enormous buttresses still visible on its east and south walls are testimony to a concern about subsidence (Fig. 18). It could be linked to the fire of 1241 – the right date for the style of the rebuilding – which may well have been particularly serious in the claustral ranges nearest the monastic kitchen. It may also be relevant that major work on the refectory is documented in the abbacy of Peter Wyche (1258-61),[53] possibly the result of subsidence. We have argued above that the refectory had probably been built in the twelfth century perpendicular to the cloister, following mature Cistercian planning, so it would have run south towards the river, parallel with the east range undercroft.

The undercroft is often called the monks' day room, but, in common with similar spaces in many medieval monasteries, its precise function is uncertain. Excavations on the site of the day room at Rievaulx Abbey found rosary beads, plates, coins, buttons, pens and a writing tablet, which Peter Fergusson interprets as showing a multi-purpose character of usage over the 400 years of its existence.[54] At Stoneleigh, the only utilitarian feature remaining is a fourteenth-century ogee-headed recess for a lamp, in the fourth bay of the west wall, above a Gothic door which led west out of the undercroft, now blocked (Fig. 2G). The two-light Gothic traceried window now in the fourth bay of the east wall is quite incongruous for a medieval monastic undercroft, and must have been inserted here after the Dissolution to provide more light for a change of function to cellars or services (Figs 18A, 21). Clearly it is a genuine medieval window, though somewhat restored, and has been re-used from a more important part of the monastery, possibly the east chapels of the church. It is in the Decorated style, dateable by its details to *c.*1290-1320, which could place it amongst the works by Abbot Hockele but more probably those in the abbacy of his predecessor, John de la Sale (1292-1308).[55] Its significance lies in the fact that it is the only medieval traceried window to survive intact, apart from those in the gatehouse.[56]

Several discoveries in the recent programme of field archaeology shed additional light on other features of the conventual buildings. To the south of the east range, nearer the river, the footings of a large diagonal wall were uncovered close to the south-east corner of the conservatory (Appendix, 2.4). It could have been part of the latrine block linked to the dormitory or part of a main drain from the south end of the monastery. An L-shaped building on a diagonal alignment in approximately this position appears in the 1597 and 1749 estate maps (Figs 23A-B, 120), perhaps a post-Dissolution structure built on medieval foundations.[57] A second discovery has been a short length of substantial wall foundations inside the north end of the eighteenth-century west range (Appendix, 2.3). This is most likely to relate to the former north wall of the monastic west range, and further scrutiny of its evidence may aid our understanding of why, according to the plans, the present west range is not exactly parallel with the medieval fabric of the east range, nor perpendicular to the north range (Plan 1, Fig. 34).[58] Cistercian monasteries are noted for the precision of their claustral layout, so possibly this anomaly has been created by the eighteenth-century rebuilding: but why change the alignment? This issue can only be noted in passing and requires further research.

Thirdly, in the courtyard of the house, footings were traced running parallel with the east range between the chapter house door and the processional door to the church (Appendix, 2.2). These are the foundations for the outer wall of the cloister walk to the cloister garth, and their thickness (0.8 metres) suggests that they carried a modest stone structure, presumably a series of open arches or window tracery, but that the cloister was unlikely to have been stone vaulted. The find also permits us to establish the width of the east cloister walk at about 3.3 metres. Any clear traces of the roof creasing against the walls appears to have been tidied away after the Dissolution, but the survival of the processional door indicates the minimum height of the cloister (Fig. 12). An area of badly worn inlaid tiles discovered *in situ* at the south-east corner of the cloister may provide a dating clue to new work being undertaken on the cloister, possibly in the first half of the fourteenth century (Appendix 2.2).

✌ ✌ ✌

The courtyard forms the most tangible link today between the monastery, with the inward-looking cloister at its heart, and the present house with its outward-looking ranges grouped around this former monastic space. It is to the sixteenth- and seventeenth-century predecessors of this house that we must now turn our attention. There is no consensus in the existing literature about the chronology of its development in the hundred years or so following the dissolution of the monastery in 1536. All physical evidence for the south and west ranges in this period appears to have been swept away,[59] and the style of such relevant features that survive in the east and north ranges is generally not capable of being dated closely. Furthermore, there is no relevant documentary evidence relating to the Leigh family's occupation of the site, following its joint purchase by Sir Thomas Leigh in 1561, until two inventories of 1626 and 1639; and the information they provide is not unambiguous with regard to the architecture.

Opinions have therefore varied as to whether most of the conversion work still extant in the east and north ranges should be attributed to the tenure of the first Sir Thomas (1561-71); or to his widow, Alice, still resident until 1603, perhaps in conjunction with her son, the second Sir Thomas; or to the latter alone, between 1603 and his death in 1626, perhaps continued after 1626 by his grandson, the third Sir Thomas.[60] The answer, of course, is probably a composite of these dates, as one remodelling improved on a previous one. Several authorities favour the second Sir Thomas as builder, and, where dates are proffered, they tend to be towards *c.*1600

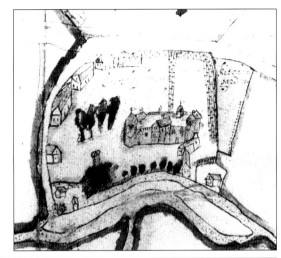

FIGURE 23A
Stoneleigh Abbey:
Goodwine estate map, 1597,
detail showing the house
(SBTRO, DR 671/3)

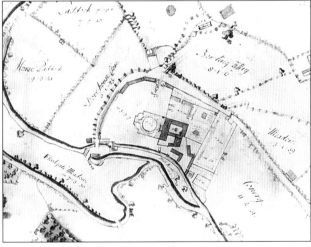

FIGURE 23B
Stoneleigh Abbey:
Thomas Wilkes estate map,
1749,
detail showing the house
(SBTRO, DR 671/24)

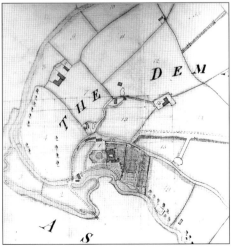

FIGURE 23C
Stoneleigh Abbey:
Matthias Baker estate map,
1776,
detail showing the house
(SBTRO, DR 671/30a)

or after 1603.[61] However, it has always seemed strange to this author that a house so close to Kenilworth Castle, the subject of Lord Leicester's major works to accommodate Queen Elizabeth's famous visits between 1565 and 1575, should not have been considered by most historians to have been rebuilt during the same years. Significant new evidence which appears to corroborate this earlier dating has come from the recent scientific testing of roof timbers in the east range, cut from trees most likely to have been felled in the years 1568-70.[62] It would therefore seem that new work on the east range was commenced by the first Sir Thomas, and was probably well advanced by the time of his death in 1571.[63]

Before assessing this hypothesis in more detail, the state of the monastic site between the depradations of Henry VIII's commissioners and 1561 should be considered. The first recorded resident after the Dissolution is a farmer, Thomas Dadley, who was leasing the abbey in the later 1540s and 1550s.[64] From his time survives a description of the site, the architectural parts of which are worth giving in full below, for their interpretation has proved controversial.[65] Additionally, an inventory of Dadley's goods made in 1558 would seem to apply to the same property.[66] The description reads:

> Md there is standynge wthyn the Scyte of the seyde late monastary wheryn the
> ffermer Thomas Dadley nowe dwelleth a fayre longe howse buylded of a longe
> range of Stone and Timbre and Covered wth tyles and theryn havinge dyvers
> romes benith and over the same a fayre haule, a fayre longe chambre and one
> other fayre chambre adioyninge to the Sowthende of the seid chambre a
> buttree underneth in a manner of a seller, a great hawle hole Roofed a howse
> called the Cloyster chamber, a fayre kytchinge wth a Chymney, all wch doo yett
> remeyne builded of Stoone substantially and much glased wth dyvers other
> stoone walls yet remeyning of howese wasted
> Item a fayre Gate howse well buylded of Stoone and covered wth Tyles
> conteyninge in it iij Over Romes and ij nether Romes wth iij Chymneys

From this, we learn of three main surviving elements – a habitable 'fayre house' consisting of a 'long range of stone and timber', a gatehouse, and various 'other stone walls' of the monastery in ruin.

Different authors have construed this document to mean either that Dadley's 'fayre house' was the former east range of the claustral buildings, or that Dadley actually lived in the gatehouse.[67] However, various reasons point instead to the former west range of the monastery as being the most likely location of Dadley's residence, whilst the church, the east range and probably parts of the south range lay in ruin. First, the east range was almost certainly roof-less, because we now have the dendrochronological dates of c.1568-70 for some of the trusses.[68] These must relate to the rehabilitation of the east range for domestic use. We can also be certain that the church was unserviceable, having been at least unroofed and generally despoiled, but that it had not been demolished because enough remained after 1561 to be cannibalized into the new house.

Secondly, the evidence at Stoneleigh strongly suggests that by the late medieval period the abbot had his lodgings in the west range, and that this would be the obvious pre-existing 'house' for Dadley to occupy. Examples of such lodgings and their retention as the core of post-Dissolution residences may still be seen at Lacock Abbey, Wiltshire, and Newstead Abbey, Nottinghamshire, both Augustinian houses.[69] Such lodgings already possessed their own hall, the focus of the household, making this the most obvious model for conversion for a new proprietor of relatively modest means, rather than the adaptation of the church or refectory into a hall, as was carried out for major courtiers at the Hampshire abbeys of Netley and Titchfield.[70] The practice of living in the west range may have been more common for the heads of houses in some of the other monastic orders, such as the Augustinian canons, but precedents exist in Cistercian houses, as at Hailes, Gloucestershire, and probably Rufford, Nottinghamshire.[71] At Stoneleigh, such an arrangement would also have placed the abbot in closer proximity to the guesthouse accommodation in the outer court.[72]

Thirdly, if Dadley's house occupied the west range, the former monastic kitchen would have been at its southern end, as is implied in the document quoted above.[73] This was the usual position for the kitchen in Cistercian houses, to the west of the refectory in the south range and thus adjacent to the west range (as reconstructed in Fig. 2). This would further suggest that the 'greate hawle hole Roofed' was the monks' refectory still standing, presumably set perpendicular to the south range as in mature Cistercian plans (see Fig. 2R).[74] It would have been a ground-floor hall[75] in contrast to the 'fayre haule' in the west range, and it would seem that it did not survive in this form beyond the 1550s, if we may judge from the documents. The inventory of the goods of Thomas Dadley, taken in 1558, lists only one hall, and the same is true of the Leigh inventories of 1626 and 1639.[76] Overall, Dadley's house probably resembled the conversion at Hailes Abbey, where the post-Dissolution L-shaped house encompassed the west range and the immediately adjacent parts of the south range.[77]

Thus the likely basis for the planning of the Leighs' first house becomes clearer. In brief, it was entered through the west range, containing the hall and some apartments, linked by a first-floor gallery in the north range to further apartments and accommodation in the east range. The south range was the least important, probably given over to servants and services, and parts of its medieval fabric modified substantially. In practice, it is assumed here that the main accommodation was arranged essentially on a 'U-plan', with the good apartments split between the east and west ranges. Also it would seem, from the jumble of architectural features left in the former cloister, that the house was primarily outward-looking, in the vein of newly-fashionable Elizabethan great houses like Longleat.[78]

To appreciate the detail of the house which preceded the major eighteenth-century rebuilding by Francis Smith (hereafter the pre-Smith house), we may reconstruct a tour of it, starting at the west range and moving clockwise around the other three ranges. It is contended here that the main entrance was at the west, that this arrangement was retained in the eighteenth-century rebuilding and only finally moved to the north side in the early nineteenth century. Illustrations of the house and its setting in the surviving estate maps of 1597 (Fig. 23A, the most schematic), 1749 (Figs. 23B, 120) and 1766 (Fig. 23C, the most precise) are generally helpful to this hypothesis, though not decisive.[79] Both the eighteenth-century plans show gardens to the east, to the north-east and apparently to the north as well, with a kitchen garden further to the east; and the essentials of this topography are present in the 1597 map (Fig. 23A). The two eighteenth-century maps also indicate that entry to the immediate environs of the house was by way of the medieval gatehouse and strongly suggest that the route continued into the walled ornamental forecourt in front of the west facade.[80] Both also show the eighteenth-century stairs entering the west range and, though the 1749 map depicts pairs of prominent gateposts in several places on the north side (Fig. 120), they do not seem to make sense in signifying a major north entrance to the house.[81]

The depiction of the house on the 1597 map has no such details (Fig. 23A), but, given the overall continuity of topography in all three maps, the existence of a west entrance to the house in the sixteenth century seems likely. Thus, the Elizabethan visitor would almost certainly have ascended steps into the former abbot's hall on the first floor, raised over undercrofts, as may still be experienced at Lacock Abbey. To the right (south) on entry would have been the services and kitchen, and to the left, beyond the high end of the hall, several apartments. These would be 'The Great Chamber', 'The Withdrawing Chamber' and 'The Best Compast Window Chamber', included in the inventory of Sir Thomas Leigh II, taken in 1626.[82] The 1639 inventory of furniture, taken in his son's time, describes this withdrawing chamber as 'next unto the Gallery',[83] which apparently places it at or near the north-east corner of the west range, close to the entrance into the gallery in the first floor of the north range. Therefore the best chamber was most probably sited alongside the withdrawing chamber, in the north-west corner, with a prominent bay or oriel window – the 'compast window' – perhaps facing west. The best chamber, which also incorporated an inner chamber, was almost certainly the bedroom of the best suite, judging from its list of furnishings. The state bed chamber continued to be sited at the north end of the principal floor in the new eighteenth-century west wing, though then linked directly to the gallery (Plan 2, 'Library').[84]

A useful clue to the width of the west range of the post-Dissolution house is contained in the estimate of 1714 by Francis Smith of Warwick to build the new west front.[85] The statement there, that 'The Garden Front to be returned about 14 Foot', clearly implies that this was to be a new front added to the existing west range.[86] A return of fourteen feet on the north side of the present building reaches the mid-point of the north-west corner room, the Card Room (Fig. 34 C).[87] Confirmation that this marks the approximate western extent of the medieval west range is provided by the discovery of the foundations of the west wall of the church more or less on the same north/south axis during the recent archaeological fieldwork (Appendix, 1.3). When the old west range was entirely demolished in 1720, its materials appear to have been reused as infilling in the cores of the new walls, for all the lower interior wall surfaces are finished in brick.[88]

The main room in the north range was the first-floor gallery, functioning as the primary link between the good accommodation in the west and east ranges, and also perhaps as a long gallery.[89] It is the only gallery of which we have knowledge at Stoneleigh, and is assumed to be 'The Gallery' listed in both the 1626 and 1639 inventories.[90] It ran almost the complete length of the former church south aisle, fitted into its upper part by walling in the arcades to the nave and dividing it longitudinally into two floors. There may have been a room at its western end, a survival of a late medieval arrangement whereby one end of the abbot's lodging in the west range continued into the south-west corner of the nave, somewhat analogous to the situation at Newstead Abbey.[91] This could be a reason why parts of the church escaped demolition at the Dissolution, in the same way that the church's west facade at Newstead was spared. The facts that the gallery utilizes the south aisle rather than the site of the north cloister walk, and that the west facade of the church is apparently aligned with the west range (as explained above) lead one to this conclusion. The most obvious way to link the west range effectively to the gallery would be adapting the medieval arrangement of an overlapping room.[92]

On the ground floor of the north range the main feature was a loggia, containing a grotto. Humphry Repton commented on the grotto in his Red Book (1809) as one of the pre-existing features of the house,[93] but its date is uncertain. It might have belonged to the Carolean period when grottoes first became fashionable in this country, like the best surviving example at Woburn Abbey, attributed to Isaac de Caus, c.1620-40.[94] Evidence for the loggia remains in the four classical round-headed arches on the ground floor, the style of which suggests a date not later than the middle of the seventeenth century (Figs 10B, 11B).[95] It is not easy to explain why the easternmost arch is further away from the others (Fig. 3), unless it led into a separate ground-floor space. Originally some of the arches would have been open to the garden beyond, facing north, following Italian custom and like the loggia containing the grotto at Woburn. A housing cut into the westernmost arch shows that at one stage it was filled with a wooden fitting, perhaps an openwork screen. The arches have since been blocked, perhaps when C.S. Smith remodelled the north range in 1836, but possibly earlier:[96] at Woburn, the grotto was considered too cold by the later eighteenth century and doors were fitted.

Presumably the loggia and grotto were originally entered through a fifth, central arch underneath the external stairs, removed in 1836, which led up to the gallery (Fig. 25). The purpose of these stairs was apparently not as a main entrance, but to link the interior of the house with the north gardens shown in the 1597 and eighteenth-century estate maps. Stairways with double flights of steps were appearing in courtly circles in Carolean England, especially in conjunction with garden settings,[97] but on stylistic grounds the Stoneleigh example appears to be no earlier than the second half of the seventeenth century. Thus, it was added in front of an existing loggia, and it may be significant that it is not until the Baker map of 1766 that a projection in approximately this position is shown on a plan of the house (Fig. 23C).[98]

The replacement of the north range on a grander scale was already intended in the eighteenth century, as is obvious from the unfinished stonework on the north-east return of Francis Smith's west wing. There one can see toothing intended to link to new work and an east-facing door (blocked) at the level of the gallery roof (Fig. 24A).[99] However, it was not until 1836 that these earlier arrangements were finally swept away, in a much more modest scheme carried out by C.S. Smith. In a major re-orientation of the house, the north range replaced the west range as the main entrance, overturning three hundred years of tradition. The gallery floor was removed and the interior of the north range remodelled to create the tall ground-floor corridor we see today, accessed from a new north porch stylistically in keeping with the older architecture (Fig. 3).

Moving now to the east range, more accommodation and fabric from the post-Dissolution house exists here than anywhere else, albeit in a labyrinth of rooms resulting from frequent modifications, including the latest adaptation of the range into four houses (Plans 1, 2, 3).[100] Mrs. Austen recounted the same difficulty in 1806:[101]

> ... as to the offices, which were the Abbey. Mr. Leigh almost despairs of ever finding his way about them. I have proposed setting up direction posts at the angles ...

The basis of the arrangement is on two floors, with attic rooms above, and with a tower block of three floors plus an attic at the north-east corner, fitted into the south transept of the former church (Figs 1, 27).

In the sixteenth and seventeenth centuries the family and guests would have entered the corner tower block on the first floor from the north gallery, arriving in a lobby[102] adjoining the main stair (Plan 2B). The north elevation of this block is the one smart architectural set-piece surviving from the pre-Smith house, with three tiers of three windows each, terminating in a low gable treated somewhat like a pediment with classical mouldings (Fig. 27). The adaptation of the transept to an apartment block is the most distinctive feature of the house conversion, and, if the fundamentals of this design go back to about 1570, then it is an early manifestation of

FIGURE 24
Stoneleigh Abbey: west range, north-east return to north range (© R.K. Morris, 1990s)

FIGURE 25
Stoneleigh Abbey: north range, north side before 1836 (Thomas Baker, watercolour *c*.1820)

FIGURE 26
Stoneleigh Abbey: east wing, east elevation, general view (© Frank Knight International)

the fashionable tendency towards the 'high house' in the region.[103] Locally the outstanding example is Leicester's contemporary New Building at Kenilworth Castle, to provide the private apartments for Queen Elizabeth's visits.

The size and closeness of the windows in the north elevation, commanding a prospect of the north garden, must signify the location of some of the best accommodation. Three self-contained suites are indicated, and the large window on the first floor on the east side of the corner block implies that the first-floor suite was the best of these (Fig. 7). Looking further along the exterior of the east range, the groupings of paired windows on the first floor must signify several more good chambers (Figs 18, 26). Even in the Elizabethan period there may have been views onto an east garden, and the eighteenth-century estate maps seem to indicate a mount garden here, circled by trees (Figs 23B–C).[104] How the main chambers and rooms of entertainment listed in the inventories fit into this architectural framework is far from clear. The interpretation of inventory evidence, for rooms other than the most obvious, poses problems even where houses of this period have come down to us in a much more complete state, as at Elizabethan Wollaton Hall and Hardwick New Hall.[105]

Both the inventories of 1626 and 1639 list a 'Hayre-coloured' chamber,[106] a red chamber, a great wainscot chamber and a summer chamber in the same sequence after the best chamber (mentioned above). They were each provided with inner chambers, and it would seem that the blue chamber which appears in 1639 after the 'hayre-coloured' chamber had been converted from the inner chamber of the latter. In addition, between the red chamber and the great wainscot chamber, both inventories list the withdrawing chamber to the three chambers[107] and the gallery. The mention of the gallery at this point suggests that these various chambers are located in its general vicinity. There is no satisfactory way of interpreting this information to reconstruct an entirely logical route through the house by those making the inventory.[108] The interpretation suggested here is that all these chambers were in the east range, with the 'hayre', blue, red and withdrawing chambers in the north-east corner block and the great wainscot and summer chambers beyond on the first floor of the east range.[109] If we restrict our analysis to the fabric that actually survives, then one additional piece of information in both inventories favours this interpretation. After the withdrawing chamber to the three chambers and before entering the gallery, the prisors record the minimal contents 'In the Space and going up the Stairs'.[110] It is reasonable to assume that this refers to the main staircase sited (as now) in the north-east corner block, and that all the good apartments listed after the best chamber might therefore have been in this area of the east range.

The layout of the partition walls in the corner block suggests a suite of three rooms – a withdrawing chamber, a main chamber and an inner chamber. This arrangement is now best represented on the second floor (Plan 3C).[111] Some of the later house plans of the Elizabethan architect, Robert Smythson, include guest suites with this tripartite grouping of rooms; for

FIGURE 27
Stoneleigh Abbey: north-east corner block, north elevation
(© R.K. Morris, 2001)

example, on the top floors of his 'hour-glass' plan and his 'square house with small internal courtyard' (withdrawing chamber, bed chamber, and closet or inner chamber).[112] Such luxury guest suites were to become increasingly popular during the seventeenth century.[113] It would be tidy to be able to link some of the groups of chambers in the inventories to this layout, but only the best chamber is explicitly given its own withdrawing chamber and inner chamber, and this suite was surely located in the west range.[114]

So the details of the documentary and fabric evidence for the good accommodation are frustratingly difficult to reconcile, though the general disposition is clear. During the later sixteenth and seventeenth centuries, important suites of chambers occupied the better parts of the east range, namely the corner block and the first-floor rooms in the northern and central areas of the range. On the other hand, it is likely that chambers for household members dominated the southern part of the range and probably some of the ground-floor accommodation. After the main rooms of entertainment, both inventories continue with a considerable list of chambers like the steward's chamber and chambers assigned to named persons, especially females (for example, Lady Dudley's Chamber in 1626 and Mrs Congleton's in 1639), which could well have been located here. Well down this list in 1626 and 1639 is 'The Mount Chamber', which may have looked on to a mount in the east garden, a feature apparently depicted in the 1749 and 1766 estate maps (Figs 23B–C). If so, this reference would provide valuable evidence that such a feature existed in the garden by 1626 and may also suggest that all the chambers listed immediately preceding the mount chamber were in the east range as well.

Later, the east range became associated primarily with the offices and servants' rooms, as mentioned by Mrs Austen, and this has conditioned modern attitudes to the relative importance of the different ranges. The social demotion of the east range was confirmed during the eighteenth century, after the building of the new west range, but this trend may have started in the later seventeenth century, if that is the date of the new hipped-roofed kitchen block at the south end (Figs 1, 18K).[115] After 1924 the kitchen was moved to the former chapter house, where later twentieth-century visitors encountered it.[116] Originally, one assumes the kitchen was at the west end of the south range, on the site of the monastic kitchen.

The south range is the hardest of all to interpret because of the almost complete lack of evidence for the medieval and post-Dissolution periods. However, there are good reasons for assuming that buildings remained on the south side and that the courtyard was thus always enclosed. First, Stoneleigh Abbey had seventy hearths in the 1660s, more than any other Warwickshire country house.[117] Combe Abbey was assessed at fifty-one hearths, but the conversion at Combe utilized only three sides of the former cloister (see further below). Secondly, the drawing of the house on the 1597 estate map, and the plans of it on the eighteenth-century maps, all show a south range. Its elevation is in full view in the 1597 depiction, with a tall gabled building in the centre, projecting southwards at right-angles (Fig. 23A). This is most likely to be the monastic refectory still surviving as a structure, probably the 'greate hawle hole Roofed' documented in about 1550.[118] Presumably its shell had been converted into other accommodation in the meantime, as it is not identifiable as a 'hall' in the various documents after the 1540s;[119] and it has disappeared entirely by the time of the 1749 map, confirmed by further plans in the 1760s. At a comparable example, Lacock Abbey, the refectory was retained and subdivided into chambers, and the hall of the house was in the west range. At Combe Abbey, which was Cistercian and is a monastic conversion very comparable in some ways to Stoneleigh,[120] the great hall remained close to the position of the medieval refectory, in the range opposite the church site.[121] However, Combe was approached not from the west but the south, where the church and cloister walk had been completely removed and a U-shaped house with an open courtyard created to welcome the visitor. Thus the retention of the refectory position for the hall makes more sense in the house conversion there.

At Stoneleigh, we may be almost certain that some of the service accommodation listed in the 1626 and 1639 inventories was in the south range and the adjoining parts of the east and west ranges. This would include the larders, scullery and bakehouse, and rooms such as 'The Clerk of the Kitchen his Chamber' (1626); also the female rooms, such as 'My Ladies Chamber' and 'The Young Ladies Chamber', for which a location in the southern half of the east range is a possibility. By the mid-eighteenth century at the latest, the south range had been reduced to little more than a corridor, as shown in the 1749 estate map and plans of the 1760s. In 1813 the architect Thomas Hopper proposed deepening it to create extra servants' accommodation, work subsequently undertaken by C.S. Smith, probably in the 1830s.[122]

So far, very few specific dates have been offered for the parts of the pre-Smith house described above. How much of this house arrangement might go back to the earlier years of Queen Elizabeth's reign? Or is the house substantially of the seventeenth century? The only secure evidence for an early rebuild by the first Sir Thomas in the 1560s is the recent scientific dating to c.1568-70 of roof trusses towards the north end of the east range.[123] Such work high up on this area of the buildings make it very probable that the shell of the pre-Smith house described above was being created at this time: with the north-east block converted from the transept and the long gallery from the south aisle, as the vital link between the east and west ranges.   Otherwise, no other features of the fabric can be dated unequivocally to the sixteenth century, though some of their details are suggestive. In particular, similarities can be noted with mouldings employed in Leicester's works at Kenilworth Castle (c.1570-75). The large ovolo (quarter-round) moulding of the cross-mullioned windows which characterize the north-east block and the north gallery (Fig. 3) is very close in size to that on the Kenilworth windows.[124] Likewise, the small ovolo moulding framing the round-headed arches of the north gallery range (Fig. 11B) is extensively used at Kenilworth for door frames and fireplaces. Nevertheless, the

FIGURE 28
Stoneleigh Abbey: north-east
corner block, main staircase
(© Frank Knight International)

FIGURE 29
Stoneleigh Abbey: north range, south side elevation, detail: blocked window and chimney-breast
(© R.K. Morris, 2001). The letters relate to references in the text.

overall form of the Stoneleigh cross-mullioned windows, with relatively broad lights, suggest that they belong in the first half of the seventeenth century,[125] when the ovolo mullion continued in use. Equally, if the round-headed arches were executed as part of the grotto on the ground floor of the north range, then they are unlikely to predate the early seventeenth century, as we have seen. On the other hand, if they belong to a pre-existing garden loggia, they could be sixteenth-century and even from the time of the first Sir Thomas.[126]

Another instance of a feature spanning the fashions of both the Elizabethan and Jacobean periods is the compass window of the best chamber, listed in the inventories. Although no longer existing, we can be confident that this was a bay or oriel window with star-shaped projections. The remains of an early oriel window of this type may still be seen on the south exterior of the great chamber at Kenilworth Castle, c.1570-75, but the form was especially popular in the time of the Jacobean surveyor, John Thorpe, who included a compass bay window in his design for the south elevation of Aston Hall in 1618, lighting the great parlour and the great dining chamber above.[127] Either of these important local examples might have served as a precedent for Stoneleigh, but no more can be said with certainty than that it must predate its first mention in the 1626 inventory.

Other features survive which can be assigned more positively to the seventeenth century on stylistic grounds. This is most evident for the main type of window in the east range and for the two old staircases there. The first-floor windows of the east elevation have ogee mouldings for their stone frames (Fig. 26), a moulding more characteristic than the ovolo for stone window components in the first two-thirds or so of the seventeenth century; as seen, for example, in the mullioned and transomed windows of this period in the west range at nearby Combe Abbey. Presumably the wooden cross-mullioned frames for casements in the apertures (Fig. 18W) are replacements for a similar arrangement in stone, for casement frames of this type could date from c.1660 to as late as c.1750 on the basis of local examples in Warwick.[128]

The two wooden seventeenth-century staircases in the eastern part of the house are probably in their original positions. One rises in the south-west corner of north-east block and must be the main stair to the best chambers east of the gallery (Fig. 28, Plans 1-3D). It is of the open-well type made fashionable in Jacobean times by more lavishly ornamented examples at Knole (Kent, c.1605-08) and Hatfield House (c.1611), with its balustrade panels carved with urns and swirls of foliage in a robust provincial style (Fig. 28). The second stair lies more or less in the centre of the east range on the courtyard side (Plans 2-3M), and in its upper stages the balustrade panels are carved with open strapwork, a simple version of much grander Jacobean examples like the great staircase at Aston Hall, probably of about 1630.[129] This Stoneleigh stair could be of a similar date, whereas the north-east staircase might be contemporary or as late as the 1660s. Some authorities have linked the latter, and even an interior refurbishment of the east range, with the date of 1655 moulded on a lead rainwater-head on the north facade of the north range.[130]

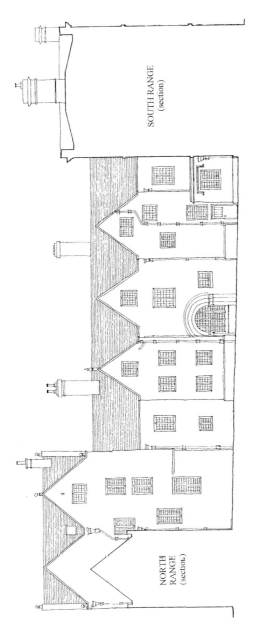

FIGURE 30

Stoneleigh Abbey: east range, west elevation (© R. Melville & Partners, 1993)

However, both staircases, though indubitably seventeenth-century, have been fitted into architectural settings which could be earlier. This is particularly evident in the courtyard elevation of the north-east block, where the stepped arrangement of the windows reflects the presence of a large staircase inside (Fig. 12, right) and where the use of chamfer mouldings contrasts with most other window mouldings around the house. Plain chamfer mouldings could as easily be of Elizabethan as of seventeenth-century date. Similarly, stepped windows with chamfer mouldings identify the position of the second stair in the projecting bay in the courtyard, one of a pair of bays added each side of the chapter house door apparently to provide a loosely symmetrical three-gabled composition to this elevation of the east range (Fig. 30). Thus, on the courtyard side of the house we may have the survival of Elizabethan architectural fabric, perhaps going back to the time of the first Sir Thomas, into which new staircases were fitted by his seventeenth-century successors to keep up with changing furniture fashions. None of the other wooden fittings surviving in the house, all in a Jacobean style, is of assistance in elucidating the architectural history.[131]

On the other hand, it is important to recognize that the fabric surviving from the post-Dissolution house is a promising field for archaeological analysis. It is not just a series of architectural set-pieces from set dates, but in places retains fragments from several pre-Smith phases juxtaposed. A particularly good example is the courtyard elevation of the north range, centred on the 'outdoor fireplace' with pediment, which has puzzled some writers (Fig. 29B).[132] Here we see at least three phases of alterations. First, and earliest, is the round-headed aperture in the wrong position to be a medieval nave window, and thus more likely to belong with works to convert the aisle to residential use. It is either a twelfth-century window frame which has been repositioned, probably in the sixteenth century, or possibly a new-made classically-inspired window of the kind appearing in the early seventeenth century, such as the windows inserted into the great hall at Ashby de la Zouch Castle.[133] Subsequently, the window was blocked and disused when a fireplace for the first-floor gallery was built in this area (Fig. 12A). Probably the cross-mullioned windows, almost certainly seventeenth-century, were introduced at the same time. Their raised position suggests that the gallery was being heightened,[134] and probably that the facilities beneath were being improved, which should explain the mysterious pedimented feature (Fig. 29B).[135] This is likely to be seventeenth-century too and must originally have been a door giving access to the ground floor, perhaps part of a passage between the courtyard and the north garden. It is difficult to tell whether it is an integral part of the projecting chimney-breast or has been appended to it later; but it was retained when subsequently the aperture was blocked, perhaps when C.S. Smith reordered the north range in the early nineteenth century.

Another significant example of archaeological phasing is discernible in the east elevation of the east range. We have already noted that there is a clear break between the masonry of the

FIGURE 31
Stoneleigh Abbey: east range,
2nd floor, a roof-truss
(© R.K. Morris, 2000)

FIGURE 32
Stoneleigh Abbey: pieces of Gothic window tracery excavated by
Warwick Museum Field Archaeology Section: scale 10 cm. (© R.K. Morris, 2001)

ground floor and the upper floors (Fig. 26) and also that the ogee stone frames of the first-floor windows should be of the seventeenth century. They are presumably contemporary with the new masonry of the upper floors, because the stones of the frames are in course with the wall stones.[136] We are therefore presented with the apparent anomaly of roof trusses in the northern bays, scientifically dated to c.1568-70, juxtaposed with a masonry cladding of fifty to one hundred years later. Nor, in fact, is the roof construction uniform, because at least one undated truss of a different design is exposed in the attic of the centre bay, with a reused timber for its principal rafter (Fig. 31, Plan 3N). Clearly there is an archaeological sequence to be unravelled here, but essentially what seems to have happened is that Elizabethan accommodation in the east range had been given a new exterior facade in the following century.[137] Conversely more of the Elizabethan fabric may survive on the courtyard side, as we have seen, especially as the arrangement of gables there is not entirely in sequence with those of the east facade (Fig. 1).

Facades with plain gables were going out of fashion for major courtier houses in the later sixteenth century. One has only to compare their use still at Longleat before 1572 with the elaborate shaped gables on the garden front of Kirby Hall, Northamptonshire, for Sir Christopher Hatton, 1575-91.[138] By such standards, Stoneleigh's use of simple gables surmounted by spheres is surprisingly *passé* for a great house in the seventeenth century. The same judgement may be passed on the curious Gothic-style hoodmoulds over each cross-mullioned window in the north-east corner tower and the north range, which are usually encountered only in provincial gentry houses (for example, Gawthorpe Hall, Lancashire, 1600-05) and vernacular architecture.[139]

In conclusion, Stoneleigh still retains in its east and north ranges significant evidence from the house created and occupied by the first three Sir Thomas's (1561-1671). Most of the visible architectural features and fittings belong to the seventeenth century, and probably mainly to the time of Sir Thomas III, the first Baron Leigh (1626-71). In particular, the year 1655 on a rainwater hopper may provide a clue to the sort of date when the architecture of the east and north ranges and the north-east block was being given its final form. Nevertheless, the recent scientific breakthrough in obtaining dates in Queen Elizabeth's reign for timbers from the house roof and gatehouse doors has added substance to the belief that the conversion of the monastery into a substantial courtyard house must have been begun by the first Sir Thomas (1561-71). He is the one most likely to have needed to tidy up the ruins of the church, adapting the aisle and transept to a gallery and apartments, and it has been argued above that the essential framework and organisation of that Elizabethan house survived through to the early eighteenth century.

The main loss has been the pre-eighteenth-century west range, containing the hall, great chamber and best suite of rooms. Nonetheless, as Geoffrey Tyack has observed, the buildings which survive from this period are surprisingly plain, in contrast to the accumulation of expensive personal possessions listed in the inventories of 1626 and 1639.[140] This may reflect the relative priorities of the Leigh family in this period, and a lack of interest in fashionable architecture emanating from London; a trend hardly reversed by the third Baron Leigh when he employed the local architect, Francis Smith, in 1714.[141]

Finally, we must guard against complacency. Far from being definitive, the building history presented above remains superficial in many respects and highlights gaps in our knowledge, some of which may be filled by a future opportunity to inspect fabric previously inaccessible. The house has an archaeology which is as yet not fully understood, and this applies both to fabric above ground and to field archaeology beneath the floors and in the gardens and park.

A P P E N D I X
Field archaeology at Stoneleigh Abbey 1998-2001

Some opportunities for field archaeology have been provided at the Abbey during recent work carried out for Stoneleigh Abbey Ltd and Historic Houses Rescue. These have been restricted to a series of watching briefs undertaken by Warwickshire Museum Field Archaeology Section (WMFAS). What follows is a brief handlist compiled by the author of finds relevant to the architectural history mainly of the medieval church and monastic buildings.[142] References are to the site (SLA), area or feature codes of WMFAS, or to their interim Archaeological Recording Reports for 1999 (SLA Report No.). The approximate locations of finds outside the house are marked on Figure 33.

1. The Church

1.1 North Transept and North-East Crossing Pier. Substantial foundations almost 2 metres thick located about 10 metres north of the north-east corner of the house (SLA 327) are likely to be part of the footings of the north-east pier of the crossing (Fig. 33 A). A smaller shallower foundation wall about 5 metres to the east (SLA 326) is thought to relate to a post-medieval garden wall rather than to one of the medieval east chapels of the transept (Fig. 33B). Its likely continuation was traced further north (SLA Report No.18, SLA 586), so it may relate to the feature shown dividing the north and north-east gardens in the 1749 and 1766 estate maps; probably the same one indicated very schematically in the 1597 map. Skeletal remains were found a short distance to the east of 326 (SLA 343), at a depth which suggests they could be medieval, but no further evidence about dating or context is available.

1.2 South Transept Chapels. A trench directly adjacent to the east wall of the east range revealed a short section of the dividing wall between the two east chapels of the transept (SLA Report No.17, SLA 584, Fig. 33C).

1.3 Nave. To the north of Francis Smith's west range, the substantial foundations (about 2.3 metres wide) of a wall running north/south were revealed in two places (SLA Report No.14, SLA

279 and 450, Fig. 33D). This almost certainly locates the west wall of the nave. The westernmost limit of the foundations was about 4 metres east of the west range west wall, and at their northernmost extent about 10 metres from the north wall.

2. The Conventual Buildings

2.1 The Chapter House. Inside, the removal of the modern floor make-up revealed (a) the base of the northernmost shaft of the west door, with traces of red and white polychromy on it (SLA Report No.11); (b) that the column in the centre of the room sat on a base which was roughly square and had a small rebate cut out of one edge (SLA Report No.14, and Bryn Gethin, personal communication). There was not enough archaeological investigation around the base to corroborate or negate the possibility that the column might be a secondary insertion.

Outside, a trench directly adjacent to the present east wall of the east range revealed a small amount of masonry contiguous with the chapter house north wall (SLA 582), interpreted as evidence for that wall continuing to eastwards (SLA Report No.17, Fig. 33E). A further section of stone wall running north-south was recorded about 13 metres east of the east range east wall (SLA 583), interpreted by WMFAS as perhaps belonging to the east wall of the chapter house (SLA Report No.17, Fig. 33F).

2.2 The Cloister. On the site of the east walk, some footings of the wall to the garth were located in line with the processional door into the former south aisle of the church (SLA 321, Fig. 33G). The construction, of mortared sandstone blocks, was about 0.85 metres wide, and indicated that the walk was more than 3 metres wide internally.

In the south-east corner of the courtyard, part of a pavement of inlaid tiles belonging to the cloister was identified *in situ* (SLA 528). Preliminary research by Bryn Gethin has identified parallels with decorated tiles from Kenilworth Abbey and Nuneaton Priory, thought to be of the fourteenth century.

2.3 The West Range. Work on surfaces below ground inside the west range of the present house uncovered 'the remains of massive stone walling with tooled blocks' in the northern part of the basement, in what is now the Residents' Store Room (SLA Report No.13, Fig. 33M).

2.4 Miscellaneous. To the south-east of the conservatory, and approximately in line with the east wall of the east range, part of the footings of a large wall was recorded, about 1.5 metres thick and running diagonally north-west to south-east (in SLA trench C2, Fig. 33J). Its location and alignment suggests it might relate to the latrine arrangements for the monastic dormitory.

2.5 Guest Range. Directly east of the gatehouse, some of the foundations were revealed of the thirteenth-century guest range, described further in Chapter 2 (SLA Report No.11, Fig. 33K).

3. Loose finds

3.1 Worked stones. Four fragments from stone windows were discovered *ex situ* in excavations to the east of the gatehouse (Fig. 33K,L). The best piece is a length of diverging glazed tracery,

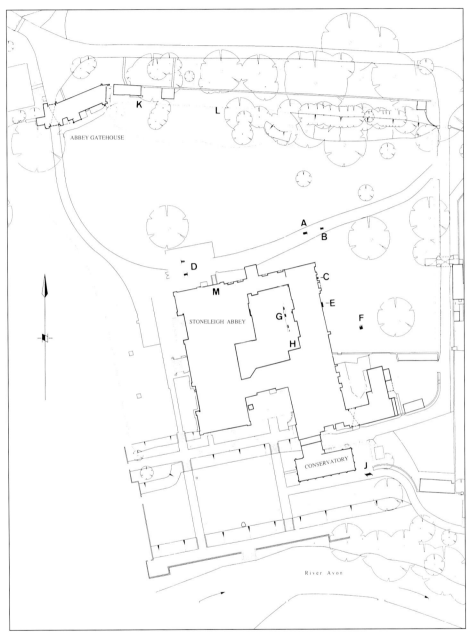

FIGURE 33
Stoneleigh Abbey: plan of the house and immediate surroundings, showing relevant field archaeology by
Warwick Museum Field Archaeology Section (from a plan by R. Melville & Partners).
The letters relate to references in the text.

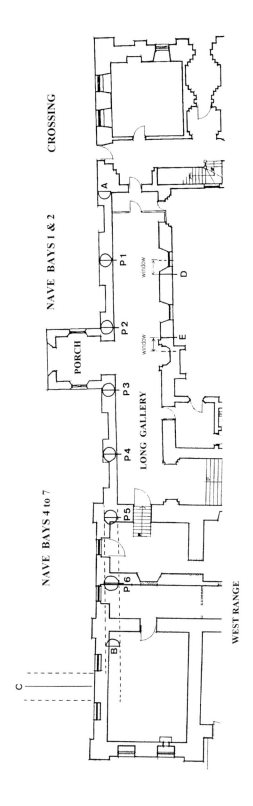

FIGURE 34

Stoneleigh Abbey: north range, plan, detail: with the locations of the medieval
nave south arcade piers and south aisle windows reconstructed
(from a plan by R. Melville & Partners).

Key: A – east respond of arcade
B – west respond of arcade
C – approximate centre axis of nave west wall
D – eastern window, west jamb
E – western window, east jamb
P – pier

with the springings for cusped patterns on each side (SLA 99; Fig. 32, centre). It was found in excavations at the east of the former guest range (Fig. 33K) and probably derives from it (see Chapter 2, Period 1). Stylistically its likely date span is from the late thirteenth century to *c*.1325. The other pieces were all found further east (Fig. 33L). A length of window mullion and a piece of cusped tracery belong together (SLA 98 trench I1.250; Fig. 32 left and right respectively) and may not originally have been glazed. The stylistic date of the mullion profile is of the first half of the fourteenth century and is similar in general design to one used in the gatehouse works of the 1340s. The fourth stone is a damaged piece of jamb for a glazed window (SLA 98 trench I1.186). It has a deep chamfer profile, is probably of fourteenth-century date, and shows signs of having been reused.

All these pieces are located in the WMFAS store at The Butts, Warwick, and profile drawings of them are in the author's Warwick Mouldings Archive.

3.2 Medieval floor tiles. An assemblage of about 150 tiles, most of them with inlaid decoration, was recovered loose in the house, but their exact provenance is unknown. They are from the fourteenth century and in pattern are similar to examples from other midland sites, like Kenilworth Priory. They were at the WMFAS store at Warwick at the time of writing.

Acknowledgements

This paper has been in gestation since the late 1970s when I first took small groups of History of Art students from the University of Warwick to study the Abbey. We were permitted to see only a few parts of the pre-eighteenth-century interiors, accompanied by Mrs Lee, Lord Leigh's housekeeper. Even now, twenty-five years on, I am aware that there are still parts I have never seen or not studied properly. Inevitably over such a long period of time, many more debts of gratitude have accumulated than I can acknowledge here. For expediting access to the house, I should like to thank the late Robin Chaplin; the staff of the former Stoneleigh Abbey Estate Office, especially Mr Spencer, Major Gordon-Duff and Mrs Elliman; Shahab Seyfollahi and Victoria Flannigan of Stoneleigh Abbey Ltd; Philippa Williams on behalf of Historic Houses Rescue; Professor Richard Higgott and Colin Richmond-Watson. I have benefitted enormously from all the other contributors to the 1999 symposium, both from their papers and from subsequent discussions; and also from the assistance of the Warwickshire Museum Field Archaeology Section (especially Cathy Coutts, Bryn Gethin and Nick Palmer) and Julian Munby of Oxford Archaeology. I am grateful to Nick Doggett, Bryan Sitch, Roberta Warman and Lucy Worsley for assisting me with information about other sites; to Hilary Izzett (a Warwick student in 1978), Mairi Macdonald, George Demidowicz and Nat Alcock for assistance with the documents; to Rodney Melville and partners, especially David Cattell and Steven Coulstin for supplying me with excellent plans; and to Alan Watson and Harry Sunley for photography. Lastly, this paper would probably never have seen the light of day without the encouragement and forebearance of Robert Bearman.

CHAPTER TWO

An Archaeology of Hospitality:

THE STONELEIGH ABBEY
GATEHOUSE

Rochelle L. Ramey

Today's visitor to Stoneleigh Abbey sees an extensive scatter of isolated buildings of varying dates and from a wide variety of architectural genres. But for the name of the estate, it is all too easy to forget that this imposing secular mansion and its grounds were once the setting for a religious community. When its chequered history is recalled, it is with a sense of distance; for our modern, predominantly secular, society, there is little that is familiar in the current published illustrations and descriptions of medieval monastic life. In their day, however, monastic houses such as Stoneleigh attempted, through the provision of hospitality, to make their way of life accessible to secular visitors, who were thus able to experience, appreciate and understand what is now presented as foreign.

Although a vast amount of literature on medieval monasticism has been produced, examining both textual and structural remains, most of it, until quite recently, has overlooked daily life beyond the claustral house and church, for

> ... the relevance of the inner or outer court, of the agricultural areas, and of
> individual structures like the guest houses, mills, almonry, or gatehouse,
> looked peripheral; at best they were treated as vernacular architecture, at
> worst as crude farm yard structures.[1]

The true irony of the absence of scholarship in these areas is that the activities which took place therein were a central aspect of monasticism, and critical to its welfare. Although the focus has lately shifted to an interest in non-claustral areas, we are still reluctant to examine in detail the social context of these 'peripheral' structures. It was primarily in these external regions of the site that the drama of hospitality, for example, the meeting of secular and religious cultures, was enacted. Hospitality found various guises and expressions in medieval society, ranging from charity to the poor, to generosity for the benefit of the affluent. One of the most fundamental doctrines of the Christian faith, maintained throughout the medieval period, was based on New Testament scripture:

> Come, ye blessed of my Father, inherit the kingdom prepared for you from the foundation of the world. For I was an hungred, and ye gave me meat: I was thirsty, and ye gave me drink, I was a stranger and ye took me in (Matthew 25: 34-35).

The recognition of the divine, however, was not necessarily the dominating principle behind monastic hospitality – a generous hand also reaped the rewards of donations of land, money, rights and exemptions, as well as novitiates (new recruits), critical to maintaining monastic life, facts of which the Cistercians were well aware. A form of reciprocal generosity, hospitality was not simply the provision of food, drink, accommodation and gifts. At its most refined level, it oversaw the very visual and symbolic exchange of social roles within a household, whereby the guest became host. Hospitality therefore provided the vehicle for both the reaffirmation and negotiation of social positions or value in medieval society.

Since hospitality reflected such a significant part of the monastic life, it was logical that there be institutionalized control mechanisms for managing interaction between the visitor and the claustral house. Arguably the most effective means of monitoring and directing such encounters was through the buildings in which visitors were received, the gatehouses, guest houses, superiors' lodgings and their associated service structures, although additional areas of the precinct to which visitors had visual or physical access might also reiterate the same messages and meanings imparted by buildings constructed specifically for their use. Several hundred gatehouses survive in varying states of preservation in England, of which twenty-five belonged to Cistercian houses. In the case of guest houses and superiors' lodgings, identification is complicated by the similarity of the structures and the lack of established criteria for differentiating between them; earlier research on Cistercian abbots' lodgings, however, has established that their preferred position was south-east of the cloister,[2] while guest houses were most often free-standing and to the west or north-west of the cloister or church. Of approximately one hundred tentatively identified as either guest houses or superiors' lodgings, twenty-three were Cistercian, and most of the remains are ruinous. This paper, by examining one relatively complete example, the Stoneleigh Abbey gatehouse, designed and constructed expressly for the purpose of managing interaction between secular and monastic spheres, attempts to highlight some of the messages which these buildings communicated to medieval visitors.[3]

Buildings and personnel

The monastic gatehouse was the first structure which a visitor or guest encountered. Scholars have traditionally regarded it as a symbol representing seclusion and isolation, a deliberate attempt to shield the monastic life from the secular.[4] The gatehouse is considered primarily in terms of its ability to restrict access to the courtyard, signifying sharp dichotomies of inside/outside, or secular/religious. Such a representation, however, simplifies the social role of this structure for it is within the gatehouse that the sophistication of medieval building becomes apparent: for example, the further away from the monastic church a gatehouse was positioned, the greater the probability that it would be constructed directly west, north-west or north of the church, and aligned so that the gate passage overlooked the church, particularly its west front.[5] Conversely, the closer the gatehouse was to the church, the more likely it was that the passage would be positioned perpendicular to the west front.[6] This observation, however, only scratches the surface – a sophisticated vocabulary of structural features and decorative embellishments also served to manage visitors' attention, and sought to summarize their relationship with the monastic house.

Standard arrangements of domestic guest accommodation encompassed at least two distinct structures, the superior's lodging, and the guest house. These were normally positioned either within or abutting the claustral ranges, or stood apart in the courtyard. The internal arrangement and use of space in both instances was in many ways identical to that found on manorial sites of the period, comprising a self-contained complex often including a hall, great chamber, parlour, bedchambers, a chapel and services such as a kitchen, buttery, pantry and stables. Both households included numerous support staff, employed to maintain the various departments; as in secular houses, servants were yet another physical manifestation of the wealth and generosity of the host, and thus those who were a visible presence in visitors' spaces were fitted with the livery of the house. The distribution of visitors between these households was a complicated matter, dictated by the status of the guest and the expense of providing hospitality, and, to a certain extent, variable over time and between monastic orders. The twelfth-century chronicle of Jocelin of Brakelond states that the guest house was reserved for religious visitors while the abbot entertained secular guests of significant social status. However, late thirteenth- and late fourteenth-century account books, from Beaulieu Abbey and Selby Abbey respectively, indicate that the monastic guest house was accommodating a variety of individuals, including knights and members of the royal family and their retinues.[7] The guest house constructed in the mid thirteenth century at St Alban's appears to have been specifically devoted to such a purpose.[8]

The guest house was overseen by a guest master, a respected, trustworthy monk appointed as caretaker and host, and responsible for the maintenance of the house and the entertainment of its occupants.[9] While the presence of a guest master is known from monastic documents, the

FIGURE 35
Stoneleigh Abbey Gatehouse, south elevation, following restoration

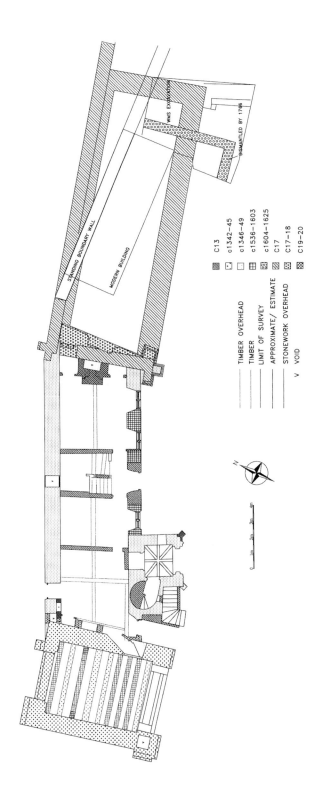

F I G U R E   3 6 A

Stoneleigh Abbey Gatehouse, phased ground-floor plan of gate and guest range (© Rochelle Ramey)

physical identification of chambers for this individual, either in the guest house or elsewhere, is less certain. The increasing tendency in later monasticism towards privacy for individual monastic inmates suggests that guest masters, at least on some sites, were able to live independent of the claustral house. The accounts of Selby's guest master, for example, which include the purchase of candles for lighting his 'office' and the purchase of reeds for strewing the floors of the 'rooms of the office', suggest a series of chambers dedicated to this function.[10] While the lodgings of the superior have been identified on many monastic sites, the standing remains of guest houses, and thus of guest masters' chambers, are more elusive, and much is left open to speculation. Of particular interest is the social position of this individual as host when his guests outranked him.

The Stoneleigh Abbey gatehouse

The Stoneleigh Abbey gatehouse (Fig. 35), the most complete survival from Stoneleigh's monastic history, is a two-storey structure incorporating a guest range extending to the east (Figs 36A, 36B). This dual nature makes the building particularly useful as a case study for examining monastic hospitality. Within the monastic plan, the gatehouse was positioned approximately 45 metres north of the west front of the monastic church (Fig. 33), thereby guaranteeing the medieval guest a full view of the religious focal point of the monastery. Published descriptions of the building have dismissed the easternmost part of the attached domestic range as 'wholly an addition of seventeenth-century date, much repaired in the nineteenth century',[11] although Nikolaus Pevsner was able to make some distinction between what he saw as seventeenth-century refacing to an original fourteenth-century upper hall.[12]

Before restoration works undertaken by Stoneleigh Abbey Limited began, a programme of detailed stratigraphic recording on the gatehouse was undertaken, using archaeological techniques such as computer-rectified photography and hand measurement to record and stratigraphically analyze the standing material stone by stone. Through such methods, it has been possible to dismantle conceptually the present structure and trace its development back to its original medieval state, and to understand its intended form, including its arrangement and use of space, and its role within the monastic site. This has revealed why the standing gate and guest range were constructed in their particular forms, in what manner they elaborated on pre-existing guest buildings, and how their organization and use of space could influence, and be influenced by, the inhabitants and guests of the monastery.

Period 1: the early guest range

Period 1 is represented by the eastern gable wall of the domestic range (Fig. 37) and by a fragment of return wall at the eastern end of the northern elevation (Figs 38, 36A). These remains are dated to the late thirteenth century on the basis of both stratigraphic and stylistic evidence. The uppermost blocked window is cut by the line of the dendrochronologically-dated Period

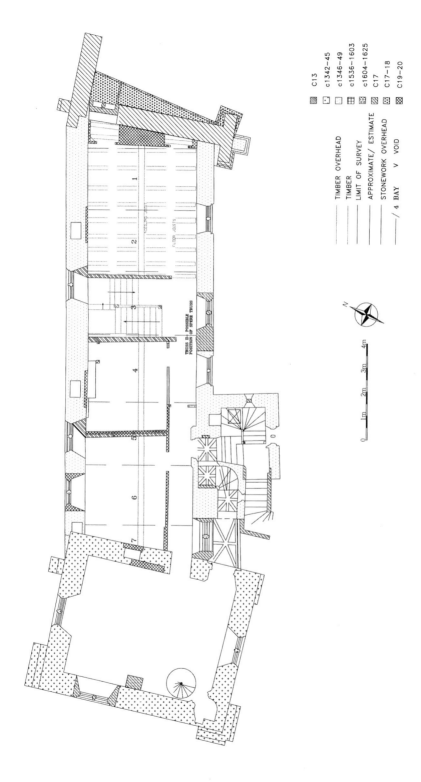

FIGURE 36B

Stoneleigh Abbey Gatehouse, phased first-floor plan of gate and guest range (© Rochelle Ramey)

3 roof of the surviving guest range, while the western buttresses are clearly enveloped by Period 3 fabric (Fig. 39). Capitals found *in situ* in the eastern face of the gable wall are identical in profile to late thirteenth-century capitals excavated from nearby Kenilworth Priory.[13] The gable remains represent the western extent of a large two-storied structure, now destroyed, projecting further east. Excavations in 1999 by the Warwickshire Museum Service detected the foundations of this building and demonstrated that its full external east-west dimensions were 18.3 metres in length, by 7.3 metres in width (internal dimensions 16.7 x 5.7 metres)[14] (Fig. 36A). Externally, surviving remains high in the gable wall indicate that the building was decorated along its length with a stringcourse of carved grotesque heads, three of which survive (one on the north, and two on the south). No evidence remains of the means of physical access. The building was lit from the gable at first-floor level by a pointed window, internally flanked by the above-mentioned capitals surmounting jamb shafts, and by an additional window in the apex. Stonework decorated with red ivy leaves and scrolled vines, a rare example of Cistercian paintwork, was found collapsed into stonework blocking the first-floor window.

The fragmentary remains of the Period 1 structure leave its function somewhat unresolved, but its basic form, position and decoration, as well as the building's physical relationship with the Period 3 range, support its interpretation as a guest structure. Although Stoneleigh Abbey was founded in 1155, some of its less important buildings, like those of other monastic houses, may have been constructed from timber, and only rebuilt in stone over a long period of time. At Fountains Abbey, the wealthiest Cistercian house and also the quickest to erect stone buildings, between twenty and forty years passed before the first stone guest chambers were constructed, and a timber aisled hall followed shortly thereafter.[15] Late twelfth-century remains in the eastern range of the main house at Stoneleigh indicate that, as expected, the foremost concern was to complete the claustral living quarters and the church. Thus, in spite of its later thirteenth-century date, the Period 1 structure may yet have been the first such stone domestic guest building erected on the site.

The combination of guest structures found in these early years of the Cistercian order is demonstrated by a comparison with Fountains, as well as with non-Cistercian, and even non-monastic buildings. The standard arrangement for a self-contained household consisted of the components of hall, chambers, and services – throughout the twelfth and thirteenth centuries in particular, this was often arranged as a ground-floor aisled hall with a detached, juxtaposed two-storey chamber block and service structures.[16] Current research into the conditions for, and occurrence of, first-floor halls in monastic visitors' buildings suggests that such spaces, though making an appearance in the twelfth century, as in the Aula Nova represented in the Canterbury Waterworks plan, were generally not commonplace except in specific conditions, namely, where the hall replaced or reused earlier standing fabric.[17] At Stoneleigh, there are, therefore, two likely interpretations of the Period 1 structure – either it

C– CUT	PG/ · – PEG	▲ VENT
F– FILL	TL/ – TILE	LEVELS
SL– SLATE	BRK/ – BRICK	● EMPTY PEG HOLE
CH– CHAMFER	PH/ □ – PUTLOG	PROJECTION
W– WINDOW	TB/ – TIMBER	VOID
D– DOORWAY	MO/ MORTAR/ RENDER	

TOOLING
MASON'S MARK
--- PROFILE
LIMIT OF SURVEY

0   1m   2m

FIGURE 37
Stoneleigh Abbey Gatehouse, east elevation of early guest range (© Rochelle Ramey)

was a first-floor guest hall over storage or living accommodation, or, more probably, a detached chamber block accompanying a since-destroyed ground-floor hall. Further excavation or the use of ground-penetrating radar on the area of open ground between the guest house and the site of the church might resolve this issue.

Period 2: the gatehouse

The gatehouse is a two-storied, pitched-gable structure positioned approximately 17.25 metres to the west of the thirteenth-century guest house remains. There is conclusive structural evidence that the gatehouse proper was a free-standing structure, namely, the form of a projecting corbel on the western elevation, a stringcourse concealed at second-floor level within the domestic range on the east, and a region of disrupted sandstone facing at the south-east corner (Fig. 36A). That a gatehouse had existed on this site from the later twelfth century is clear from the incorporation into the present structure of stonework from that period (Fig. 23 and above, p. 35). However, dendrochronological sampling on the timber of the gate passage[18] has yielded a date between 1342 and 1345, and this corresponds favourably with the chronicles of Stoneleigh, which recount the involvement of of Robert of Hockele (abbot, 1310-1349) in the gatehouse's re-construction.[19] As the building neared completion, however, Hockele altered his plans, and commissioned the construction of an adjoining guest range, linking the gatehouse with the thirteenth-century guest building further east. Hockele's original intentions will be discussed below, while the alterations to these plans will be considered in Period 3.

Contrary to observations published in 1951,[20] both the north and south, or outer and inner, façades of the gatehouse (Figs 35, 38) are almost wholly original, with only minor monastic and post-monastic insertions. Set high in the gable of the northern elevation is a badly weathered sandstone block bearing what are reputed to be the remains of the shield, helm and crest of the founder, Henry II.[21] Both façades retain large two-light windows divided by mullions and transoms, but, while that on the outer face contains curvilinear tracery with cusped heads and mouchettes, the inner is formed from simpler reticulated tracery. This difference between the outer and inner faces can also be observed in the mouldings of the arches over the passage – that on the outer face is moulded, while the arch of the inner face is flat (the lower order is a later addition).

While fourteenth-century monastic houses of various orders were experimenting with prominent polygonal turrets or broad expanses of wall as the backdrop for sculpted decoration on the outer façades of their gatehouses, the Cistercians were unusually consistent in employing a simple, pitched-gable design, a visual and structural arrangement which had persisted from the twelfth century. Though already an old form by the fourteenth century, it yet effectively portrayed what the Cistercians perceived as their monastic image and still encouraged a very particular and deliberate relationship between their visitors and their house.

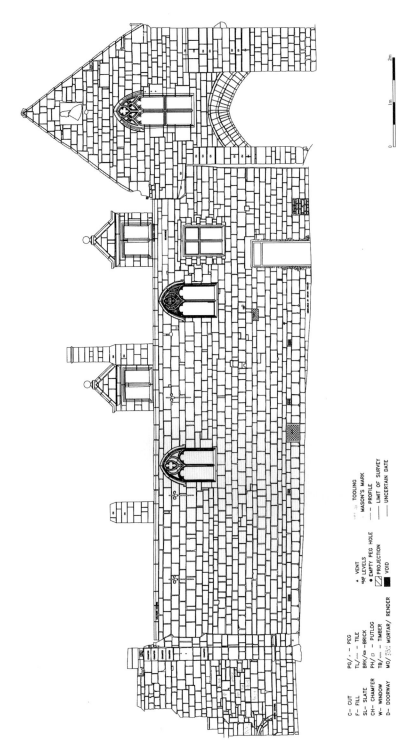

C– CUT   PG/ – – PEG
F– FILL   TL/ — – TILE
SL– SLATE   BRK/▭ –BRICK
CH– CHAMFER   PH/ ▢ – PUTLOG
W– WINDOW   TB/ — – TIMBER
D– DOORWAY   MO/ ░ MORTAR/ RENDER

▲ VENT
LEVELS
● EMPTY PEG HOLE
▨ PROJECTION

·· TOOLING
· MASON'S MARK
— – PROFILE
— – LIMIT OF SURVEY
— – UNCERTAIN DATE
▮ VOID

F I G U R E 3 8

Stoneleigh Abbey Gatehouse, north elevation of gate and guest range (© Rochelle Ramey)

The inner façade at Stoneleigh and elsewhere received a less decorative treatment, with no armorial shield and less decorative forms of tracery and mouldings. This contradicts claims that inner and outer façades were treated in the same manner due to a two-way regulatory function of keeping monastic inhabitants in and strangers out.[22] The messages of affiliation and patronage, continuity and permanence, which Stoneleigh imparted to onlookers by means of its north façade, particularly through the arms of Henry II, were applicable to the general public, and perhaps specifically to those who would not enter the courtyard, such as individuals receiving alms at the gate. The façade was capable of commanding such attention primarily through the comparative lack of impressive decorative structures outside the walls of the abbey. In an environment where precinct walls regularly attained over ten feet in height, the closer the viewer ventured towards them, the less visible the buildings within would become. Thus a visitor with the intention of penetrating such barriers instinctively sought out the means of entry. The concentrated decoration above head-height on the gatehouse indicates an intention to direct the viewer's attention upwards, both on account of the religious associations with the heavens, and, in the case of guests, in preparation for their visual encounter with the monastic church.

While the roof timbers of the gatehouse have been replaced through centuries of structural repair and alterations, including the construction and dismantling of a dormer window on the west and a clock tower centred over the roof, the timbers of the gate passage are, at least in part, original, with a felling date of 1342-45.[23] A combination of dendrochronological sampling and structural analysis has demonstrated that the gate passage was initially divided into two sections, a lobby to the north and a gate hall to the south, by the inclusion of a timber post and brace archway, originally positioned one further joist south than at present.

Through the careful placement of the gatehouse and alignment of the gate passage (Fig. 33), the visitor's view was channelled forwards, through the passage and into the courtyard. In more concentrated efforts to achieve this effect, some builders embellished gatehouse passages with repetitive schemes of blind arcading, as at Evesham Abbey, St Mary's Abbey in York, and Durham Cathedral, for example, or ceiled the lobby more decoratively than the gate hall, as, for instance, at Reading Abbey and Whalley Abbey. Furthermore, by the careful placement and alignment of the passage overlooking the west front of the church, a critical knowledge of the layout of the rest of the site was imparted. With only a basic recognition of the points of the compass, the liturgical alignment of the church also indicated the most likely layout of the various domestic and service ranges radiating from the cloister. The standard monastic plan thereby encouraged and facilitated, rather than discouraged, outsider access.

The unblocking of a doorway in the south-east wall of the gate passage (Fig. 36a) demonstrated that the south-east corner of the gatehouse was originally flanked by a turret containing a spiral stair, ascending to a heavily moulded doorway leading through to the upper

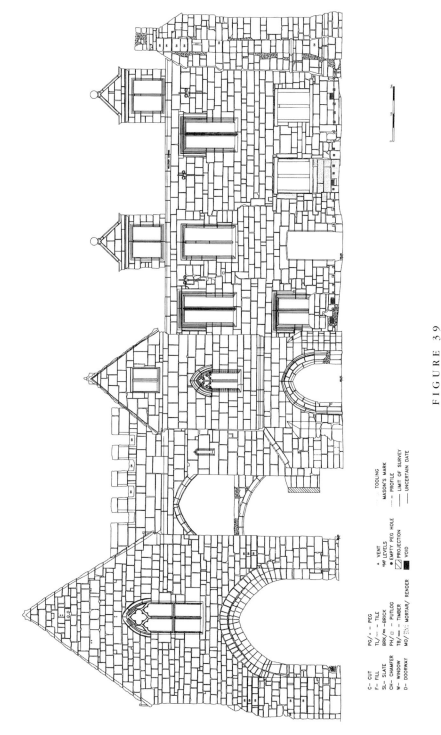

C – CUT
F – FILL
SL – SLATE
CH – CHAMFER
W – WINDOW
D – DOORWAY

PG/+ – PEG
TL/▭ – TILE
BRK/▬ – BRICK
PH/□ – PUTLOG
TB/▬ – TIMBER
MO/▨ – MORTAR/ RENDER

· · · · TOOLING
▲ VENT   MASON'S MARK
᠁ LEVELS   – – – PROFILE
● EMPTY PEG HOLE   ─ · ─ LIMIT OF SURVEY
▨ PROJECTION   ─── UNCERTAIN DATE
▨ VOID

F I G U R E   3 9

Stoneleigh Abbey Gatehouse, south elevation of gate and guest range (© Rochelle Ramey)

floor of the gatehouse. In this respect, as in others, the gatehouse as originally designed was intended to resemble the outer gatehouse at Maxstoke Priory, an Augustinian house located approximately ten miles north-west of Stoneleigh. While demonstrating the existence of a route to the first-floor chamber, however, the re-opening of the doorway did not confirm that an additional access was angled north-east into a ground-floor space for the use of a porter, prior to the construction of the guest range in Period 3. On the basis of comparative structural and documentary evidence from other monastic sites, Cistercian or otherwise, such a ground-floor space would be expected.

The first-floor chamber over the gate was lit by the large windows described above. Analysis of the western elevation has demonstrated that a projecting corbel originally supported a wall chimney stack, with a fireplace opening into the first-floor space. This was probably removed in the seventeenth century, when alterations to the use of space in the gatehouse and attached guest range necessitated the insertion of a chimney stack between the two structures, thus making the medieval fireplace redundant. In the south-west corner of the room is a garderobe closet, discharging down a chute concealed by the extensive buttressing on the south-western corner of the building (Fig. 35), and lit by a small quatrefoil oculus on the western elevation. The standard of decoration and the provisions for comfort mark this chamber as one meant for the accommodation of an individual of significant standing. While the spatial relationship between the thirteenth-century guest building and the gatehouse leave much of the Period 1 and 2 provisions for hospitality open to speculation, the Period 3 evidence, described below, suggests that this chamber was the guest master's.

Period 3: the guest range

Following quickly upon the erection of the gatehouse was the construction of a guest range, linking the gatehouse with the Period 1 guest building, and comprising a first-floor hall over living or storage space, a two-storied entrance porch, and a vaulted passage connecting the range to the first-floor chamber of the gatehouse (Figs 36A, 36B). Stratigraphic and stylistic evidence, in conjunction with dendrochronological sampling of the roof, has indicated a completion date of around 1349 or 1350.[24] These additions, and the requisite modifications to existing structures, altered not only the way in which the gatehouse chamber was accessed, but also the nature and use of space in and around the gate and the thirteenth-century guest range. The northern elevation of this range still represents primarily Period 3 work (Fig. 38). Minor insertions and alterations included the seventeenth-century addition of dormer windows lighting an added second floor, and the respective nineteenth- and twentieth-century insertions of a window and doorway towards the western end of the façade. Two Period 3 curvilinear windows are found at first-floor level, the tracery of which includes long mouchettes flanking an ogee quatrefoil, alternate with windows on the southern elevation (Fig. 39). Their positions reflect the

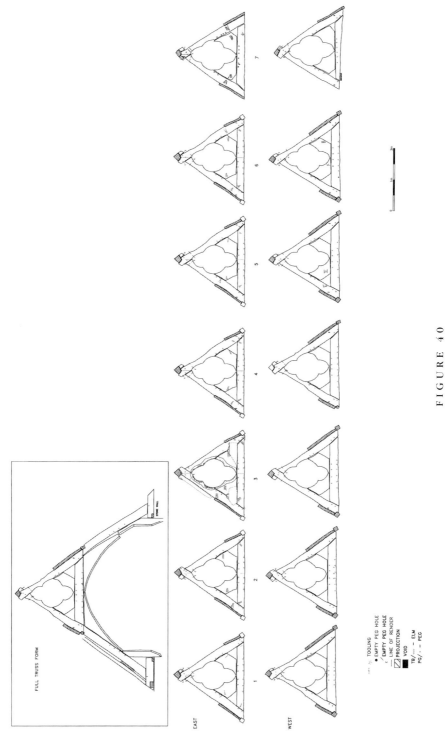

F I G U R E 4 0

Stoneleigh Abbey Gatehouse, east and west faces of guest range roof trusses (© Rochelle Ramey)

division of the hall into spatial 'bays', framed by roof trusses (Fig. 36B). Internally, each window is backed by a segmental rear arch, deep enough to provide a window seat to either side of the opening. During restoration, the internal chamfered faces of the mullions of both northern windows revealed a pattern of red-painted leaves on a whitewash background.

At the eastern end of the southern elevation, a flat expanse of wall marks the extent of the first-floor hall (Fig. 39). Period 3 material can be positively identified at first-floor level, but the dating of much of the ground-floor fabric, subjected to multiple intrusions and alterations, remains uncertain despite detailed recording. As stated above, the two first-floor windows lighting the hall alternate with those on the north – while the heads of these windows are square, they replace pointed heads identical to those on the north, carefully replicating the medieval moulding profile of the lower jambs. The seventeenth-century insertion of a second floor necessitated the insertion of dormer windows, and a doorway onto a staircase ascending to the second floor.

Although we might expect that the southern lateral wall would be constructed in line with that of the thirteenth-century range and the south façade of the gatehouse, it was instead set back by over a metre. A rib-vaulted passage, with decorative floral bosses at primary rib intersections, connected a porch to the gatehouse chamber (Fig. 36B). The embattled parapet surmounting the passage (Fig. 35) has been thus far interpreted as an addition of the nineteenth century, probably on the strength of its first distinct appearance in Repton's 1809 illustration (Fig. 71), although it should be noted that earlier drawings portray the gatehouse from a sharp south-western angle, thus obscuring this region of stonework (for example, Fig. 120). During restoration work, however, evidence was discovered for a water spout, contemporary with the parapet, channelling water away from the roof. Its blocking appears to have coincided with the seventeenth-century insertion of a doorway and adjoining staircase, to the western side of the porch, onto which the spout would have drained. This therefore suggests a pre-seventeenth-century date for both the spout and the parapet.

The dismantling of the Period 2 stair turret was a necessary prerequisite for the provision of a vaulted passage. Both the floor and vault were then tied into the south-east corner of the gatehouse. While the resulting 'bridge', supported by a buttressing arch below, appears unusual, such an arrangement, since both the present windows appear to have been inserted into original openings, permitted physical access to the gate chamber as well as visual access and light to the first-floor hall and the ground-floor space below. It is probable that a porter's chamber was provided behind the ground-floor opening, entered primarily from the gate passage, although the interior of this area has been too drastically altered to allow further investigation of this possibility.

At the northern corner of the heavily-moulded first-floor doorway into the gatehouse chamber is a carved human torso and head. The figure wears a liripipe (a long, pointed hood), but is otherwise too weathered to detect further significant detail. Of several possible identities for this individual, including a peasant or jester, the most satisfactory, relative to the structural and social context, is the medieval traveller to whom the guest house would have provided hospitality.

A plain, unmoulded archway across the passage marks the point of descent from the 'bridge', down a flight of steps lit by a small ogee-headed lancet, to a landing. From here, the passage opened into three distinct spaces (Fig. 36B). A spiral stair in the porch, probably reused after the dismantling of the gatehouse turret, descended to the ground floor of the porch. Alternatively, an additional archway at first-floor level opened into a chamber above the entrance porch. Finally, a pointed doorway opened northwards into the first-floor hall; internally this doorway projected from the main wall face on a corbel. Between the doorways of the hall and porch chamber is evidence for the position of a laver.

On account of the irregular alignment of the Period 3 range in relation to its flanking structures, the first-floor hall was divided internally into six full bays aligned north-south, with additional irregularly shaped half-bays at each end (Fig. 36B). A doorway (now a cupboard) pierced the northern end of the Period 1 gable wall, thus permitting movement between the high end of the hall and the thirteenth-century building. The bay division of the hall is dictated by a roof of seven arch-braced collar trusses, each cusped above the collar (Fig. 40). These are stabilized by two levels of cusped windbraces to either side of the roof. Chamfered posts, terminating lower on the sandstone wall, lent additional support to the tie beam of each truss – these posts were mutilated in the seventeenth century, in order to allow sufficient head room on the second floor.

Detailed recording demonstrated that the carpenters adhered to common 'grammatical rules of the language of building',[25] which not only assigned the relationships between individual timbers and trusses, but also dictated the social importance of the available space. Assembly marks were detected on the eastern face of each truss (Fig. 40) and a careful examination of surviving common rafters suggested that these also were chamfered on their eastern side only, details which indicate that the high-status end of the hall was to the east. The haphazard nature of this marking (in varying sizes and positions along the tie beams and principal rafters, or sometimes simply omitted), as well as the varying quality of joints and cusping on each structural member, suggest that this roof, though still adequate for a high-status space, was of a lower quality of construction than might be expected in comparison with other sites, and was constructed by more than one carpenter. Such details demonstrate not only the potential variability in the quality of visitors' structures, but perhaps also signify the presence of other financial priorities for the monastic house.

The overall arrangement and use of space in the new guest house was intricate. According to its position at the high end of the new hall, the thirteenth-century structure was now, if not in Periods 1 and 2, being used as a chamber block. As stated above, however, the Period 2 gatehouse chamber was also a high-status space. The retention of a heavily-moulded doorway leading into the room suggests the continuity of that character through to Period 3. However, the chamber was entered only via the associated vaulted passage, not directly from the hall. Primary access to the hall was provided from three directions, through the chamber block, through the ground-floor of the entrance porch, and through the corbelled hall doorway, though only two of these routes were intended for general visitors' use. There was a deliberate attempt to guide the visitor to the appropriate space by highlighting specific approaches to the hall; upon entering the ground-floor porch through the external moulded entrance arch (Fig. 35), the visitor gained access to the main structure through a second heavily moulded arch, not via the small, unobtrusive doorway to one side. Inside the guest range, a stair must have led up to the first floor, probably positioned at some point between bays five and seven, although post-monastic alterations have erased this evidence.

The prominence of the corbelled doorway mentioned above indicates that it was an intended visual feature of the hall, although its primary function was to emphasize the entrance into the hall from the vaulted passage. Since the hierarchy of the hall favoured the eastern end and a great chamber in the Period 1 structure beyond (Fig. 36B), both of which would normally be reserved for guests, the private vaulted passage, the chamber over the porch and the gatehouse chamber were probably reserved for a permanent occupant. The most likely candidate for this space was a guest master, an important monastic official whose role as host on behalf of the monastery was not necessarily supplanted by the social status of his guests – guests who retained the right to preside over the hierarchically dominant regions of the guest house.

Period 4: the dismantling of the Period 1 guest range

The contents of the 1558-61 survey of the recently dissolved monastery suggest that by this date, the thirteenth-century guest range had been dismantled, and a thatched farm structure erected in its place. This sixteenth-century farm building is visible in 1749 and 1766 plans of the Stoneleigh estate and in a 1749 panoramic view of the site (Figs 23, 120). This sequence of events was confirmed by the Warwickshire Museum Service's excavations on the site.[26] However, the question still remains as to whether the guest range was still standing and in use up to the time of the Dissolution, or had already been dismantled due to a lack of use or a state of poor repair.

Differences in the profiles of buttresses projecting from the south end of the east gable (Fig. 39), and in the fragmentary walling on the north, as well as similarities between masons' marks found on the same stonework and on the blocking of the first-floor window of the east gable elevation, imply that the thirteenth-century range was dismantled at some point following the construction of the Period 3 range. There is no definite evidence of when this occurred, but it seems very likely that a building constructed only shortly before the fourteenth-century guest house, and thus probably in good repair, would be retained and used, and that the dismantling of that structure would only occur once the building no longer served a useful function or was falling into disrepair. In both instances, the Dissolution might have provided the necessary conditions.

Conclusions

The programme of detailed archaeological recording undertaken on the Stoneleigh Abbey Gatehouse has demonstrated both the main phases of the building's construction and the role of the standing structures within the abbey's provisions for guests. The first identified phase of construction, the later thirteenth century, included what was probably the abbey's first stone guest house, perhaps replacing an earlier, possibly timber, structure. This two-storied stone guest house may have provided living accommodation to accompany an additional detached, ground-floor hall. The gatehouse, re-constructed between 1342 and 1345, along with the thirteenth-century block, provided favourable conditions for the creation of a first-floor hall between them, completed by 1350, and probably replacing an earlier guest hall in the area. Such a scheme retained the thirteenth-century stone structure as a chamber block, with a new doorway piercing the gable wall to permit access between. There is thus far no evidence to imply that this arrangement did not continue until the surrender of the monastery in 1536, at which time the thirteenth-century range was probably de-roofed and dismantled.

There is evidence to suggest that the internal use of space in the present gatehouse consisted of a first-floor hall above an undercroft. The latter was used either for storage or sleeping accommodation, with an additional room within the western end of the same for the use of a porter manning the gates. Accompanying this arrangement were the quarters of a guest master, a previously little-examined individual who oversaw the guest house not as a lord – as his abbot would have presided over his lodgings – but as a representative of the monastery, an intermediary between two supposedly distinct cultures. The guest master gained access to the hall and probably a first-floor study by means of a vaulted passage extending from his gatehouse chamber to the porch.

The hierarchical layout of space employed in the gatehouse, while innately manorial in its associations, was accompanied by those nuances which were part of a monastic tradition. This sent strong signals to all who entered the monastery, including suggestions of religious, political and economic dominance as well as spiritual and material largesse. These were presented at the first encounter with the north face of the gate, were reiterated with a full view of the monastic church and were expressed in the nature of the reception and accommodation of the visitor in the guest house. By emphasising specific elements of the visitor experience – for example, the accentuation of doorways which opened either inwards or outwards, were accessible or inaccessible according to specific guidelines – the monastery reaffirmed both its benevolence and its authority.

Acknowledgements

I am grateful to Stoneleigh Abbey Limited and Rodney Melville and Partners, for permitting me full access to the Stoneleigh Abbey gatehouse before and during the restoration programme. Financial support from the Royal Archaeological Institute allowed me to record in detail the roof structure over the guest hall. I would also like to thank Dr Richard Morris and Professor Andor Gomme for their helpful comments on elements of my interpretation. Further thanks go to Simon Rowell for editing a draft of this paper. My greatest debt, however, is to my supervisor Jane Grenville, for her comments on and criticisms of both this paper and of the D.Phil. research upon which it is based.

CHAPTER THREE

Abbey into Palace:

A LESSER WILTON?

Andor Gomme

In France it would be called a *Château*, in Germany a *Schloss*, in Italy a *Palazzo*. There is indeed something palatial about eighteenth-century Stoneleigh – especially in its aspirations. There may even have been an idea of doing another Chatsworth by rebuilding all four ranges round the courtyard one by one; there was certainly an intention to do, on an appropriately smaller scale, what Wren did at Hampton Court, building two adjacent grand ranges at right angles which from a chosen position hide the Tudor jumble behind and suggest an English Versailles. But the Leighs, it seems, were not people to put both feet in the water at once; or if they did, one at least was quickly withdrawn, and even the lesser grand scheme was never finished.

Things certainly began hesitantly, the first proposal being for no more than a face-lift, albeit a fairly spectacular one. In 1714, Edward, the third Baron Leigh, recently back from a Grand Tour, commissioned a design from Francis Smith for building 'the front of a house'.[1] Smith, by this time well-established in Warwick as the leading master-builder in the Midlands, estimated that this would cost £545, or, if only two storeys high, £463. For long it was assumed that the larger figure related to the building of the whole great west range of Stoneleigh, and it was often quoted as a remarkable example of the economy for which Smith was renowned.[2] More remarkable than possible: Smith was a careful businessman, and work on such terms would long before have bankrupted him. By comparison the carcase (only) of Ombersley Court in Worcestershire, which Smith built in the early 1720s and which is less than half as long as Stoneleigh's west front, cost a little over £2,000.[3] Moreover, the return walls of the 'front' that Smith was to build were to be no more than 14 feet long – obviously impossibly small for the depth of a new wing. The notorious estimate, in fact, was to be for what it said – simply a refronting job to the existing west range, a cheap way of smartening up one side of the rambling house in something like an up-to-date style.

This frugal scheme seems to have been quickly abandoned, and, in a way that was to typify the stop-go process by which the west range emerged, nothing more was done for another six years. The family, apparently, continued to live in rather cramped quarters in the east wing, which, probably at this point, was itself given a mild face-lift with a set of neatly evened-up cross-windows; and a modest service wing (removed in the nineteenth century) was built at the south end of the medieval undercroft.[4] Lord Leigh moved with caution and in 1716 tried out his mason with a farmhouse well away from the great house. It was to be finished within three months and to cost a mere £100: a note on the back of the agreement records that 'my Lord Leigh is to pay Mr. Francis Smith twelve pounds more upon finishing of the building within mentioned in case the said Lord Leigh approves of the said Building and that the said Francis Smith deserves the same'.[5] The house (now called New or Stone House Farm) was sturdily built and stands externally unaltered – simple, even a bit crude, with cross-windows that are no more than groups of holes punched through the walls: plate-tracery versions, so to speak, of those on the revamped east front (Fig. 41).

In 1720 work on the west range began in earnest. First comes a bill for £71 for pulling down the old building and digging foundations for the new, then payments roughly every month for five years.[6] By 1725, when this series of accounts breaks off, Smith had been paid just over £3,300; a year later an entry in the Cubbington parish register[7] speaks of the work as complete – a word which must be treated with much reserve. But the main structure was up and to some extent habitable: surviving account books from then until 1738, when Lord Leigh and his architect-builder died within a month of one another, imply only spasmodic mopping-up operations.

No drawings for any of this work survive, but it seems likely that the design for the refronting proposal may have largely re-emerged as the front of the west wing which Smith built. The estimate provided for 'such Breaks, Pilasters, Rusticks, Window Stuff, Door Case, Fanos [i.e. pediments], Cornish, Plint and Rails & Bannister' as its accompanying draught directed – all of which appear in plenty on the present façade. At 175 feet, the executed front is slightly longer than the refront would have been, has higher main floors, and the returns at each end are now a realistic 65 feet – none too deep for a range of such prodigious length. It is a design which stands apart in Smith's *oeuvre*, and indeed there is no other house of its time that closely resembles Stoneleigh. Massive as it is, it certainly falls short of the baroque bravura of the masterpieces of Hawksmoor and Vanbrugh: its very repetitiousness marks it as provincial in the limiting sense. Yet, while it lacks also the festive exuberance of Thomas Archer, the grandeur of Heythrop, which the Smith brothers had built to Archer's design a decade or so earlier, stayed in Francis's blood. Certainly baroque paradox and tension are present, however little Smith may have known of their origins in seventeenth-century Rome. The façade is very long and proportionately not very high – 62 feet – yet verticals are everywhere emphasized (Fig. 42). The huge Ionic order rises from pedestals the height of the full basement through all three

FIGURE 41
Stone House (or New House) Farm, Stoneleigh

FIGURE 42
Stoneleigh Abbey: west range from the south-east

storeys, so that, as in many of Smith's stylar houses, only the pilasters – great square pillars clamping the three main projections – carry a full entablature; and there is no horizontal between basement and cornice to counteract the visual upward thrust. The windows are tall and their apparent height is increased by the pediments which meet the sills above in projecting panels so that there is no flat wall visible except as a series of vertical strips between the windows. The effect is to imply a giant order across the whole façade. The design has been accused of gaucheness, but Smith should surely be credited with knowing what he was doing in creating this glowering concentration of tensed energy, reinforced by the sense of compression induced by the recessed sections of the façade which seem to brace themselves to keep the dominant projecting blocks apart. What is really perplexing is that Smith was working simultaneously on this aggressively anti-Palladian design, on the serenely poised Sutton Scarsdale and on the arrestingly fanciful Chicheley. Hostile critics might charge him with a lack of principle – but they all come off.

The west wing was designed to provide a set of rooms of a size, splendour and elegance impossible in the cramped layout of the old house, but they were for family use – not a set of state rooms as, for example, at the slightly later Wolterton, where we know that the family lived in the rustic and went up two floors to bed, bypassing the main floor altogether,[8] or at Holkham, where the family lived – and live – in what is essentially a separate house, leaving the whole grandiloquent centre for show. The Leighs lived from the start in as much of the west range as was ready and were, intermittently, eager to bring more rooms into family use. The old house was to be relegated to subordinate quarters or even quite other activities: a plan of the 1760s shows the upper floor of the east range given over to servants' rooms and the undercroft used as a brewhouse.

How much of the west wing was habitable by 1738 is still in question. In the basement the undercroft of the hall provided a spacious and surprisingly well-lit servants' hall (Fig. 43: and see Plan 1, Vaulted Chamber). The chapel was provisionally fitted up, for years later, when it was achieving its present form, the joiner George Eborall's first job was to take down the wainscot and the organ, after which he altered the gallery and the seats and new-framed the ceiling.[9] But the problem of access to the west wing from the rest of the house – which would have been of less moment had the family been able to move across entirely – had not been sorted out; and it remained almost isolated. As late as 1806, as we know from a letter from Jane Austen's mother,[10] the old gallery along the north front opened into the state (or crimson) bed-chamber (now the Library, Plan 2) and the other rooms in the north-west corner had become an access corridor, apparently the only one there was. But at least some of the rooms were in use during the short lifetimes of the third and fourth barons: even after an extensive sale in 1750, the rooms north of the hall (now the Saloon) were fully furnished, and their present character and decoration plainly date from Francis Smith's time. All have the lustrous stylar wainscot of various

FIGURE 43
The former Servants' Hall (now the Vaulted Chamber)

FIGURE 44
The former Dining Room (now the Brown Drawing Room), c. 1950

orders which was the mark of a conservative but still swagger taste in the 1720s. In the largest
– the great Dining Room (now the Brown Drawing Room) – the almost overbearingly massive
Corinthian order, pilastered on the long walls and with three-quarter columns at the ends,
was not to the taste of Mrs Austen's time (Fig. 44). The Silk Drawing Room (now the Card Room)
is more intimate: it has only pilasters and those only for the chimney-piece. The order is
composite and rather stiff, as that order tends to be.

The state bedroom, which Mrs Austen found alarming – 'just fit for a heroine' – was
greatly altered in the 1830s when its adjoining dressing room was opened into it to form the
Library, but the chimney-piece survives and has the most interesting order of all, a modified
composite with the volute horns turned inwards (Fig. 45). This was a popular motif of Smith and
his associates, which came to England via the favourite baroque pattern book of the day,
Domenico de Rossi's *Studio d'Architettura Civile*.[11] Stoneleigh's capitals are distinctive in
incorporating the Leigh crest and a coronet, but otherwise very like those at Ombersley,
where the wainscot is similar enough to give confidence that the same team worked in both
houses. From comparisons with authenticated work at Davenport and Badminton, the principal
carver can be identified as Edward Poynton, both for wainscot capitals and exterior stonework.
The principal Ombersley joiner was the highly talented and well-trusted Thomas Eborall
(George's elder brother), whose work is recorded in most of Smith's houses of the 1720s and
'30s. That he was in charge of joinery at Stoneleigh – perhaps somewhat to his disadvantage –
is confirmed by entries in Lady Maria Leigh's accounts as her husband's executrix, referring to
Mr Eborall's bond of £260 on which five per cent interest was being paid (and even that was two
years in arrears).[12]

The two rooms south of the hall are quite different from those to the north, the wainscot
more routine and of deal. In Mrs Austen's time the first was the dining parlour (now the Parlour),
and that at the end the breakfast parlour (now Queen Victoria's Bedroom) where, she reported,
'we generally sit, and reason good 'tis the only room (except the chapel) that looks towards the
River'. These rooms may be among miscellaneous work done in the 1740s; but the great staircase
is certainly of Francis Smith's time and doubtless made by Eborall (Fig. 46). Again a favourite
type of Smith's – three slender balusters on an open string with ogee-moulded soffit – elegant
but manly, and used, with small variations, in almost every country house he designed.
Already in the 1720s it was a type on the way out and rejected by the Palladians. Yet Smith
must have imbued his pupils and assistants with a special fondness for it, for Nathaniel Ireson
was using it in the 1740s and David and William Hiorn twenty years later still. The appreciative
client presumably chose the completion of Smith's main work on the west wing as the occasion
to commission a handsome (though anonymous) portrait of his architect looking surprisingly
young for a man then in his middle fifties.

FIGURE 45
Capital in the former
State Bedroom,
on the first floor

FIGURE 46
The principle staircase

Mysteriously, however, the client seems to have lost interest as soon as the great wing was up. He had originally had yet more ambitious plans: a note by the fifth Lord Leigh refers to a proposal for a library 'where my grandfather intended building towards the Garden'.[13] This seems to refer to the north range of the house, where there is indeed telling evidence that the west range was designed to be followed by another: quoins at the north-east corner of the west range are clearly in an unfinished state – only rough-hacked at their edges (Fig. 24) – and indicate a proposed extension eastwards along the north front. This is confirmed by a blocked doorway facing east above the level of the roof of the existing north range: the door must have been intended to lead into a new north range with rooms at the same level as those in the west. Nothing came of this: even the hall was, as later evidence makes abundantly clear, left unfinished. For the time being the Leighs' *batissomania* had evaporated: there was no shortage of money, for Lady Leigh is said to have died 'immensely rich'. Lord Leigh apparently just lost interest in his great new works, preferring, it seems, to go on living in the east range which was evidently re-wainscoted at about this time. For the years between 1726 and his death in 1738 architecture at Stoneleigh seems to have come to a standstill.

After her husband's death, Lady Leigh apparently continued to hold the purse strings, even though her son Thomas, the fourth baron, was of age and though she herself moved out to Guy's Cliffe, just outside Warwick. Despite her wealth, she was evidently concerned not to be extravagant on the house, and most of the payments recorded from her reign were probably for maintenance and other routine work. It was only when she died in 1743 that things at Stoneleigh started moving again. Two works of note can be identified from Thomas Leigh's short life.[14] One was the building of a large dog kennel, an essential item in any landed estate in hunting country – too near the house, as it turned out: it was taken down and rebuilt further away as early as 1766, to be rebuilt yet again in 1818. The recasting of the chapel at the hands of George Eborall and the Worcester stuccoist, John Wright, with some work by the gifted Warwick carver, Benjamin King, for which he was but grudgingly paid, has lasted better. Its overall form dates from the first building of the west wing and takes advantage of the fall of the land towards the south to be on two floors – like that, for example, at Wimpole Hall – an updated version of the old medieval double-decker, in which a gallery at principal floor level is for the use of the family, while the body of the chapel, a floor lower, has a common entrance for servants and those of lower estate. Eborall redesigned the gallery and made a pulpit and pews,[15] and Wright devised and executed a decorative scheme for the walls and ceiling.

Wright was a competent craftsman, in the swim of his time: for the routine of window- and door-frames, cornices and so forth he had a limited proto-rococo vocabulary which blossomed into what he called 'Festoons' – long drops for the bare patches of the walls, made of scrolls adorned with conventional shells (Fig. 47). His precisely itemized bill[16] tells us that in addition to tabernacle frames, some for the windows and doors, some blank, Wright supplied

FIGURE 47
The chapel: John Wright's plaster-work

FIGURE 48
The chapel: John Wright's centrepiece for the ceiling

'Twenty Braggotts to Kneeing Ditto', 'Twenty Pendant Floroones under Ditto' and forty ornaments to the top and lower kneeings. Braggets can sometimes, it seems, mean wooden or leather armatures for plasterwork, and the kneeing may possibly refer to the projecting corners to his frames;[17] but squaring the numbers of these items with anything visible in the chapel has so far defeated observation. Wright's more ambitious work in the ceiling is easier to identify: for the centre he made a sunburst which he described as 'a Blaze and Blunt Rays with Nine Cherub heads in the clouds' (Fig. 48). This is sandwiched between two panels – at the gallery end 'a large figure of Hope and Angel attending with the Anchor and 2 Boys and 3 Cherubs' (the 'boys' are fledgling angels, and the cherubs merely heads), and over the altar what should be 'Four Angels sounding the Resurrection & four other figures supposed coming out of their Graves the scene a Church yard' (Fig. 49). In fact there are two trumpeting angels, two resurrecting figures and a cherub (or perhaps a boy) playing hide-and-seek behind a tombstone whose perspective Wright has failed to master. The execution is passable, though Wright had a justifiably modest opinion of his own skill at figurework: the figures look rubbery and are not anatomically very plausible.

The phrasing of his bill suggests that the conception was probably Wright's own; but during the nine years between Francis Smith's death and 1747, when he himself died, Francis's eldest son William was the master in charge. His ill-fated client died only two years later, having lost several children in infancy as well as his first wife, and leaving a young widow in charge not only of the estate but of her stepson, his seven-year-old heir, who eventually went mad, had to be confined and died without issue. Thomas Leigh's death left a legacy of debts to craftsmen amounting to at least £1,200; independently of this, Smith, who had already been paid £258 in 1746, was still owed £635.[18] It is hard to suppose that the chapel and dog kennel can explain more than a fragment of this amount. What – assuming that the debts were not of extravagantly long standing – can it actually have been for?

Possibly the orangery could account for a part, though there is no mention of it in any account, and stylistically it could well have come fifteen years later. There is no shortage of rooms upstairs that would have needed doors, wainscot, plastering and fireplaces. But the finishing of most of these cannot have preceded that of the hall, which at this point evidently did not have a permanent ceiling. What then of the hall itself – by far the largest single item, in terms of both architecture and decoration, yet to be done in the west wing? William Smith undoubtedly made designs for the hall and estimates: at the foot of a bill submitted in January 1745 he added a slightly querulous note: 'I have charg'd Nothing for the desighns and Estimates of the Hall nor any profitt out of the work at the Chapel or the Dog kennell or any thing else'.[19] It sounds as if work on the hall was to proceed without delay; and, furthermore, one William Smith design for the hall still exists – in a portfolio of drawings gathered together by the fifth Lord Leigh and the authorship attested not only by the style of draughtsmanship but by Lord Leigh's listing it in

FIGURE 49
The chapel: the resurrection scene on the ceiling

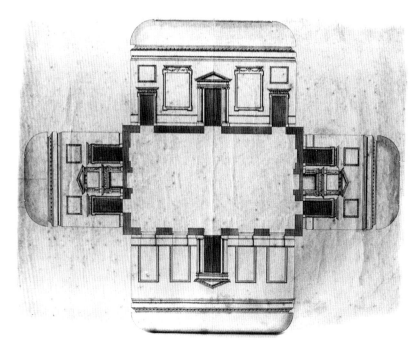

FIGURE 50
William Smith's design for the Hall (now the Saloon) (SBTRO, DR 671/33)

his index as 'Mr. Smith's design for coving the Hall' (Fig. 50).[20] This Mr Smith must be William, not Francis: the tabernacles on the east wall are exactly like those in the chapel (and others in the 'ballroom' at Stanford Hall, created by William in about 1743), the east and west doorcases – perhaps straight out of Batty Langley – are thoroughly Palladian, the secondary doorcases are exactly like those at Radburne of two or three years earlier, and the double-decker integrated chimney-pieces, in a style quite foreign to his father's, are in the generic Palladian that William used at both Radburne and Stanford.[21]

The design is not much like the room we now have; in fact the conception seems utterly different – static, with an uninviting formal symmetry, revealing all at a glance. But its very existence rules out the possibility that the hall in anything like its present form dates from before William Smith's time. Might he, nevertheless, have made the very different design that was finally built? That it is the unexecuted design that has survived is not in the least surprising: it did not have to be worn to pieces by craftsmen working from it. The hall is, of course, far richer than any other known room by Smith, and in a somewhat different idiom; but even the ballroom at Stanford was hardly anticipated in his previous work. Perhaps it, or the related saloon at Hawkstone Hall in north Shropshire, should be seen as the flexing of imaginative muscle in preparation for something greater. The character of the room is by and large right for the 1740s: it has a clear architectural form, to which rococo decoration is subordinate. Smith had used a colonnade to screen one end of the hall at Radburne and intended one at Catton, and, though at Stoneleigh the colonnades that we now see at each end are only incipient, the columns and the great beams they appear to carry define formally distinct sections of the room, leaving a perfect square within which can fit the perfect figure of the circle which is the room's climax. The conception is neither rococo nor neo-classical, but essentially of the Renaissance (Fig. 51). The order is Corinthian – taken from the Vitruvian order as exemplified in the baths of Diocletian, and already present at Stoneleigh in the great dining room, where Francis Smith would undoubtedly have taken it from John Evelyn's translation of Roland Fréart's *Parallel of the Ancient Architecture and the Modern*. Whoever designed the hall used the same order, carried out now in plaster and making a learned allusion for the benefit of those with a sound classical education: the neck of the capital appears as a woven basket surrounded by acanthus leaves (Fig. 52). Vitruvius's story of the origin of Corinthian, graphically illustrated in Fréart's engraving which the craftsman must have had in front of him, is too good not to tell once more:

> A freeborn maiden of Corinth, just of marriageable age, was attacked by illness
> and passed away. After her burial, her nurse, collecting a few little things which
> used to give the girl pleasure while she was alive, put them in a basket, carried
> it to the tomb, and laid it on top thereof, covering it with a roof-tile so that the

FIGURE 51
The Hall, now the Saloon

things might last longer in the open air. The basket happened to be placed just above the root of an acanthus. The acanthus root, pressed down meanwhile though it was by the weight, when springtime came round put forth leaves and stalks, and the stalks, growing up along the sides of the basket, and pressed out by the corners of the tile through the compulsion of its weight, were forced to bend into volutes at the outer edges.

Just then Callimachus, whom the Athenians call katatexitekhnos for the refinement and delicacy of his artistic work, passed by the tomb and observed the basket with the tender young leaves growing round it. Delighted with the novel style and form, he built some columns after that pattern for the Corinthians, determined their symmetrical proportions, and established from that time forth the rules to be followed in finished works of the Corinthian order.[22]

The principal doorcase, despite its broken pediment, is still in a restrained baroque, not at all rococo. It could have been suggested by designs by or after Inigo Jones, which since 1727 had been available in engravings by Kent and Flitcroft in a book which had clearly impressed Smith; the subsidiary doorcases might even have come from the same plate.[23] Yet, even if the hall had been left after Smith's death for his successor William Hiorn to finish, is there not after all too much rococo for even the later 1740s, and too much that is fully developed? Perhaps one could accept the splendid frieze (Fig. 53), which is not too unlike the one that Charles Stanley is assumed to have made for Okeover Hall, Staffordshire, in 1746; but the overmantel frames, and especially their cresting, would surely be prodigious for a date before 1750. Besides, there are no payments to any stuccoists at this period, nothing since those to Wright for his work in the chapel. Nor does Wright's name figure among the copious debts left after Thomas Leigh's death. The scale of these remains a mystery, for the evidence is that the main works still remained to be done.

In 1749 Edward, the new Lord Leigh, was only seven: once again there was a dowager firm of purpose in charge and once again a clamp-down on building – this time for a much longer period during which the trustees set aside £300 a year to keep things in repair, justifying the sum on the grounds that the house was 'a very large building and great part is very old'. Life at Stoneleigh must have been much damped down, with the great west wing left not only unfinished but probably largely unused.

Then suddenly, in the autumn of 1763, the house was full of workmen again, with a new architect in charge. William Hiorn, Smith's former pupil and assistant, who with his brother had stepped into prime position in Warwick when William Smith died, still had a large part to play;

FIGURE 52
Capitals in the Hall, now the Saloon

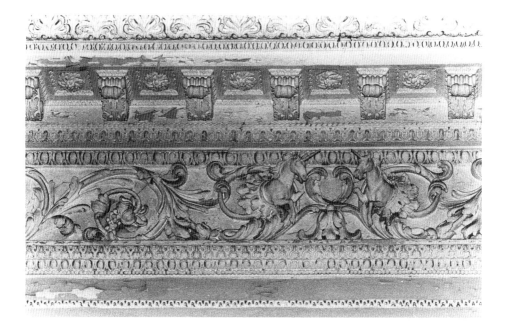

FIGURE 53
Section of frieze in the Hall, now the Saloon

but it is Timothy Lightoler who now issues directives to craftsmen and receives week-by-week reports on what they have done. Enormous amounts of money were spent during the next two or three years: the accounts are certainly not complete, but they include well over £2,000 to masons, carpenters and other building craftsmen (all this in a building whose carcase had been standing for forty years), and four times as much to London firms for furnishing and decorations, which did not include stuccowork. Among these were William Gomm and Son, cabinet-makers, who, among other things, made to Lightoler's design a pretty rococo communion table for the chapel, now in the Victoria and Albert Museum.[24]

Ambitions were far greater still: the fifth Lord Leigh clearly wanted to outmatch or trump his grandfather with a great new range of his own in a newly up-to-date manner, prepared in drawings whose cool professional precision characterizes a group of three elevations and two plans for a north range to rival the west and to include one, or maybe two, more great rooms – at a time when the hall had still not been completed and the furnishing of the rooms upstairs was barely begun.[25] The elevations all duplicate the existing north return of the west range, sandwiching between the two a colonnaded and pedimented Palladian frontispiece whose correct entablature, necessarily reducing the top-floor windows, clashes awkwardly with the broken entablature of the baroque outer sections (Fig. 54). The plan of the principal floor that goes with one of these shows a double-apsed music room; above was to be an equally large library – into which, had it ever been built, the blocked door referred to earlier would now have opened. The proposal provided a more logical connexion between the east and west ranges than existed at the time, or indeed exists today, but envisaged the family as having abandoned the old east wing to the servants, though its front was nevertheless to be made symmetrical by duplicating the existing high gables with a pair at the opposite end (Fig. 55). There were also plans for a huge elliptical stable, which, like so much else at Stoneleigh, came to nothing. Indeed, externally, apart from the duplication of an early eighteenth-century laundry block on the south side, little changed before the 1830s, when C.S. Smith reorganized the north range and made a grand approach to the state rooms via the Gilt Hall.

The style of the later drawings in the portfolio is hardly to be distinguished from that of known drawings by one or other of the Hiorn brothers. But the Stoneleigh stable plan is signed 'Timo Lightoler Invnt', and several other drawings are identified as Lightoler's in Lord Leigh's index. So, though there is a fireplace design inscribed by William Hiorn, it seems reasonable to assume that most, if not all, the others are Lightoler's. The 'Scheme for altering the Plaid Parlour' (the Parlour) is in a hand easily recognizable as his by comparison with the signed set of drawings prepared at exactly the same time for Platt Hall, Manchester (Fig. 56). The overmantel is in a frilly rococo which one finds again in the drawing room at Platt, inspired surely by the draughstmanship of a Hiorn design for Gopsall Hall, Leicestershire.[26] Lightoler had moved to Warwick from his native Lancashire before 1750 and cannot have failed to have come

FIGURE 54
Stoneleigh Abbey: design for new north front, 1760s (SBTRO, DR 671/33)

FIGURE 55
Stoneleigh Abbey: design for new east front, 1760s (SBTRO, DR 671/33)

FIGURE 56
Timothy Lightholer's
design for the
'Plaid Parlour',
now the Parlour
(SBTRO, DR 671/33)

immediately into contact with the Hiorns, who had by then taken over from the Smiths as the leading master-builders in the town. Like William Hiorn, he was a carver by training; and, though mid-eighteenth-century architectural draughtsmanship has so much in common that identification is risky without outside documentation, the near-identity of their hands suggests that they may have been in close collaboration long before the 1760s, when Lightoler was architect in charge at Stoneleigh and Hiorn had evidently picked up his old post as principal contractor.

Hiorn made a number of plainish chimney-pieces for the upper floors: he must have done something to make Lord Leigh suspicious, for the bill for them is inscribed with a minatory note from his lordship: 'Mr. Hiorn, You are acquainted that my servants are never allow'd to take any money as vails, acknowledgements, or presents. Upon discovery of bribes both tradesman & servant will be turn'd off'.[27] Mr Hiorn was not turned off, but he was not considered up to making the best chimney-pieces, which were designed by Lightoler and put into the hands of a flamboyant carver named Devereux Fox, whose most idiosyncratic piece is that in the north-west room on the first floor: he described it as having '2 Boys in the Middle with a bird, and french work tree work swags of fruit and flowers'.[28] This piece was charged modestly at £14 16s.1d. – less than Hiorn charged for a plain one. Fox's figure therefore probably refers to the carving alone, Hiorn's including also the marble. For Fox's most important work at Stoneleigh the underlying architecture was provided by John Bastard the younger of Marylebone, whose other contribution was two statuary stools for water closets with brasswork complete. Bastard and Fox presented a joint bill and may therefore have been in partnership. Between them they made 'by the order of Mr Timothy Lightolder' two Portland stone chimney-pieces for the hall, for which they charged £99 11s.0d. the pair, plus packing and carriage to the inn – implying that the chimney-pieces were made in London (Figs 57, 58).[29] The bill is dated 14 November 1764, and Fox's minute description can be confirmed phrase by phrase from top to bottom: no client should be in doubt about what he was paying for.

> In the Cornice the little Oge with three Leaf Grass, the Ovolo in Bedmould
> with Eggs and Tongues; in the frize each side of Tablet, Groops of Laurel and
> Oak Leaves, with Acorns and Berrys tied together with Ribbons, the Torus to
> the plinth of the Terms with six raffled Floors and double Tongues, the Terms
> with Hercules Heads, with a Lyon mask'd in the top with the Skin hanging
> down over the Shoulders tied in a Knott, and hanging down in the front.

The Herculean theme is, as Fox perhaps deliberately implies, especially to be noted, and is one that we must return to; but at last there is a certain date for something in the hall, with, moreover, Lightoler's name firmly attached as designer. There are supporting documents. Lightoler's set of instructions to the carpenter Thomas Stokes, dated 22 October 1763, is indeed

FIGURE 57
Hall, now the Saloon:
south chimney-piece

FIGURE 58
Hall, now the Saloon:
north chimney-piece

most instructive: he drew out a structural plan for framing the hall and another of a typical 'partition truss' (Fig. 59), explaining:

> Timber to be prepear⁴ for the truss partitions to Go over the Hall to Geather
> With all the Cross partitions the Whole to be well and Close fram⁴ and well
> Strap¹ as shewn in the drawings the flooring Joysts not to Dovetale in to the
> Beame but Lap¹ and joyted as shewn at A and Spiked at the top. let the Ciling
> Joysts be lap¹ 1 Inch under the Beame and Spike⁴ up and the ends to be
> Spliced as shewn at B to provent the Ciling from Cracking. to take Grate ceare
> that all the ends of the timbers have proper bearings on the Walls and that the
> leay [they lie] on Boulstars of Oke; and an Arch turnd over the ends of all the
> Beams so larg as not to tutch them but to admit the eyeor [air] to pass freeley
> round them.[30]

Such detailed instruction from architect to craftsman marks a turning point: no medieval carpenter would have allowed anyone else to tell him how to frame a floor. Lightoler added little sketches to help Stokes, perhaps over what were then novelties. Oddities which need some explanation are the pecked vertical lines running across the right-hand half of the framing plan (two between each pair of beams, or girders), which Lightoler's legend tells us indicate 'pieces of Boards let in betwixt the Joysts as tight as possable the whole depth of them that those are Eaquall to a Beame'. Presumably Stokes was to understand that the other half of the ceiling was to be treated in the same way, and the intention here is probably to create something similar to what was known as a bridging floor, which (as Francis Price explains in his widely-used handbook, *The British Carpenter*) is 'framed with a binding, or strong joist, in every three or four feet distance, and flush to the bottom of the girder'.[31] In view of the size and consequent weight of the plaster ceiling which the joists were to carry, and the need to prevent cracking, additional cross-bracing was probably felt necessary and these boards were perhaps a cheaper or easier way than putting in full binding joists.

The mighty 'truss partitions' with which Lightoler proposed to divide the space over the hall suggest at first a man on a boy's errand. But they were designed to be more than partitions: the legend on the framing plan explains that the girders near the ends of the hall 'need no truss in them as the Columns stand underneath'; that is, unlike the inner girders, they were thought to have adequate support from below, whereas the latter had to be partially hung from the upper truss, made up of counterbeam, bressumer and principal braces, and resting on 'king pieces' within the walls.[32] The practice of suspending large ground-floor ceilings from roof trusses was not new: this was a sophisticated variation probably developed from partition trusses shown in Price's book.[33] To fit the trusses shown on the framing plan, Lightoler at first devised a symmetrical layout of rooms on the first floor with a central vestibule entered through a Venetian

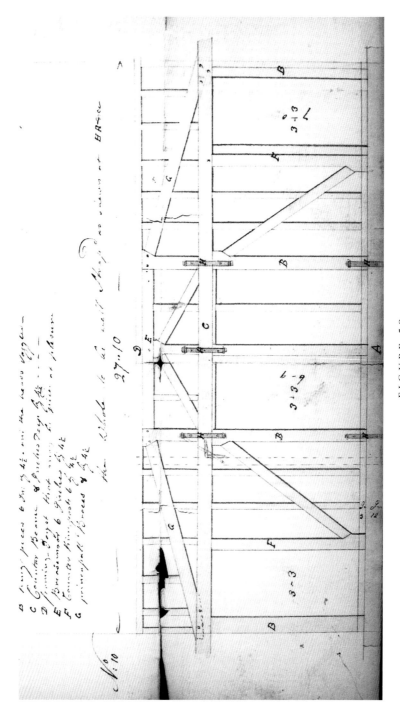

FIGURE 59

Constructional details by Timothy Lightoler for the first-floor truss partition
(SBTRO, DR 18/3/47/51)

door or serliana. This, however, went ill with the approach to the chamber floor up the great staircase, which takes off opposite the main door of the hall, turns along the outer east wall and returns some 7 feet to the north of its starting point (Figs 60, 61). Lightoler evidently decided that it was more important to make the serliana the visual focus of the upper flights of the staircase (reflected in a Venetian window above the stair itself) than to stress its purely symbolic relation to the hall. In so doing, however, he so re-ordered the layout of first-floor rooms that the truss partitions could no longer be used. Perhaps after all they were unnecessary.

Lightoler's note about why the end girders over the hall need no truss establishes that there were then, or were to be, columns beneath them. How many, though? And how long have they been there? For at least the last century and a half the end bays have each been marked off by two columns standing only a foot or so from the side walls. They cannot have been there before the 1760s, because Lightoler made a design for the hall which is no more than William Smith's coved design with a new rococo trim (Fig. 62). Either, then, Smith's hall had been built and Lightoler was trying to smarten it up, or, finding the unexecuted design, he was using it as the base for a first shot at something better. The latter is more likely, since Lord Leigh refers to both simply as 'designs'. No drawing now survives which shows the hall as we have it, but four plans among the Lightoler/Hiorn drawings in the portfolio indicate a screen of *four* columns under each of the end beams. One of these is a further development of the Smith design – in which this time only the middle section of the room, between the controversial beams, is to be coved. There are attached columns along the long walls, and – faintly outlined in pencil on the plan – tetrastyle colonnades marking off the end bays. Two other drawings are designs for a now evidently flat ceiling, in both of which the great beams are marked with circles indicating the positions of four columns. That the full colonnades were not simply an unexecuted proposal and that they did once exist is documented in a letter from C.S. Smith to the Honourable Mrs Leigh (dated 18 October 1836) in which he refers to 'the old pillars lying prostrate'; he reveals that they were of wood and that those allowed to remain were to have new shafts of scagliola.[34] At the points on the soffits of the beams where the columns used to stand are plaster rosettes coarsely moulded in a manner inconsistent with the rest of the stucco work in the room; they were evidently made in the 1830s to cover scars left by the removal of the inner pairs of columns. Lightoler's note about the trusses suggests that he was counting on the sets of four to support them, though it is doubtful if the columns would have been of use to him in carrying a major load; for underneath the hall is the servants' hall, and the columns stood above vulnerable points of a vault too shallow to contain within it a strongly braced truss.

Experiments were clearly going on in the 1760s which show that the eventual design of the hall was still not decided, though by November 1764, when the Herculean fireplaces arrived, the overall decorative scheme had presumably been determined and was perhaps already in progress. The succession of drawings might seem to point to Lightoler as the hall's main, if

<FIGURE 60
Timothy Lightholer's design for the
landing (SBTRO, DR 671/33)

FIGURE 61>
Timothy Lightholer's design for the staircase
(SBTRO, DR 671/33)

FIGURE 62
Timothy Lightholer's design for the Hall,
now the Saloon (SBTRO, DR 671/33)

FIGURE 63>
Timothy Lightholer's drawing for the chapel door
(SBTRO, DR 18/3/47/51/7)

not only, begetter. Details are persuasive: the rococo frames of the overmantels, which must post-date the chimney-pieces at least in the making, the lesser doorcases which at first suggest Inigo-Jones-inspired William Smith but on closer inspection show unSmith-like details – leatherwork up the sides and coy sprigs of acanthus curling round the foot of the architrave. There is indeed a Lightoler drawing for the chapel door which shows the same little curls (Fig. 63).[35] The main doorcase may look unexpectedly robust for Lightoler's generally rather lightweight sensibility; but he does include some bold pieces in *The Modern Builder's Assistant*, and the Smith drawing (with an unbroken pediment for this doorway) proves that the present one cannot have survived from his father's time (Fig. 64). So is it all Lightoler? If yes, it points to an architecturally more resourceful interior designer than one might have expected from the evidence of other rooms he is known to have designed: the dining room at Platt, for example, or that at Burton Constable, or the state dining room at Warwick Castle. It is true that these are not very like one another either; but none of them suggests a mind that naturally turns to bold interior architecture rather than applied decoration. The known presence of William Hiorn may provide the explanation. A few years before the hall at Stoneleigh was conceived, he and his brother had designed and built Foremark Hall, near Repton in Derbyshire (Fig. 65). The hall, running transversely across the entire centre of the house, has a colonnade near each end, creating subordinate spaces within the long room similar to those originally at Stoneleigh, though more modest in scale; and the saloon, parallel at one end of the house, is articulated under the main beams by columns near the ends – oddly enough just as at Stoneleigh now.[36] Obviously there are drawings missing from the Stoneleigh sequence, some at least of which must have been used in the final construction of the hall; the likelihood is that the two architects worked together on it, Hiorn providing the architectural bones while Lightoler evolved the decorative layout.

The decoration – hardly an adequate word for what makes the Stoneleigh hall so memorable – has, however, so complete a scheme of its own and is at the same time so closely tied in to the room's architectural form that the master stuccoist must have been intimately involved in its creation: he cannot simply have been called in once the structure was complete. As hinted already, it is devoted to Hercules; but it seems that the architectural layout was being thought out before he came on the scene. Of the two surviving drawings for the tripartite ceiling, the more fully worked-out has for its centre a scene, evidently intended for plaster, of a chariot in the clouds drawn by two lions (Fig. 66). Lions traditionally drew the chariot of Cybele, great mother of the gods; but this one has two figures in it – both female – with a spray of palm leaves, symbols of some triumph which the surrounding cherubs confirm with their garlands and flowers. The centre of the other drawing is a blank, but the sketch in one of the end panels must surely portray a very youthful Hercules struggling to tame the Cretan bull – the barest hint of what was to follow.

FIGURE 64
Hall, now the Saloon: doorway to staircase

FIGURE 65
Foremark Hall, Derbyshire: the Hall

Throughout the eighteenth century, individual mythological scenes or single figures had, of course, been popular in paint or stucco for the decoration of English ceilings and overmantels. The selection of subjects seems in many cases as random as the quality of craftsmanship is variable. By contrast, the sequence which fills the hall at Stoneleigh, not only consistent in both style and subject but displaying a clear-cut thematic structure throughout, stands out as a complete work of art of a kind which in this country is rare indeed.

The popularity of Hercules as the type of virtue or courage triumphant over difficulties and danger makes it surprising that he does not figure more often in English country-house mythology, kept alive as it must have been not only by grand tours but by regular reading of authors as diverse as Homer and Cicero. Sculpturally as well as verbally, he had been frequently absorbed into Judaeo-Christian imagery – appearing, for instance, among Old Testament heroes and prophets on Giotto's campanile at Florence and the Certosa at Pavia – and the achievement of his famous labours was regularly displayed as a model of quasi-Christian determination. Clive Aslet persuasively suggested that Joseph Spence's poem, *The Choice of Hercules*, could serve as a model for the Stoneleigh scheme:

> The poem opens with Hercules being approached by two fair women: 'This striking sacred awe; that softer winning love.' They are respectively Virtue and Sloth. Virtue, like Minerva, a helmeted and spear-carrying figure whom Spence has already associated with men climbing craggy hills, urges Hercules to pursue his Labours in order to be worthy of Jove. Sloth, equally, holds out the attractions of the flower-strewn path. Virtue encourages the hero to sacrifice to be sure of heavenly protection. The final reward, after the Labours, is reception on Olympus: 'among the Gods, a God'. Perhaps one may therefore describe the Stoneleigh overmantels as representing The Choice and The Sacrifice, while the Labours around the walls are the prelude to being received by the gods in the ceiling.[37]

It is not quite as simple as that. Unquestionably, the north overmantel shows us the Choice, even though its layout is reminiscent of Roman representations of Hercules in the garden of the Hesperides (Fig. 58). Hercules, leaning indolently against a tree, has evidently not yet made up his mind to follow the call of Virtue, who points imperiously upwards to a tempietto perched on top of a precipitous crag: the flowery path of Sloth leads, with perhaps unconscious irony, through gentle meadows to a Palladian mansion. This, in any case, is not the start of the story: in the ceiling above this scene is a vignette of the infant Hercules strangling the snakes which the vindictive Juno had introduced into the room where he and his twin brother, Iphicles, were sleeping. Presumably the main figure, at her ease in the clouds, is Juno, though she looks curiously unconcerned at the failure of her plot. There are six subsidiary doors in the room with

FIGURE 66
Timothy Lightholer's design for the Hall (now the Saloon) ceiling (SBTRO, DR 671/33)

FIGURE 67
Hall, now the Saloon: the labours of Hercules

a sopraporta over each in the form of a large oval medallion, modelled for the most part with a ferocious power matching the violent activity of Hercules's Labours, five of which are included – in order, as one goes round the room from north to south, killing the Nemean Lion, the capture of the Erymanthian Boar, bringing back Cerberus from Hades, killing the Lernaean Hydra, and catching the Cretan Bull (Fig. 67). There is no obvious reason for the selection of these five out of the traditional twelve or for moving away from the traditional order. Almost all the Labours demanded a combination of strength, courage and cunning; so perhaps the choice depended less on the symbolic significance that any one might have and more on what the stuccoist thought would make a telling show.

The sixth medallion is reserved for a quite different episode and becomes the first of three scenes near the end of Hercules's life on earth. He has mortally wounded the centaur Nessus, who attempted to rape Hercules's wife, Deianeira, while ferrying her across the River Evenos. She stands by the dying centaur, holding a cloak which he persuades her will act as a love-potion if dipped in his blood. The modelling of this scene, though no less expert, lacks the tumultuous energy of the plaques of the Labours and prepares for a different kind of intensity in the closing scenes. The south overmantel does, as Aslet said, depict a sacrifice – not just any sacrifice, but a special one, after Hercules's victory over his enemy Eurytus, an occasion for which he has sent his acolyte Lichas to ask Deianeira for a new cloak(Fig. 57). Hercules had kidnapped Eurytus's daughter, Iole, and made her his mistress, and Deianeira, seeking to regain his love, sent Lichas with the cloak fatally dipped in the treacherous centaur's blood. He is shown arriving with it, on the right; the small figure on the left may be Hercules's son, Hyllus, into whose charge he later gave the luckless Iole. Hercules, visibly now an old man though still holding his club, will put on the cloak for the ceremonial sacrifice already burning on the altar. The resulting catastrophe is shown in the ceiling panel immediately above: Hercules writhing in agony as he tries in vain to tear off the poisoned cloak (Fig. 68). It is perhaps the most brilliantly observed and executed of the whole series, the muscular tension in the limbs and pain in the face expressed with astonishing naturalness and force.

It is not, of course, the end; but the beginning and the end of his earthly life frame the stupendous apotheosis in the middle where Hercules finally receives the reward for his Labours – being presented to Jove amid a voluptuous concourse on Olympus, where he will be finally reconciled with Juno, on Jove's left and identifiable with the lounging goddess who long ago watched him strangling the snakes (Figs 69, 70). The relief in this great tableau is for the most part fairly low and there is none of the tense physicality of the smaller panels, but the lovingly sensuous moulding of naked flesh is wonderfully supple, inescapably the product of a lifetime's study and experience. How naturally the gods stand or sit or lie, and how truly the moulding follows the contours of the muscles and flesh, how well the body is known. Is there somewhere on a ceiling in Italy or France a painted apotheosis that might lie behind this one in stucco?

FIGURE 68
Hall, now the Saloon: the death of Hercules

FIGURE 69
Hall, now the Saloon: apotheosis of Hercules

Raphael's 'Council of the Gods' in the loggia of the Villa Farnesina was doubtless well enough known to prompt many imitations and developments, and there must be no shortage of mythological coronations that might have been distantly suggestive, from Henri II's Ronsard-inspired royal Olympus at the Château de Tanlay to Minerva crowning France in the former petite galerie at Versailles; but nothing really close has proposed itself.[38]

The apotheosis is the climax of the room; but before moving finally to consider the authorship of this amazing masterpiece, there is one further suggestion to make about the symbolism of the whole series. The story clearly starts at the north end of the room and ends – on Earth – at the south, with the centre reserved for Olympus. But next to the scenes of Hercules's sacrifice and death is the door that leads, through the end of the Parlour to the chapel (Plan 2): Hercules, who has been portrayed as a quasi-Christian model of courage and pertinacity through a series of hugely demanding trials, was one of those who, like Orpheus, triumphed over death to visit Hades and return victorious – in his case with Alcestis, also a paradigm of self-sacrifice. There is, of course, no hint of that story in the Stoneleigh stuccowork; but is it an accident that Hercules's earthly death is near the entrance to the promise of another resurrection? Paul and Barnabas exhorted the disciples at Iconium and Antioch to continue in the faith, since 'we must through much tribulation enter into the kingdom of God'.[39] That certainly seems to be the message that the whole great sequence conveys: the tempietto to which Virtue points at the moment of choice might suggest a Christian church to those who had been on the Grand Tour.

Who, then, could have created it? Two names that have been put forward can be dismissed immediately. Giovambattista Cipriani was paid eight guineas in 1765 for eight (or, according to his own receipt, seven) designs for the hall, and the notion has persisted that he designed, or even carried out, the stuccoing. There are not eight, or seven, of anything in the hall, though it is not impossible that he sketched ideas for a Herculean series, which the stuccoist may have been given as a prompt to his work. But the executed panels are so obviously conceived in three dimensions that he can have learnt little from the 'feeble and gaudy' painter (as Redgrave called him[40]), whose designs at a guinea a piece must have been very small beer. John Wright died in 1753, so he cannot have been involved. A more plausible claimant is Robert Moore, who first appears at Stoneleigh in the 1740s as one of Wright's journeymen, paid at the remarkably high rate of 3 shillings a day.[41] In the 1760s he is back as his own master and in 1765-6 was paid at least £605 – a little more than twice as much as Wright received for the chapel and hence not nearly enough for the total of plasterwork now known to have been done at this time, which, in addition to the hall, includes the staircase hall and numerous rooms on the first floor.[42] So there must be missing payments to someone, and Moore is the only known plasterer whose name is recorded among the Stoneleigh accounts at this period. Moore's character as a stuccoist is chameleonic: he did routine classical at the Shire Hall in Warwick, gothick at Arbury, Jacobean

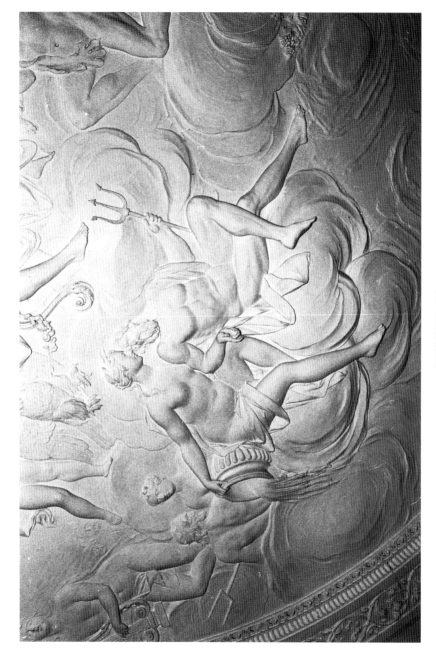

F I G U R E 7 0

Hall, now the Saloon: apotheosis of Hercules (detail)

in Warwick Castle – all of it pre-designed by an architect and all of it somewhat repetitive abstract work. On the other hand, there seems no good reason to deny him the trophies on the walls of the staircase hall at Stoneleigh. Lightoler made some fussy and confused sketches for the walls, which only distantly resemble what was carried out (Fig. 61), and very likely Moore himself designed the existing layouts, which are reminiscent of the walls of the chapel on which he had worked as Wright's journeyman. The finely wrought trophies, with emblems of the hunt mixed in with shells, scrolls and ribbons are also very like those in the saloon at Hagley, where Moore (but not Moore alone) worked in the late 1750s under the direction of John Sanderson.[43] For ceilings Lightoler seems to have preferred delicate scroll and leafwork with Chinese touches and miniature figures executed in very low relief. It was probably Moore who did similar work on Hagley saloon ceiling and also the more thorough-going chinoiserie in the Chinese room on the first floor at Stoneleigh. The staircase ceiling, on the other hand, is purely abstract – stylistically inconsistent with the walls but in touch with the formalism then newly introduced by the younger Joseph Rose working under the direction of Robert Adam.

This is all excellent work, but utterly unlike the great figurative scheme in the hall – not only because that is figurative but because it has the robust naturalism and physicality of a different and older tradition. Moore may have done occasional figurative work, but if he did the cavorting cherubs on the ceiling of the Hagley saloon, he was not even up to Wright's reach-me-down parodies of skills which were no longer being fostered as the living taste of the time. At the topmost level – that of the Hercules series – these skills could only survive as late as the 1760s in the hands of a master drawing on long experience of a rich tradition then at the point of passing. At this point, against a huge shift in sensibility, no-one *could* learn to master this manner at such a level of accomplishment. The decline in figurative plasterwork is almost everywhere marked at this period, not only in provincial craftsmen like Wright but in those of greater reputation. To look at the contemporary work of Giuseppe Cortese is to be reminded of what happens when lesser men try to keep alive a style which is dying because the sensibility which informed and gave it life has yielded to something very different. His figure of Justice, for example, executed in 1762-3 on the ceiling of the courtroom in the guildhall at Beverley, is well sculpted, with especially good drapery, but in no sort of relation to the clouds she is supposed to be sitting on, and the clouds themselves are mere slabs of putty. There is an unattributed Judgment of Paris at Merly House, Dorset, of about the same date: no more than paraphrases of human bodies, the goddesses' breasts just token pudding basins by contrast with the lovingly understood flesh of a river goddess at Stoneleigh. A master steeped in an older sensibility could still bring it off. Furthermore, the technique employed in casting the scroll frames throughout the hall and the brilliantly undercut friezes, which are all refinements on Wright's craftsmanship, depends on extensive use of reverse casting moulds as in traditional English work, very different from the direct modelling by means of 'poussir-irons' used in the figure panels: there must have been at least two hands at work on the plaster in Stoneleigh hall, and it is the one trained in English technique who is most likely to be Moore.

So, though Moore's is the only stuccoist's name we have in the books, and though it may seem folly to look for someone else, we must. He might just be English, trained, as the Perritts of York were, in the 'Italian' tradition'; but probably not, because, like the Perritts, they had mostly moved on with the times. It is happily no longer fashionable to assume that any decent plasterwork in England must have been done by 'Italians' – who mostly came from the Italian-speaking Swiss cantons, though some were Danish or German. When John Wright, conscious of the limitations of his own skills, told Lady Luxborough that 'where more elegance is required he employs an Italian under him',[44] all we can be certain of is that the talented subordinate was not English. If Wright acted in this way, so also might his one-time journeyman, so that the absence of a second stuccoist's name in the accounts may not signify. Indeed, there is suggestive evidence that Moore may have done just this at Hagley. The saloon there may be entirely his, but, whatever else Moore did in that house, he did not do the hall overmantel, which, in a gesture of prophetic helpfulness to historians, Francesco Vassalli had the foresight to sign. Nevertheless, unlike Moore's, his name does not appear in the Hagley accounts. Since, plainly, the same man did not do both the babes on the saloon ceiling at Hagley and those in the hall, perhaps Vassalli had the Hagley hall to himself. Like many artist-craftsmen, he had a way of conserving his talents: nearly identical medallions at Townley Hall (Lancashire) and Shugborough (Staffordshire) were made at least eighteen years apart and might have been done at any point in his long career, which had started in England at least as early as 1715 when we know he was at Duncombe Park.[45] So he was in his sixties or even more at the time of the Stoneleigh hall. At this point, however, Vassalli was certainly still at work, for in 1763 Philip Yorke, visiting Shugborough, enthused over his new ceiling in the dining room there:[46] Apollo at breakneck speed in his chariot accompanied by the racing Hours. Apollo's breast and the naked back of one of the Hours have the same vivid muscularity of the sculpting at Stoneleigh, and, though most of the hours are clothed in deeply ruched drapery, one knows from its movement and flow that there are again muscular bodies underneath. The shallow relief of the landscape on the right brings us back to that in the 'Choice' overmantel at Stoneleigh.

The Hercules series at Stoneleigh is perhaps the supreme masterpiece of baroque stucco sculpture in England – created in a brief Indian summer long after the main flowering period had ended. Of the 'Italians' who brought it to this country, almost all had died or long gone back to the Continent; their surviving English followers had gone on to other things, and none of their successors had inherited to the full the mastery of physique which above all characterizes this art in its higher reaches, nowhere more magisterially than at Stoneleigh. Of the finest masters there remained only Vassalli, still living near Shugborough in 1763, not too far away; and the great Stoneleigh roundel can only be his apotheosis, as it is those of Hercules and of Stoneleigh.

Francis Smith's work at Stoneleigh closely overlapped that at Sutton Scarsdale. In both cases the aim was to re-fashion a sixteenth-century house so thoroughly that it became an aristocratic mansion. The early house at Sutton Scarsdale evidently had an H-shaped plan, and around this Smith wrapped four new ranges (one of them open to allow access to the offices, rather as that on the south side of Stoneleigh) and so created what was virtually a courtyard house *de novo*. At Stoneleigh he had the four ranges of the converted monastic cloister to work on: as in so many other grandiose schemes, the ambition was never fulfilled, and baroque Stoneleigh is a torso of what it might have been – rather like mid seventeenth-century Wilton. It may seem presumptuous to offer the magisterial Jones-inspired Wilton as a comparison with Stoneleigh; but Wilton too had started as a sixteenth-century conversion of a medieval conventual cloister, and it seems highly likely that the intention was always to rebuild the other ranges behind its great suite of state rooms in the new south front. In architectural terms doubtless Stoneleigh is not a serious competitor; but a more modest Elizabethan conversion than at Wilton and the failure to complete either of the eighteenth-century schemes have left the overall history of the house much more physically visible. Although Stoneleigh has nothing remotely to compare with the courtly splendour of Wilton's state suite, it has in its one great room not only plasterwork superior to any at the more famous house but an overall conception more humanely eloquent than anything the other has to offer.

Acknowledgements

This paper is a revised version of two others, the first given at the Society of Antiquaries in 1988 and printed in *The Antiquaries Journal*, lxviii, part ii, 1988, 265-86, the second at a conference on The Later Eighteenth-Century Great House, at Rewley House, Oxford in 1997 and printed in a volume of the same title, edited by Malcolm Airs. I am grateful to the editors of both volumes for permission to re-use material from them.

CHAPTER FOUR

STONELEIGH ABBEY IN THE NINETEENTH CENTURY

Geoffrey Tyack

In 1789 the fifth Lord Leigh died, leaving Stoneleigh Abbey to his sisters and their issue, with remainder to 'the first and nearest of my kindred being male and of my name and blood'. In due course this proviso led to complications, but in the short term the estate passed peacefully to Lord Leigh's sister, Mary. She died in 1806, having left Stoneleigh to the Leigh family of Adlestrop, in Gloucestershire, where about a century later, in Edward Thomas's words, an express train was to pause unwontedly in late June.

The Leighs of Adlestrop were descended from Rowland Leigh (d. 1596), eldest son of the Thomas Leigh who first bought Stoneleigh. They were thus the senior branch of the family, but they had always been less wealthy and less grand than their Stoneleigh cousins. The first of the family to take possession of Stoneleigh was the Reverend Thomas Leigh (1734-1813), rector of Adlestrop and Broadwell, and younger brother of James Leigh (1724-74), who had employed Sanderson Miller to carry out Gothic alterations at Adlestrop Park between 1750 and 1763. He would have been an obscure footnote in the history of Stoneleigh were it not for two things. First, his cousin Cassandra was the mother of the novelist, Jane Austen, and left an account of a visit to Stoneleigh with her daughter in 1806, shortly after Mary Leigh's death:

> The House is larger than I could have supposed – we can now find our way
> about it, I mean the best part, as to the offices (which were the old Abby [*sic*])
> Mr. Leigh almost dispairs of ever finding his way about them – I have proposed
> his setting up <u>directing Posts</u> at the Angles. I will now give you some idea of the
> inside of this vast house. You go up a considerable flight of steps. into a large
> Hall; on the right hand [is] the dining parlour, within [i.e. beyond] that the
> Breakfast room where we generally sit, and reason good tis the only room

> (except the Chapel) that looks towards the River. – on the left hand [of] the hall
> is the best drawing room, within that a smaller, these rooms are rather gloomy,
> Brown-wainscot and dark Crimson furniture; so we never use them but to walk
> thro' them to the old picture gallery [in the east range]. Behind the smaller
> drawing room is the state Bed Chamber with a high dark crimson Velvet Bed;
> an <u>alarming</u> apartment just fit for a Heroine; the Old Gallery opens into it, -
> behind the Hall and Parlour [is] a passage all across the house containing 3
> staircases & two small back Parlours. There are 26 Bed Chambers in the new
> part of the house, & a great many (some very good ones) in the old.[1]

Second, Thomas Leigh brought in Humphry Repton in 1809 to suggest improvements to both grounds and house. Repton's proposals for the house, though not carried out, throw considerable light on what actually happened at Stoneleigh over the next three decades, and help us understand the rationale behind the house as we see it today.

Repton admired Stoneleigh Abbey as 'a curious specimen of the architecture of every date' from the tenth century to the eighteenth, but he thought that the house presented several severe inconveniences. In particular, the interior layout of Francis Smith's west wing (Plan 2) was not 'conformable to the present manner of living, which consists of large rooms arranged <u>en suite</u>... with the best apartments looking to the best view'. He liked the large number of spacious rooms, but thought that they were 'oppressed by the comparative great size of the Hall [the present Saloon], which separates instead of connecting the two ends of the house'. The two rooms at the north end (Cassandra's 'alarming apartment' - originally the State Bedroom and Closet, now the Library and Card Room) had 'all the dignity together with the gloom of those Cedar Parlours occasionally mentioned in the works of Richardson, when society existed without the Music, the Pamphlet, or News Papers, of the present day'.[2] His criticism of the early eighteenth-century interiors was echoed by Mary Berry, who visited the house in 1810 and bemoaned the fact that the wealth of the Leighs had descended to 'people who have done no good, encouraged no improvements, employed no fine arts, collected nothing'. As for the Abbey, it was:

> one of the worst-contrived large houses of fourteen windows in front that I
> ever saw; most of the rooms are oak boxes, floored and lined with oak, there is
> not even a pretence to a library in the house; and the present possessors, an
> old clergyman and his old sister are perfectly encumbered with the wealth, to
> which they succeeded in a late period of life, and which obliged them to leave
> a comfortable parsonage, where they had passed their best years.[3]

Repton suggested rebuilding the south range so as to incorporate a new dining room, and proposed a picturesque Italianate treatment, rather than the more common neo-classical manner

FIGURE 71
Humphry Repton's impression of Stoneleigh Abbey after proposed improvements, from the Red Book
(SBTRO, DR 671/76a, fol.20)

FIGURE 72
Humphry Repton's proposals for cottages on the estate, from the Red Book
(SBTRO, DR 671/76a, fol.29)

of the time. This might reflect the fruits of his close – but recently acrimoniously terminated – partnership with John Nash, who, in some of his influential villas, had taken to heart the advice of Richard Payne Knight:

> The best style of architecture for irregular or picturesque houses, which can now be adopted, is that mixed style, which characterizes the buildings of Claude and the Poussins: for as it is taken from models, which were built piece-meal, during many successive stages: and by several different nations, it is distinguished by no particular manner of execution, or class of ornaments; but admits of all promiscuously, from a plain wall or buttress, of the roughest masonry, to the most highly wrought Corinthian capital: and, in a style professedly miscellaneous, such contrasts may be employed to heighten the relish of beauty, without disturbing it by any appearance of deceit or imposture.[4]

In his Stoneleigh Red Book Repton alluded to this passage when he wrote: 'Instead of taking over models from Temples and other Buildings of which we hardly know the use... it would surely be better to imitate those graceful and picturesque combinations, which we admire in the works of the best painters, such as Gasper [sic] Poussin, and Claude de Loriane, and in Garden scenery the graceful Watteau'. Such a scheme is shown in a view of the 'improved' house from the south-west, showing an arrangement of Italianate terraces around the house, a colonnade, and a low urn-topped tower of a kind which was to become common in the domestic architecture of the Victorian era (Fig. 71).

For the cottages on the estate, however, Repton proposed the 'purest style of the wooden Gothic': in other words the neo-vernacular 'Old English' style pioneered by him and Nash and used, for instance, in Apsley Lodge at Woburn, Bedfordshire a very early example of what later became known as 'stockbrokers' Tudor'. In particular, he suggested building a row of mock timber-framed cottages near his proposed new bridge taking the main drive over the Avon, remarking that it should be 'an article of humanity and policy as well as of Economy to provide [labourers'] habitations within reasonable distance of their work' (Fig. 72).[5] This was a clear criticism of the eighteenth-century practice of removing villages in order to provide an uninterrupted view of a country house, though, as a Cistercian monastery, Stoneleigh had never had a village close at hand. In the event, the bridge was built in the classical, not the Gothic style, and it went up to the designs of the great engineer, John Rennie, in 1815.

Nothing came of Repton's schemes, and the house remained untouched until after the death of the Reverend Thomas Leigh in 1813. He was succeeded by his nephew, James Henry Leigh (1765-1823), son of James Leigh of Adlestrop, who had died in 1774. Almost immediately he commissioned designs for lodges and other improvements to the grounds from William Porden, architect of the Dome at Brighton Pavilion (1804-8), and from another fashionable Regency architect, Thomas Hopper.[6] These remained unexecuted, but Leigh and his wife re-furnished the house in the Regency taste, spending £13,862 on furniture, pictures, plate, china and wine between 1813 and 1823. The work was largely finished by 1819, and much of the furniture survived in the house until recently. Purchases included chandeliers, carpets, chintzes, wallpapers and eighty-two yards of crimson velvet for curtains and furniture covering. There were also substantial payments to the sculptor, Richard Westmacott, for chimney-pieces, to Mr Wyatt of 360 Oxford Street for pier glasses, to William Cooke of Warwick and others for upholstery, and to John Alcott of Coventry for taking down marble chimney-pieces from the early eighteenth-century Watergall House, demolished in 1814-15, and re-erecting them at Stoneleigh.[7]

The main architectural work carried out by James Henry Leigh was the building of a new stable block and riding house in the years 1815-19.[8] For this he went not to a fashionable London architect but to a local man, the Birmingham-born Charles Samuel Smith. He had been trained under Jeffrey Wyatt (later Sir Jeffrey Wyatville), one of the sons of the architect James Wyatt, and built up a practice in the rapidly expanding Leamington Spa, where he designed the Pump Room (1813-14), the Regent Hotel and the upper Assembly Rooms (since demolished).[9] These are, or were, in the classical style, but the stable block at Stoneleigh is in Tudor-Gothic, chosen no doubt to allude to the origins of the house as a sixteenth-century private residence. Built of local red sandstone, it embodied major changes in stable-design which followed the growing popularity of thoroughbred racing horses in the late eighteenth century, with loose-boxes, accommodation for grooms and a spacious riding-house for indoor horsemanship, complete with a gallery from which the horses could be observed by visitors to the house. The stables themselves are arranged in a semi-circle, inspired by the stables at Belvoir Castle, in Leicestershire, which Smith had seen, with coach houses occupying the building in the chord of the arc and the riding house next to the entrance, which is surmounted by a crenellated tower (Fig. 73). A covered way (since demolished) leading to the north front of the house was built in 1819-22. The cost, excluding the covered way, was £8,055. Smith also prepared designs for a number of estate cottages and lodges, including Grecian Lodge at the main entrance to the estate (1815) and some essays in the neo-vernacular style which Repton had proposed a few years earlier (Ruin Lodge and Thickthorn Cottage in 1818, Mary Lodge and Deerkeeper's Lodge (Figs 117-118, for example), some of them thatched, though built of local stone rather than of mock-timbered construction.[10] He also designed the fanlight over the Norman arch to the courtyard of the house in 1821.

James Henry Leigh died in 1823 and was succeeded by his son, Chandos Leigh (1791-1850).[11] Chandos did nothing to the house for fifteen years, possibly because his mother (who died in 1843) was still in control. She was eager to revive the Leigh peerage on her son's behalf, but she was challenged by an alternative contender, George Leigh of Blackrod, in Lancashire, who in 1813 had claimed descent from the fourth son of the first Lord Leigh. His case was argued in a

FIGURE 73

Stoneleigh Abbey, the stables and riding school: drawn and lithographed by John James Brandard, c. 1830

FIGURE 74
The Long Gallery

FIGURE 75
The Gilt Hall, *c*.1950

book of 1832,[12] but his claims were found to be fabricated and in 1839 Lord Melbourne's government gave the title to Chandos Leigh. The alterations carried out by Chandos Leigh between 1836 and 1839 were clearly related to his peerage claim, and were finished in the year of his elevation. But they also put into effect some of the ideas first broached by Repton for making the house more comfortable. One important change was the introduction of a hot water system. Another was the transference of the main entrance from the west to the north range, built out of the south aisle of the monastic church. Thomas Hopper had prepared a classical design for a new entrance in the north range in 1836,[13] but, as had happened with the stable block twenty years before, he was dropped in favour of C.S. Smith, who had already drawn up designs for remodelling the north range in both the classical and 'Old English' styles in 1813, when the idea of turning the gallery there into a library was being discussed.[14]

In a letter of 1837 Chandos Leigh made it clear that he wanted the work to be economical but substantial, and in 1838 he told his mother that 'economy [is] certainly after the expenditure of so much money our object';[15] the cost to 1838 (when the work had largely been finished) was £7,184. He opted for the neo-Tudor style, allowing some of the masonry of the north range to be kept and its outward, though not, alas, its internal, appearance preserved. Smith had recently supervised work in the 'Old English' style at Charlecote for George Hammond Lucy, and he was currently building Grove Park (since demolished) in a similar idiom for another local peer, Lord Dormer; the neo-Tudor style was also being used by William Stratford Dugdale and his architect, Edward Blore, at Merevale Hall, near Atherstone. The work in the north range entailed removing the floor of the long gallery and the seventeenth-century external flight of steps leading to it (Fig. 25), and the creation of a new ground-floor entrance protected by a gabled porch. This leads into a Long Gallery (Plan 2) with a plaster rib-vaulted ceiling and walls lined with Jacobean-style panelling, some of it brought from the recently-demolished Fletchamstead Hall, another of the Leighs' houses (Fig. 74). At Stoneleigh, as at Charlecote, much of the internal effect of the new work depended on the decorators and craftsmen employed. They included the stained-glass artist, Thomas Willement, the guiding spirit behind the interiors at Charlecote, who designed a series of heraldic windows in 1837 showing the descent of the Leighs from royalty;[16] the plasterer, Francis Bernasconi; and the Warwick woodcarver, James Willcox, who was responsible for the panelling and whose work can be found in several early Victorian country houses in Warwickshire.

Access from the entrance hall to the west range is gained by an enclosed flight of steps built out into the courtyard. This leads to a second hall known as the Gilt Hall after the lavish gilt furniture presumably acquired by James Henry Leigh and formerly displayed there. This is a spacious classical room, with some of Willement's armorial stained glass displayed in one of the windows, and is divided by Tuscan columns from the Billiard Room in the west wing, next to the main staircase, formerly described as the Coffee Room and, in the early nineteenth century, a parlour (Fig. 75 and see Plan 2).[17] From here a lobby leads into Chandos Leigh's new Library,

FIGURE 76
The Library

FIGURE 77
The Saloon, *c.*1950

created out of the former state bedchamber (Cassandra Austen's 'alarming apartment') and its closet, with two round arches cut through the wall separating the two.[18] This dark room, with early eighteenth-century panelling taken from Watergall House,[19] not only catered for Chandos Leigh's scholarly interests it also, together with the neighbouring Billiard Room, created a 'male domain' of the kind which was then deemed to be essential in an up-to-date country-house establishment (Fig. 76).

The two drawing rooms flanking the new Library to the west – latterly known as the Silk and Velvet Drawing Rooms, and now the Card Room and Brown Drawing Room – were unaffected by the alterations. The former entrance hall, however, at the centre of the west front now became another reception room, called the Saloon, by the simple expedient of removing the central columns which had had the effect of chanelling visitors through to the staircase; the remaining columns were encased in scagliola. In a letter to his mother Chandos Leigh argued against cluttering the room with excessive amounts of furniture – she had proposed introducing cabinets – and early photographs show it largely clear of furniture, save for the superb early eighteenth-century chairs which had been in the west range since it was first occupied (Fig. 77). Beyond, the Dining Room (now the Parlour) and Morning Room (used as a breakfast room when Cassandra Austen visited the house, and now furnished as Queen Victoria's Bedroom) remained unchanged, as did the Chapel.

Smith, like Repton before him, originally hoped to construct a new south range,[20] but it was hard to argue the practical necessity for this in a house whose main problem was that it was too large. So the south range remained as it was: a corridor with a study and other rooms leading off it, with a passageway between the west range and the kitchens and domestic offices underneath. It was, however, re-faced in stone, and some work was also done to improve the kitchens.[21]

Lord Leigh died, of apoplexy and paralysis, at Bonn in 1850, and was succeeded by his son William. Educated at Harrow, he had gone to Trinity College, Cambridge, and had unsuccessfully contested North Warwickshire for the Liberals in 1847. He married a daughter of the second marquess of Westminster and became Lord Lieutenant of Warwickshire in 1856, having been described two years before as 'the handsomest, most good-natured, least assuming person possible'.[22] His first alteration to Stoneleigh Abbey came in 1851, when he employed William Burn, one of the most talented and prolific of all Victorian country-house architects, to design a handsome conservatory on the south front and 'other works' (Fig. 78).[23] Then, in 1858, he employed the fashionable firm of Moxon & Co. to decorate a suite of five upstairs rooms in the west range at a cost of £5,661 for a visit by Queen Victoria and Prince Albert *en route* to open Aston Hall, Birmingham, to the public.[24] According to the journal of Lord Leigh's daughter, Georgiana, the rooms, on the southern side of the west range, were chosen as the best *en suite* and the easiest to shut off from the rest of the house. They were decorated in white and gold, with green silk damask hangings for the Queen's bed (which survived in the house until the

FIGURE 78
The Conservatory

FIGURE 79
Queen Victoria's Bedroom, on the first floor, *c.*1950

1960s) and Chinese silk wall hangings in the adjoining sitting room and antechamber (Fig. 79). The Silk Drawing Room downstairs was also given over to the Queen's use and was newly furnished with crimson velvet curtains and amber silk damask.[25] The visit, coming not long after the social and political difficulties of the 1840s, was treated as a celebration of the virtues of *noblesse oblige*; in the oleaginous words of H.T. Cooke's *Guide to Warwick Castle*: '… every one, both high and low, rich and poor, was entertained by the noble owner, in the most hospitable manner, so as to call forth, even from majesty itself, expressions of congratulation'.

In many ways Queen Victoria's visit marks the apogee of Stoneleigh Abbey as a great aristocratic house. Lord Leigh was the largest landowner in Warwickshire, with an estate of 14,891 acres bringing in by the 1870s an annual return of £23,043 (increased to £32,013 if his estates outside the county are taken into account).[26] The house was modernised, well-furnished and well kept-up. As part of the 'Shakespeare Circuit' it was accessible to visitors, and was described and celebrated in many publications. When Lord Leigh died in 1905, at the age of eighty-one, he left a fortune of £224,000 and an estate which was still, despite the recent depression in agricultural prices, largely intact. But this was soon to change, and the twentieth century was to bring vicissitudes of a magnitude which would have been difficult to anticipate when the Queen and her entourage were greeted by Lord Leigh and the local populace in 1856.

PART TWO

PEOPLE

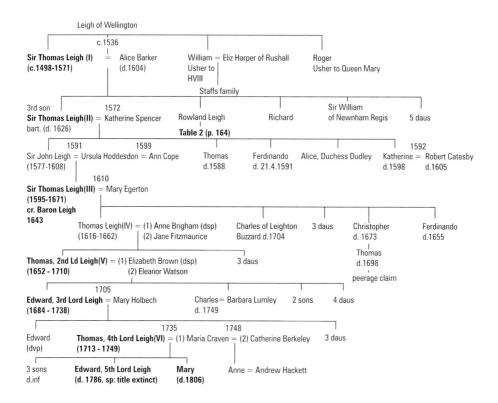

T A B L E   1
The Leighs of Stoneleigh, to 1806
(owners of Stoneleigh in bold)

CHAPTER FIVE

'Not unmarked by some eccentricities':

THE LEIGH FAMILY OF
STONELEIGH ABBEY

Mairi Macdonald

As with many families which came to prominence in the aftermath of the Reformation, the Leighs of Stoneleigh, whilst acquiring large estates and local influence, played a very modest role in the national scene. They never held high office nor, before the nineteenth century, did they marry into the upper reaches of the nobility, preferring, or being relegated to, establishing links with families of similar standing in Warwickshire and surrounding counties. Their progress can be seen as a steady consolidation, strained periodically by the untimely deaths of elder sons and the drain of providing for daughters. Nevertheless, by 1873 the Leighs were the largest landowners in Warwickshire, with 14,891 acres and an annual income from their Warwickshire estates of £23,043. Their total income from land, including extra-county property, was £32,013.[1]

The sixteenth-century Leighs claimed descent from families of the same name settled in Cheshire from the thirteenth century, but their immediate ancestry had lived in Shropshire for the preceding three generations. Richard, grandson of Sir Piers Leigh of Lyme in Cheshire, settled in Wellington, in Shropshire, and it was his great-grandson Thomas (I) who, having made his fortune in London, bought the Stoneleigh estate in the reign of Elizabeth.[2]

Thomas (I) became a freeman of the Mercers' Company in 1526 as 'late apprentice to Sir Thomas Seymer'.[3] A portrait of him in late life, aged seventy has the addition: 'Vixit annos 73' (Fig. 80) and, as he died in November 1571, his birth can therefore be placed in or around 1498. By 1536 he had married Alice Barker, alias Coverdale, the niece and heiress of a fellow mercer, Rowland Hill, also with Shropshire origins. Thomas rose steadily through the hierarchy of the Mercers' Company, granted his livery in 1536, elected one of the four wardens in 1544, and serving as master of the company in 1553-4, 1558-9, 1563-4 and 1568-9. He made similar progress in civic affairs, being chosen alderman for Castle Baynard Ward in October 1552, moving to Broad Street Ward in 1556 and finally to Coleman Street Ward in March 1558. He served as sheriff in

FIGURE 80
Sir Thomas Leigh (*c*.1504-1571), founder of the Leighs of Stoneleigh Abbey

FIGURE 81
Dame Alice Leigh, née Barker (d. 1603), wife of Sir Thomas Leigh

1555-6 and in October 1558 was elected Lord Mayor of London, in which capacity he escorted the new Queen, Elizabeth, into the city.[4] Knighted during his mayoral year (before 9 February 1559), he was, as 'my most suer and faithfull frende Sir Thomas Leigh knight and Alderman of London ... in whom I have no manner doughte', made the residuary legatee and sole executor of his friend and probable patron Sir Rowland Hill, who had himself been Lord Mayor in 1549-50.[5]

Leigh must not been seen purely as a country boy made good in the capital, for he had connections with the court and city which stood him in good stead. According to the Heralds' Visitation of 1619, one brother, William had been an Usher to King Henry VIII and another, Roger, fulfilled the same function for Queen Mary. Likewise, he seems to have had an uncle and namesake who left him well-provided; on his death in November 1545, Sir Thomas Leigh of 'Hogston' [Hoxton] beside London in the county of Middlesex, esquire, left his house called 'Hogsdon' to his nephew, Thomas Leigh, eldest son of his brother William, with remainder to William Leigh, younger son of William. Later, on 20 December 1570, Sir Thomas Leigh of Stoneleigh is found sealing and subscribing his will 'at my housse at Hogston'.[6]

It may have been this inheritance, combined with the profits of a successful business, which encouraged Thomas Leigh to invest in land from the 1550s onwards, a time when many former religious estates were on the market. His wife Alice had brought him lands at Longborough in Gloucestershire from her uncle, and in 1553 Thomas added the nearby manor of Adlestrop, lately belonging to the abbey of Evesham, which he bought from the Crown for £1,429.[7] His first Warwickshire acquisition was Thickthorn, in Ashow, the lease of which he bought in 1555. Then, on 15 March 1561, letters patent were issued to William Cavendish, cousin and heir of Charles, duke of Suffolk, to convey to Rowland Hill, knight, and Thomas Leigh, knight, the site of the monastery of Stoneleigh with divers lands, granges, mills and woodland in Stoneleigh, Ashow and Bubbenhall. Letters patent confirming the subsequent conveyance were granted to Sir Thomas Leigh and Alice his wife on 26 January 1562.[8]

By 1565, a survey of Sir Thomas Leigh's estates showed that, in Warwickshire, he now owned, as well as Stoneleigh, lands and manors in Newnham Regis, Newton, Churchover,[9] Leek Wootton, Church Lawford, Thurlaston, Rokeby and Dunchurch. In Gloucestershire and Worcestershire his holdings comprised the manors of Adlestrop, Bledington, Maugersbury, Middle Littleton and Longborough and, further afield, he owned the manor of Swinford, in Leicestershire, all former religious estates.[10] A settlement dated 20 March 1569, confirmed by his Inquisition *Post Mortem*, gives further details of his holdings and of his family shortly before his death. In addition to the property in Warwickshire, Gloucestershire and Leicestershire specified above, he held (as leaseholds from the Mercers' Company) a capital messuage and four tenements in Old Jewry, London; also a capital messuage in the parishes of St Olave and St Stephen, and messuages and lands in Hoxton, Spitalfields, Kilburn and Holloway in Middlesex. Most of this real estate was settled on his wife, Alice, for life but to be divided thereafter between five of their children: Kilburn and Islington to Richard; Stoneleigh, Stareton and Ashow to Thomas; Newnham, Churchover, Church Lawford, Newton and Kingswinford to William; premises in the city of London to daughter Isabel and the Gloucestershire estates to son Rowland. Alice also had absolute settlement to her of the manors of Littleton and the Hoxton and Spitalfields premises. His will, proved on 14 December 1571, mentions four daughters, Mary, Alice, Katherine, Winifred and Isabel, all married by the time of their father's death and already provided for by marriage settlements.[11] Richard, the second son, was settled in London and little is known of him subsequently.[12] Sir Thomas's will further includes the usual charitable bequests to the poor and for the repairing of roads, with a specific bequest to the Mercers' Company of 'one fair cup with Maidenhead' which was to be used at the election of the warden. This beautiful gilt and enamel cup survives and is still so used. It bears the inscription 'To elect the Master of the Mercerie, hither am I sent, and by Sir Thomas Leigh for the same entent'. Thomas was a supporter of the Protestant cause, as one would expect from his association with Hill, the first Protestant Lord Mayor of London. By his will he bequeathed his soul '... trusting assuredly by the merits of his most blessed death and passion to be one of the number of his elect and saved children and remain with him in the Kingdom of Heaven' and his body to be buried according to the 'laudable custom of the Church of England'. He died on 17 November 1571 and was buried in the Mercers' Chapel in London where an inscription testified to his virtues.[13]

After the death of Sir Thomas (I), the fortunes of his children, other than Thomas (II), the inheritor of Stoneleigh, need not detain us long, but it is worth mentioning that the elder line, descended from Rowland and settled in Gloucestershire, were to re-enter the picture in the late eighteenth century on the failure of the Warwickshire branch. Sir Francis Leigh, the grandson of William Leigh, who inherited Newnham Regis, was created earl of Chichester in 1644, the title passing by special remainder to his daughter and sole heir, and the estate eventually, through female heirs, to the dukes of Buccleugh.[14]

There is no evidence as to how much time Sir Thomas (I) spent at Stoneleigh, but Alice Leigh, who survived her husband twenty-one years, lived there for most of that time and was buried at Stoneleigh in 1604. During her widowhood she established the almshouses in the village, for five poor men and five poor women, who were to be unmarried.[15]

On his father's death, then, Stoneleigh Abbey and the greater part of the Warwickshire estates passed to the third surviving son, Thomas (II) who, in 1572, married into another family of rising gentry. His bride was Katherine, daughter of Sir John Spencer of Wormleighton and Althorp, and a series of settlements by Alice and Thomas confirmed the estates to the heirs of Thomas and Katherine and provided for a jointure of £600 to Katherine.[16] Their son, John, was born shortly thereafter: by the settlement of 19 November 1588, on his marriage to Ursula Hoddesden, daughter and heir of Sir Christopher Hoddesden of Leighton Buzzard, he was still under eighteen.[17] With this marriage came extensive Bedfordshire estates, destined to provide for younger sons.[18] Another marriage, potentially profitable to the Leighs, took place in 1592 when Sir Thomas (II)[19] married his eldest daughter, Katherine, to Robert, son and heir of Sir William Catesby of Ashby St Legers in Northamptonshire. Catesby estates at Chastleton, Ladbroke, Radbourne, Bushwood, Lapworth and Ashby were settled to the use of Robert and his heirs, but Katherine died before 1598 and Robert was killed in the aftermath of the Gunpowder Plot, of which he was the presiding genius.[20]

Sir Thomas (II) Leigh's career was uneventful but worthy. He fulfilled the usual roles associated with country gentry, serving as sheriff for Warwickshire in 1580-1 and again in 1594-5; he was collector for Knightlow and Hemlingford Hundreds for two taxes, the Aid for Knighting Prince Henry in 1609, and the Aid for Marrying the Princess Elizabeth in 1612. On 29 June 1611 he was created a baronet.[21] In 1605, his inherited estates in Stoneleigh, Ashow, Stareton, Leek Wootton and Fletchamstead were said to comprise one hundred messuages, sixty tofts, ten mills, 100 gardens, 3,000 acres of arable, eighty acres of meadow and 2,000 acres of pasture.[22] He also bought estates at Ardington, in Buckinghamshire, which were settled on the Spencer trustees of his marriage settlement and, more importantly, at Hamstall Ridware, in Staffordshire, which he acquired in the period between1600 and his death in 1626. By 1629 when his grandson, Sir Thomas (III), was granted a licence to alienate the Staffordshire estate, it comprised more than 2,200 acres.[23] In addition, the first marriage of John, elder son of Thomas and Katherine had brought, as mentioned above, estates in and around Leighton Buzzard. Ursula, John's wife, died after giving birth to two sons, Rowland and Thomas (III) and in 1599 John took a second wife, Ann, the daughter of Sir Antony Cope of Hanwell, in Oxfordshire, by whom he had a posthumous son, John. John the elder died in his father's lifetime.[24]

A Star Chamber case in 1622 suggests that Sir Thomas (II) had attempted some enclosure of his lands, no doubt to improve his revenue. A petition from the inhabitants of Stivichall, near Coventry, asks Leigh's pardon for throwing down fences on common land, suggesting a scenario similar to that enacted in Stratford in 1614.[25] A forerunner of this may be seen in the letters patent issued to him in April 1616 granting permission to make a park of 700 acres with free warren at Stoneleigh and Fletchamstead.[26] By his will, dated 26 October 1622, Leigh ordered his burial in the chancel of Stoneleigh Church, beside his mother and those of his children already dead. He left special bequests of personal items to his daughter, Alice, Lady Dudley,[27] and to his two surviving grandsons, Sir Thomas Leigh and John Leigh.[28] Referring to the earlier settlement of the manor of Fletchamstead on his son Sir John (now deceased) and the heirs of his body by Ann Cope, he added that he had purchased more land there, from Sir John Smith and George Matthew, which was left to his grandson John, unless his grandson Thomas (III) settled on him other lands, to the yearly value of £130, in which case the Fletchampstead estate

FIGURE 82
Thomas Leigh (1595-1672), created first Baron Leigh of Stoneleigh in 1643

would pass to Thomas (III) on whom his Staffordshire lands had also been settled. Finally he left his remaining personal estate to his wife Katherine, whom he also made his sole executrix, 'whose love and respect of me hath always been such since the time it hath pleased God first to match us together (which now is full complete forty six years) as I hold all too little for so good and well deserving a wife whose wisdom and natural care I do assure myself will always be such to our grandchildren'. A codicil dated 18 January 1626, revoked a legacy of £100 and income from land to his grandson John 'in respect that I have otherwise sufficiently provided for him', and conveyed the Fletchamstead lands to Thomas (III). He died on 3 February 1626 and his will was proved on 24 May 1626. The inventory, taken 4-5 April amounted to £4,620 10s. 4d., including the contents of Fletchampstead Hall which Dudgdale credits him with building during his mother's widowhood. A licence from the bishop of Lichfield and Coventry in October 1620 gave permission for the consecration of a chapel at the Abbey.[29]

Thomas (III), born in 1595, the son of John Leigh by his first wife Ursula Hoddesdon, matriculated at Magdalen College, Oxford, aged thirteen. Two years later, in 1610, his grandparents arranged his marriage to Mary, daughter and co-heir of Sir Thomas Egerton and grand-daughter of Lord Ellesmere, the Lord Chancellor. It was clearly intended, however, that he should continue his studies, for the marriage settlement made provision for his maintenance at Oxford and for the upbringing of Mary at Stoneleigh. The Staffordshire estates were settled upon the young couple, subject to the life interest of his grandparents, and Hamstall Ridware became their main home. Thomas (III) succeeded to the baronetcy on the death of his grandfather in 1626 and seems to have divided his time and loyalties between Warwickshire and Staffordshire until 1642 when the Staffordshire estate was settled on his own son (Thomas IV) at marriage. He served as Member of Parliament for Warwick in 1628-9 and as High Sheriff of the county in 1635-7, yet in 1632/3 he was 'of Hamstall Ridware' when he settled Fletchampstead to secure a portion of £2,000 for his daughter, Katherine, after his death and in 1635-7 was His Majesty's Axbearer or Woodward for Needwood Forest in Staffordshire.[30]

Until 1640, Thomas (III) had to pay the jointures of his stepmother and grandmother, but, on the latter's death in January of that year, part at least of his obligations were removed. On the other hand, in 1641, he made a settlement of his estates to provide for a growing family: Stoneleigh Abbey, with lands in Cubbington and Westwood Heath, were settled on himself for life with remainder to his wife Mary. All other lands were to be charged after his death, with payments of £100 annually to each of his sons, Christopher and Ferdinando, a futher £30 a year to another son, John, and portions of £2,000 each to his daughters, Elizabeth and Katherine. All lands were to pass after his death to his eldest son and heir apparent Thomas Leigh (IV).[31] Charles, a son not mentioned in the settlement, was subsequently provided for by a loan of £2,000 to buy an estate at Birdingbury and the settlement on him of lands at Leighton Buzzard.

During the 1640s Sir Thomas Leigh (III) was an active Commissioner of Array and supporter of the king. In August 1642 when Coventry shut its gates on Charles I, Leigh entertained him at Stoneleigh for three days. Nevertheless, this action seems not to have brought down the wrath of the king's enemies for Robert Lord Brooke ordered his commanders, officers and soldiers in Warwickshire and Coventry not to plunder, spoil or loot the house and goods of Sir Thomas Leigh of Stoneleigh.[32] Probably as a reward for his hospitality and loyal service, he was created Baron Leigh of Stoneleigh at Oxford on 1 July 1643. Parliament, or at least the Committee for Bedfordshire, now hardened its attitude towards him. He was taken prisoner by Sir Thomas Middleton in October 1644, but, on being sent up to London on parole, was rescued by his own party between Coventry and Stafford. By 7 October 1644 a petition from the inhabitants of Leighton Buzzard refers to the lands of Lord Leigh 'all of which are now sequestered to the use of Parliament'. The sequestration was probably provoked by his escape. On 11 October Parliament ordered that Lady Leigh should have one fifth of the rents from the sequestered Leighton estates and in a letter from the Committee at Coventry to the Committee at Bedfordshire, the Warwickshire men highly praised her honour and inoffensiveness.[33] Leigh's petition in 1646, when he offered to compound, stated that, whilst he had left Stoneleigh with the king in 1642, he had never been in arms himself, nor assisted the king with men or money. He further stated that he had spent his time partly at Hamstall Ridware and partly in the king's quarters. The implication is that Lady Leigh was left holding the fort at Stoneleigh and found herself in financial straits in her husband's absence. Leigh took the oath to Parliament and compounded for £4,895.[34]

The younger Thomas (IV), born in July 1616,[35] seems to have been educated at Cambridge and, during the upheavals of the 1640s, was a strong royalist. In 1642 he married Anne Brigham, only daughter and heir of the late Richard Brigham of Lambeth. She brought with her a portion of £6,000 and the couple had the Hamstall Ridware estates, valued at £423 13s. 4d. per annum, settled on them to provide a jointure for Anne.[36] Thomas (IV) was knighted by the king on 22 August 1642, as a gesture of thanks for his father's hospitality, being described as Sir Thomas Leigh in 1647 when he and his father were cleared of their delinquency.[37] He was assessed at £800 by the Committee for the Advance of Money in 1651 and discharged on payment of £200. This may be an indication of the financial straits into which, as his father was later to claim, he had fallen as a result of his service to the Crown. He was present in London at the Restoration, and, although barred from standing for Parliament in 1660, served as Member of Parliament for Stafford in 1661-2. He died during his father's lifetime, on 5 April 1662, and was buried at Hamstall Ridware, leaving a son, Thomas (V) and three daughters, Honora, Mary and Jane, by his second wife Jane Fitzmaurice, the daughter of Patrick, Baron of Kerry and Lixnaw.

In the years of the Commonwealth, Thomas (III) had spent his time in Warwickshire, consolidating his estates and perhaps refurbishing the house which his forebears had created in the north and east ranges of the old monastic buildings. By the 1660s, when it had seventy hearths, the house was larger than any in the county.[38] Leigh, like many other loyal county men, hurried to the side of the returning monarch in 1660. Samuel Hinton, writing to John Langley on 13 May, referred to Charles II's expected arrival in London on Tuesday. 'Will Dugdale rides all this day to be there to meet him. The Lord Leigh of Stonly goes up on Tuesday, as many persons of quality do from all places ...'. A month later it was reported 'Lord Leigh and Lord Newport sit in the House of Lords', but in August he obtained permission from the Lords to go home for a month 'for his health's sake', his intention being to take the waters at Bath.[39]

Although his son, Thomas (IV) died in 1662, Lord Leigh was not made his grandson's guardian until 1666, probably after the remarriage of his daughter-in-law, Jane.[40] Clearly, for the remaining years of his life, his concern was to deal with the financial problems left by his son, preserve as much as possible of the inheritance of his grandson and provide portions for his grand-daughters. To this end a draft Act was presented to Parliament in 1670 to enable Thomas Lord Leigh and his grandson to break the entail and sell the manor of Hamstall Ridware and other Staffordshire estates to raise portions for the daughters and to pay the debts which his dead son had incurred in the service of the Crown. The Bill was opposed in Committee and not proceeded with, other means being found to provide for Honora, Mary and Jane and to clear some of the debts.[41] There may, however, have been another reason behind the attempt to raise money from the sale of the Staffordshire estates. Leigh's grandson, Thomas (V), had been born in 1652 at Hamstall Ridware, matriculating at Christ Church, Oxford, in July 1666. In April 1669, however, he married Elizabeth, the daughter of Richard Brown of Kent, both parties being under age. The marriage broke down within a few years. According to Thomas (V)'s account, the marriage was first proposed in 1668 by his grandfather: he was only sixteen and Elizabeth had been left freehold property worth £900 a year on the death of her father in 1662, charged only with a small jointure for his widow. Negotiations foundered when Lord Leigh wanted a marriage portion rather than lands, but, according to the younger Leigh's account in 1676, his bride's mother was most anxious for the match, promising that lands could be converted to money and claiming that, through her frugality, the rental had increased by £500. Leigh decided that he had better accept a profitable though humble marriage rather than become involved in time-consuming negotiations for a nobler alliance. Shortly after the marriage Mrs Brown began to hedge about the sale of the estates and it was at this point that Lord Leigh resorted to the expedient of the Bill in Parliament for the Staffordshire sale, later alleging that its failure was due to Mrs Brown's 'false suggestions'. For some of this time, the young husband was living in Kent with his wife's family where, he would later claim, his mother-in-law encouraged his wife to be either imperious or jealous towards him. His grandfather, fearing this influence, removed the couple to Stoneleigh, but Mrs Brown followed, establishing herself at Warwick and retaining her contact with her daughter. Throughout, Mrs Brown (or

FIGURE 83
Thomas, second Lord Leigh (1652-1710)

FIGURE 84
Eleanor Watson (1659-1705), second wife of Thomas, second Lord Leigh, in coronation robes

as she later claimed, Temple, alleging a subsequent marriage with a husband, since deceased) seems to have been the provoker of the dissension, but the subsequent breakdown of the marriage and very public allegations on both sides make it hard to disentangle the true facts or motives of the parties.

Thomas (III) died on 22 February 1672, during the course of these marital upheavals, leaving his grandson 'a gentleman of very towardly hopes'. He was buried privately beside his wife (who had died in 1669) in the vault 'lately erected' on the south side of the chancel of Stoneleigh church, and by his will, made five weeks before his death, provided marriage portions of £1,333 6s. 8d. each for his three grand-daughters; they were also to receive proceeds of the sale of estates in Bedfordshire. He respited the sum of £2,000 lent to his son, Charles, to purchase an estate at Birdingbury and bequeathed to him, in addition, his leasehold estate at Leighton Buzzard, held of the Dean and Chapter of Windsor, subject to the payment of £1,500 to his son Christopher, due upon mortgage. Christopher also received £100, as did his three daughters, now the Ladies Tracy, Isham and Bromley. The residue of his estate passed to his grandson, Thomas (V), who was also made sole executor.[42] Christopher died in 1673, leaving a widow Constance and a son Thomas who died without issue in 1698.[43] Ferdinando, Thomas (IV)'s other son, had died in 1655 whilst a student at Lincoln's Inn.

After the death of Lord Leigh in 1672, his grandson's marital difficulties became more acute: Elizabeth alleged that she had been kept a prisoner by her husband, the new lord, and forbidden to communicate with her relatives; he counter-claimed with theft of property and ultimately, clandestine affairs, involving, by implication, the notorious earl of Rochester. The whole dispute evidently became a *cause célèbre*, the king intervening in an attempt to resolve matters: it ended in an action for *habeas corpus* and counter-action for defamation and perjury. Eventually, in 1677, the couple separated, she going to live with her uncle, William Andrews, in Lambeth, who received £250 for immediate payment of her debts and £500 a year for lodging and maintenance. After nine years of marriage neither party was over twenty-five years of age. Lady Leigh lived with her uncle until her death in July 1678, her husband defraying £200 funeral expenses and outstanding debts.[44]

No living child had been born of the troubled under-age marriage, although Elizabeth Leigh had miscarried in 1673 and had written to her mother in 1675 claiming another pregnancy. On her death in 1678 it was therefore essential for the new lord to remarry and produce issue.[45] In October 1679 he married Eleanor Watson, eldest daughter of Edward, second Baron Rockingham, by whom he had eight children, four sons and four daughters. Of these children, born between 1680 and 1695, four, including the eldest son, Thomas, died young, leaving, by the date of his own death in 1710, only four surviving issue, Eleanor, Ann, Edward, born in 1685, and Charles, born in 1686 and married to Lady Barbara Lumley, daughter of Richard earl of Scarborough. Charles lived on the estate at Leighton Buzzard which had been left to his great-uncle Charles, son of the first lord. He had in turn bequeathed it to his nephew, Thomas (V), suggesting it be settled on his namesake, Thomas's son, Charles.[46]

Thomas (V), who took his seat in the House of Lords on 26 January 1674 as the second Lord Leigh, was described by Hearne as 'an honest debauched Tory', being one of the peers who signed a protest against the Act of Union in 1707. He wrote on 8 March 1681 to Lord Danby that he would set aside his business affairs in the country 'and render myself in Oxford the first day of the sitting of the Parliament, with resolve to serve your lordshipp (according to my judgement) as farr as justice and honour enlargeth; and farther (I presume) your Lordship expects not from ... Leigh'. Lord Leigh ordered robes for the coronation of James II in 1686 but in 1688 was paying £200 'for the service of Princess Anne of Denmark' whose coronation he was summoned to attend in 1702.[47]

Eleanor Lady Leigh was buried at Stoneleigh on 25 July 1705. Her will, dated 17 August 1700, was clearly made during an earlier serious illness for it was confirmed by her husband 'she being so ill that it is not safe to trouble her with it'. She refers to an authorisation by her husband to dispose of her goods and, after making charitable bequests to the poor of Stoneleigh and providing for the apprenticing of twelve poor boys from various parishes, she confirms earlier settlements of lands at Tilehill on her son, Edward, and at Hunningham on her younger children, Anne, Eleanor, Charles and Lewis. Keepsakes are left to her brothers and sisters and, touchingly, she also leaves to her sister, Lady Oxenden, a heart-shaped locket containing the hair of her eldest son, Thomas, who died young. There is a suggestion that her husband may have favoured some of his children more than others, for she left her money and securities in trust to her executors to invest for her younger children and to make up the deficiency 'if my Lord provides for one worse than the other'. If they were to be equally provided for by their father, then her money would also be equally divided. By the time of the death of Thomas Lord Leigh in 1710, another child had died, Lewis in 1706, leaving only Edward, Charles, Eleanor and Ann surviving.[48]

After the vicissitudes of his early life, Thomas (V) seems to have settled into quiet domestic routines, consolidating the estates by purchase and advantageous alliances. The surviving receipts and vouchers for the estate, after the date of the second marriage, record little that is not routine or accountable: the largest single bill between 1680 and 1710 was for £92 in 1683 for tailoring, although cumulatively a large sum was spent in 1684-5 on the erection of a greenhouse and in 1710 John Burroughs presented a bill for £209 for furniture to the 'Hon. Mr Leigh', presumably Edward, shortly to become the third lord.[49]

In September 1705 Thomas (V) had arranged a local and profitable marriage for his eldest surviving son, Edward, baptised in February 1685, with Mary, the daughter and heir of Thomas Holbech of Fillongley. Leigh settled lands worth £4,000 on the couple and in return Holbech's widow, herself a substantial heiress, settled the manor and estates of Maxstoke Priory, together with Holbech estates at Bentley, Shustoke and Fillongley, on trustees for Edward and his wife. Further estates at Nosterfield Priory, in Cambridgeshire, were to be sold to pay the debts of Thomas Holbech and to raise a marriage portion of £12,000 for Anne, Leigh's youngest daughter. The mansion at Fillongley, with surrounding lands to the annual value of £20, were reserved to Elizabeth Holbech for life. The apparent imbalance in the settlement would seem to indicate that the Leighs had never fully recovered from the effects of the Civil War, and that the Holbech family were willing to pay for a marriage into the peerage.[50] By 1706 the young couple were settled at Fillongley and it is possibly for the house there that the large furniture bill referred to above was incurred. Thomas (V) had inherited the Leighton Buzzard estates from his uncle, Charles, who died in 1704, and these were used to provide a home for his other son, the younger Charles. Of his daughters, Eleanor had married Thomas Verney in 1709 with a portion of £15,000: Anne, whose portion had been secured in 1705, died unmarried in 1734.[51]

Thomas Lord Leigh's will, made less than a month before his death, is of interest mainly as an indicator of his interests and connections. Bequests to the poor of various parishes and to his chaplain, former servants and current servants are included alongside those to his sister, Mary Biddulph, who is left £100 free of her husband's control and an annuity of £20 (both sums doubled in a codicil a week before his death). The most important provision is the £800 which was left to family trustees for the endowment of a school in Stoneleigh 'for the teaching, instructing & Educating of the Children of such parents who shall from time to time inhabitt and dwell within the parishes Territoryes precincts and hamletts of Stoneley Staverton Wootton and Ashow'. Lands were to be purchased to pay a salary of £20 to a schoolmaster, to repair a schoolhouse and build a house for the master. Leigh asked his heir to permit the use of the Court House in Stoneleigh for this purpose, the trustees paying a proportion of the £800 for it.[52]

Edward, the new lord, had matriculated at Balliol College, Oxford, in 1702 with his younger brother Charles, who was later enrolled at the Inner Temple. As was common, neither proceeded to a degree, using their time at University as an informal finishing school and to establish useful contacts. Charles went on to a parliamentary career, serving variously as Member of Parliament for Warwick (1710), Higham Ferrers (1714, 1715) and Bedfordshire (1722-7, 1733-4). By the time of their father's death in 1710, both were married, and Edward was the father of another Edward. Within a few months of coming into his inheritance, he and his wife may have set off on a Grand Tour, on which he acquired the ideas which were to have such an important impact on the physical appearance of Stoneleigh. A gap in the series of bills presented by tradesmen between March 1712 and February 1713 may indicate the approximate duration of their trip, but they could have been away from Warwickshire as early as June 1711 when a second daughter, Mary, was born, but not baptised at Stoneleigh.[53] In April 1711 the remaining personal effects of their father had been divided between the brothers, Charles receiving £700 for his share in

December 1712, possibly on Edward's return. Charles may have resented the responsibilities left in his hands, or his brother's delay in fulfilling their father's will. Certainly as late as 1720 Charles was writing to Edward about matters in dispute between them and referring to the delay in implementing the provisions for the endowing of a school. He writes that he himself would be willing to give land at Leighton Buzzard for the purpose, had not the will specifically named Stoneleigh.[54] Charles also expresses his concern about the treatment of their aunt, Lady Willoughby of Parham, by her son-in-law, Thomas Arden Bagot of Pipe Hall, in Staffordshire.[55] During the first fifteen years of Edward's tenure much major work was undertaken at Stoneleigh, although this seems to have come to a halt after the major structural alterations were completed in 1726, few of the new rooms being decorated during the remainder of his lifetime. This may have been through lack of financial resources, as the estate regularly carried an arrear of rents of nearly £2,000. [56]

In 1727 Edward, the third lord, was summoned to, but did not attend, the coronation of George II. This may have been due to family dislike of the Hanoverian succession. As late as 1814 the family's alleged Jacobite leanings and its consequent effect on their public life was a matter of remark by John Britton in Brewer's *Beauties of England and Wales*:

> It is curious that a strong attachment to the Stuarts pervaded this family,
> through the whole succession of its Lords, even to the last who died near the
> close of the 18th century. They never attended Parliament, and resided entirely
> at Stoneleigh, in eccentric seclusion. Their house was ornamented with
> portraits of that fallen family ... whom the judicious had long perceived the
> propriety of discarding from political recollection. Here the Lords Leigh
> passed existence, with rural sports for employment, quite indifferent to the
> public affairs of a world, where their fanciful hereditary gratitude could not
> hope for efficient exercise. [57]

Edward Leigh, the eldest son, born in 1708 (Fig. 87), went to Oxford in 1726 and seems, by the account of his tutor, William Best and his aunt, Eleanor Verney whom he visited in 1727, to have been a youth of promise.[58] In December 1726 at the end of his first term, Best sent a letter to his father assuring him that his son 'returns from college in full possession of yt sobriety & temperance & all other good habits & qualities wch he brought with him to this place and with as much Academical learning as the time He has been wth us wou'd admitt of'. His aunt, whom he visited at Isleworth the following November, wrote: 'He seems perfectly sober and good temper'd & I dont doubt but you will be very happy in him'. His father may have had some doubts of his son's steadiness of character, for he had clearly forbidden him to visit the capital, his aunt earlier remarking 'he is so very obedient to yr commands that I believe no persuasion could have tempted him to London tho' my House is but ten miles from thence'. In

FIGURE 85
Edward, third Lord Leigh (1684-1738)

FIGURE 86
Mary Holbech (d. 1743), wife of Edward, third Lord Leigh

FIGURE 87
Edward Leigh (1708-1737), eldest son of Thomas, third Lord Leigh, as a boy

FIGURE 88
Thomas, fourth Lord Leigh (1713-1749), as a boy

the few letters which survive between father and son, those from Leigh are more relaxed and affectionate, addressing him as 'Dear Ned', and writing informally, whilst the younger man confines his news to the briefest formalities and always addresses his father as 'Honor'd Sir'. [59]

It would seem, however, that within a few years their relationship was put to a serious test. In 1733 Elizabeth Meadows, a former laundry maid at Stoneleigh Abbey, gave birth in London to a daughter Eliza, who was buried a few months later. In February 1735, a son Thomas, was born at Stretton-on-Dunsmore and privately baptised at Rugby by the minister, the Reverend Samuel Towers. In a Chancery petition, Elizabeth later alleged that she had been privately married to the young Edward at Stoneleigh on 21 September 1732 by the Reverend James Hassall, Lord Leigh's chaplain,[60] and that the son, born in 1735, was therefore the rightful heir to the barony. Towers stated that he had always believed the child to be a bastard, and Charles Leigh, the father's uncle, also described him as such when telling the vicar of Stoneleigh that he would have him reared and educated. Other witnesses were brought to allege Meadows's loose character and to refer to public knowledge of various marriage negotiations for the young Edward which had been entered into with a daughter of the earl of Halifax, Lady Betty Montague. The petition failed, but the family clearly felt a responsibility to the child. Much later, Edward, the fifth Lord Leigh, left £500 in his will in 1767 for the benefit of the family of Thomas Meadows, 'the Natural son of my late uncle Edward Leigh'. In 1765 £300 was paid for the purchase of his commission in the army, as well as further sums for uniform and kit and an annuity of £50. As late as 1798 Mary Leigh authorised an annuity of £20 to Mrs Meadows.[61]

The claim, in fact, was not made public until after the death of Edward Lord Leigh in 1738, but rumours about his son's behaviour may be reflected in his will. The larger portion of the estates were already entailed on the younger Edward, but all the unentailed estates were left to his younger son, Thomas, either immediately or in reversion after the death of his mother, together with a portion of £12,000. An intriguing sentence refers to the possibility of his eldest son marrying or co-habiting as man and wife with any daughter of the Lord Halifax or the Lord Lumley.[62] Edward, the son, had signed a will in St Paul's Churchyard, on 19 January 1736 'intending to go abroad on his travels into foreign parts'. After the discharge of his debts, he left £1,000 each to his brother Thomas, his aunt Eleanor Verney and his aunt Lady Barbara Leigh, wife of Charles, who also was to have his plate, rings and jewels; £500 went to Peter Merrick, £10 to his servant Samuel Walker and the residue to his uncle Charles who was the sole executor. There is no mention of his father nor his mother, suggesting a breach between them, and that the young man had maintained the close links he established at Oxford with his aunts and uncle. Where or when he contracted the illness is not known, but he died of smallpox at Stoneleigh on 3 August 1737 and was buried five days later, aged twenty-nine. He was probably seriously ill by late July for his father's will, redrafted on 26 July, omits all references to a reversion of unentailed estates upon Edward after the failure of Thomas's issue. He did not long survive his son, dying at Stoneleigh on 9 March 1738: he was buried there seven days later, aged fifty-three. His second son, Thomas (Fig. 88), thus inherited both the unentailed and entailed estates. Pecuniary and charitable bequests amounted to some £400, the residue of the personal estate being left to his 'dear and loving wife Lady Mary Leigh for her life'.[63]

An undated inventory, taken soon after, values the contents of Stoneleigh at this time at £4,821 16s. 1½d. Rooms mentioned include the Play Closet, the dancing room, nursery, picture gallery, new buildings and mohair room. Mary, continued to live at Stoneleigh for a few years – many of the household bills during this period are addressed to her – but she subsequently moved to Guy's Cliffe where she died in September 1743, 'immensely rich' according to the *Gentleman's Magazine*. The consequent increase in income (and possibly a freedom from her influence) encouraged Thomas, the new lord, to recommence work on the house, suspended for the previous fifteen years.

Thomas had not expected to inherit the title, having a brother five years his elder, but he had nevertheless made a most suitable marriage. In August 1735 he had married Maria Rebecca Craven, daughter of John Craven of Wyken, brother of the second Lord Craven, whose seat was at neighbouring Combe Abbey.[64] Thomas inherited the title at the age of twenty-three and was living at Stoneleigh by late 1738 when his first born son, also Thomas, was buried there. Another Thomas was buried, aged three days, in 1740. Edward, born in 1743 survived into adulthood and became the fifth lord. A daughter Mary, had been born in December 1736.

The fourth lord was a young man with a young man's interests, incurring bills of more than £100 at Warwick Races in 1740. At the same time, however, he was aware of his responsibilities, implementing in the same year the terms of his grandfather's will by conveying to trustees a piece of land near Stoneleigh churchyard for the building of a school and master's house.[65] His wife, Maria, died in 1746, but thirteen months later Thomas married Catherine Berkeley, the sister of William Craven's (his brother-in-law's) wife, who was at the time of her marriage living with her sister. The non-Stoneleigh estates were settled to provide her with a jointure of £500 and to provide portions for the younger children. Their first child, Anne, was baptised in December 1748, her date of birth being given as 28 October, possibly abroad during the couple's honeymoon tour following their marriage in December 1747. A year later, on 9 December 1749, Thomas himself was buried at Stoneleigh, aged thirty-six. He must have been ailing before this for he made his will in June 1748, leaving his new wife £500 over and above her jointure and bequeathing all the estates, which were unentailed or had been purchased by his father and grandfather, to trustees to raise a portion of £15,000 for Mary, his daughter by his first wife, at twenty-one or marriage. The residue of his real and personal estate he left to trustees for his eldest son until he came of age. A codicil, added a month before his death when he clearly knew he was dying, made pecuniary provision for his servants and decreed that his funeral was to be private, attended only by his servants, 'no Executors to be at my Funeral'.[66] His obituary in Jopson's *Coventry Mercury* makes no mention of the cause of death, merely stating that he had been confined to his bed for some weeks 'during which time he bore the Severity of his Pains with a Patience becoming a good Christian'. The piece conventionally referred to him as 'a Nobleman as eminent, for his inviolable Attachment to the true Interest of his Country, as for his Hospitality and extensive Charity'. An inventory, taken early in 1750, valued the contents of Stoneleigh Abbey at £3,353 16s. 5d., a general account of his personal estate a year later, including livestock and crops, totalling more than £5,000. The annual income from lands at his death was £6,975 10s. 6d. Ironically, the estates had been further increased in 1749 by the death of Thomas's great uncle, Charles Leigh of Leighton Buzzard, who had left all his real estate, after the death of his wife Barbara, to his nephew, Thomas Lord Leigh. Lady Barbara Leigh died in 1755 and the Leigh rental was thereupon increased by nearly £3,000 per annum.[67]

On the death of the fourth lord, the Leighs were faced with the first minority of the head of the family since the acquisition of Stoneleigh in 1561. Trustees for the young Edward, aged seven (Fig. 89), included his uncle, William Craven, who seems, in the years until Edward came of age, to have been most assiduous in his duties towards his nephew. His step-mother, Catherine, did not remain long at Stoneleigh, taking with her goods to the value of £379 1s. 7d. when she left in 1750. There is little documentary evidence as to the domestic arrangements during these years, and Edward and his step-mother may well have moved to his uncle's house. A notebook, dated 1750, entitled 'Edward Lord Leigh's 1st ciphering book' survives, but the accounts are not sufficiently detailed to give much idea as to his education. During the minority the trustees kept expenditure on Stoneleigh to a minimum, allowing £300 a year for repairs to the house and gardens with a further £210 for the Park.[68]

Little is known of Edward before 1761 when, preparatory to his going up to Oxford, his trustees applied to Chancery for an increase in his allowance. Joseph Hill, the family lawyer, writing to announce that the Lord Chancellor had agreed to £1,000 to be spent on fitting Edward out for University and to an allowance of £1,000, told Craven that great approbation had been expressed of the care taken of Lord Leigh's education 'and of his Lordships own attention to his studies which I found he was assured of before'.[69] Edward matriculated at Oriel College in July 1761 where, amongst his near contemporaries, were William Craven, his cousin, and John Chichester, brother to Arthur, earl of Donegal, a Warwickshire neighbour. His tutor was probably the Reverend John Clerk, Fellow of Oriel, to whom he left £200 in his will. Between July 1763 and 1766 receipts and vouchers record regular and often large purchases of books, music, musical instruments and scientific equipment.[70] Edward was due to come of age in March 1764 and from 1763 work was clearly being undertaken at Stoneleigh Abbey to make it a suitable home for the young lord. A major redecoration programme was instituted under the direction of Timothy Lightoler, and furniture ordered from various London suppliers. In January 1764, when Thomas Burnett of London wrote asking if the furniture and fittings which were ready could be delivered, Samuel Butler the agent replied that 'our house is now in greater confusion than ever ... as we are making great alterations in the middle part of the House'. In February Butler, writing to Lord Craven was concerned about Lightoler's costs. 'It would be a very disagreeable circumstance to his Lordship to run aground before he was aware'. There was no real suggestion that the estate could not bear the costs, merely that ready money might be found wanting. As late as April that year only the 'wrought' room and the chapel were ready for furniture.[71]

Prior to 1767 there is no evidence that Edward was anything other than completely well, and perceived so by his family and servants.[72] From the date of his coming of age, Leigh was settled at Stoneleigh, overseeing work on the house and grounds, yet still finding time to indulge in activities associated with his rank and age. In 1764 John Payton of the White Lion Inn in Stratford was commissioned to find suitable accommodation, with stabling for twenty horses, for Lord Leigh and his sister when attending the Stratford races. He was clearly interested in current affairs, arranging for the *St James Chronicle,* the *Gazetteer* and the *London Daily Chronicle* to be sent to Stoneleigh. Mary Leigh, Edward's elder sister, born in 1736, was particularly close to her brother, although spending much of her life in London or travelling to the fashionable resorts.

In 1767, when Edward was twenty-four, the future prospects for Stoneleigh and the family seemed bright. Clearly an educated and cultured young man, with a fine country mansion substantially altered and decorated to the latest taste, Edward needed only a wife to add lustre and issue to the family.[73] Before entering into negotiations for a suitable match, Leigh seems to have decided to embark upon a Grand Tour, and it is at this point that events take a darker turn. On 11 May 1767, prior to setting out for the continent, he made his will, and the fact that this will stood at his death indicates that there were at that time no doubts as to his capacity. However, a payment of £100 on 18 June 'for Travelling Expences on setting out for France' was followed, on 2 October by one of £3 3s. 0d. 'paid Dr Monro for his advice'. John Monro was at this time physician to the Bethlehem Hospital and a pioneer in the enlightened treatment of mental illness. That the October episode was no passing event is witnessed by a further payment of £49 7s. 0d. in March 1768 in respect of '17 visits in Town & 6 in the Country'.[74] No details exist as to the nature of Leigh's illness: it was presumably not violent in nature nor indeed seems to have been generally known of for several years as correspondence addressed to him bears witness. After 1768 regular consultation with Monro ceased, and in 1771 another notable figure appears on the scene, Francis Willis, to be prominent, like Monro, in the care of George III. In April 1771 the Reverend John Dodson, Leigh's 'friend and domestic chaplain', journeyed to Lincolnshire to consult with Willis. An arrangement was clearly entered into for in July Willis was paid £100 'in part of his first quarters allowance'. Between this date and late 1774, Willis was paid £1,260 annually and in addition presented accounts not only for board and lodging but for purchases on Lord Leigh's account, including in January 1772, a violoncello. None of the bills specify any items which might be regarded as medicine, referring rather to the purchase of music and visits to plays.[75]

In February 1768, Joseph Hill, on behalf of Lord Leigh, took a lease of New Grove House, Boston Lane, Ealing, fully furnished, for seven years at an annual rent of £130. Presumably Leigh and his attendants divided their time between Stoneleigh, Lincoln and the rural outskirts of London. During these years Leigh's family were concerned that he should be attended by servants who were skilled and considerate. One, King, who had proved unsuitable, was replaced in November 1769 by James Hill, on the recommendation of Dr Monro.[76]

By 1773 it was clear that Edward would not recover and his friends, family and agents decided, reluctantly, to apply for a Lunacy Commission. The writ *De lunatico inquirendo* was issued on 22 December 1773 and the formal inquisition took place at Stoneleigh in January 1774. Local men of worth were called together to declare the state of Leigh's mind and the extent of his possessions. The inquisition is formulaic declaring baldly: 'the said Edward Lord Leigh at the Time of taking this Inquisition is a Lunatic of unsound Mind and that he doth not enjoy lucid intervals so as to be sufficient for the Government of himself his Manors, Messuages, Lands, Tenements Goods and Chattels'. He has been, they declared, a lunatic for five years and upwards, a formulaic description, 'but how or by what means the said Lord Leigh so became a Lunatic ... know not unless by the Visitation of God'.[77] The document then continues, in the manner of an Inquisition *Post Mortem*, to detail the lunatic's estates in Warwickshire, Staffordshire, Leicestershire, Bedfordshire, Buckinghamshire and Cheshire, to the annual value of £11,216 with £12,200 due upon cash in hand, bonds and arrears. The valuation of the household effects at Stoneleigh and Leighton were stated to be unascertainable without inventories. These were later taken, and the value of the effects at Leighton put at £435. The valuation for Stoneleigh was not given, although in 1806 an identical inventory totalled £5,329. His 'nearer heir' and only next of kin was stated to be his sister Mary Leigh, aged thirty-five and unmarried.[78]

On 31 March 1774 the custody of Edward Lord Leigh, a lunatic, was committed to William Lord Craven and Mrs Mary Leigh, his sister. Henceforth these committees, as they were called, were responsible for his care and the running of his estates, their accounts being presented to Chancery for inspection and authorisation. From this time the family spotlight shifts from Edward to his sister Mary, his guardian until 1786 and heir after his death in that year at the age of forty-four. During this period the family were fortunate in their servants and agents: Joseph Hill and his nephew, Thomas Hill Mortimer, their lawyers, and Samuel Butler and Richard Darley, their estate agents. Whilst keeping close contact with these men, Mary Leigh and Craven seem to have been content to leave the day-to-day running of the estates to them.

Edward, the fifth lord, was buried at Stoneleigh on 4 June 1786, aged forty-four. The order of his funeral procession makes it clear that, whilst he may have been inactive for many years,

FIGURE 89
Edward, fifth Lord Leigh (1742-1786), as a boy

FIGURE 90
Mary Leigh (1736-1806), sister of Edward, fifth Lord Leigh

his demise was nonetheless treated with all the solemnity due to a peer of the realm.[79] By his will, made in 1767 before the onset of his illness, Leigh left his real estate, should he die unmarried, to trustees for his sister, Mary Leigh, for life with reversion to any sons and daughters, or, failing these, to his half-sister Anne Hacket. If both died without issue, the estates were to pass 'to the first and nearest of my kindred being male and of my name and blood that shall be living at the time of the determination of the several estates'. This clause was to lead to complicated manoeuvring and negotiations after 1806. Anne Hacket had died without issue and Mary, at fifty-one, was unlikely to marry and produce heirs. For twenty years, then, until Mary's death in 1806, there was an awareness amongst members of the Leigh family, however remotely connected to the fifth lord, that, although the title had died with Edward, there might be an opportunity to inherit the estates. This is evident in the increasing number of letters seeking to establish friendly relations, and no doubt their credentials, with Mary. In justice to the Gloucestershire branch, the Leighs of Adlestrop, who eventually succeeded, it should be noted that Edward Leigh was in friendly correspondence with one of its number, Dr Theophilus, Master of Balliol College, Oxford, as early as 1767 when he wrote of an intended visit to Stoneleigh.[80]

Leigh's personal bequests provide a fascinating insight into his friends and interests before the onset of his illness. Over and above pecuniary legacies for his sisters and their issue, he left over £9,000 in bequests to friends, many of them scholars or fellow students at Oxford. £500 went to the family of Mr Meadows, 'the Natural son of my late uncle Edward Leigh', and £1,000 to the Vice Chancellor of Oxford University and the Provost of Oriel College for the purchase or models and apparatus to illustrate the 'Mathematical Lectures and Experiments formerly read and explained in the Museum by Doctor Bradley and Mr Bliss'. More controversial was his bequest to Oriel of all his mathematical instruments and his entire library, excepting only the Stoneleigh Ledger Book and manuscript volumes relating to the medieval abbey. This bequest denuded the Abbey of the fine collection which he and his predecessors had built up: when moving books to Stoneleigh in 1806, James Henry Leigh, nephew of the Reverend Thomas Leigh, Mary Leigh's heir, described it as 'rari nantes in gurgito vasto'.[81] Mementoes were given by codicil to the duke of Beaufort, a fellow student, and to Lord Willoughby de Broke. Three violins were left to his cousin, William Lord Craven, and a fourth, 'my Urkert violin' in Craven's possession, went to Sir Watkin Williams Wynn. Leigh seems to have exemplified the well-known links between music and mathematics.[82]

For the last twenty years of her life, Mary Leigh (Fig. 90) was an extremely wealthy woman. In addition to her income from the estates, the rental of which amounted in 1786 to £13,643, Edward had left her £20,000 for her own use. She seems always to have kept a house in London, being variously described as of 'Upper Grosvenor Street' or, occasionally, as in December 1774, 'of the City of Bath' where she had gone for her health. From 1788 until her death, her

London home was Grove House, Kensington Gore, at that time outside the main centre of habitation but near enough to town to enable full participation in society.[83] Her correspondence is chiefly concerned with estate affairs but a few letters throw some light on her busy life. As with most gentry and nobility of the time, summer months were spent in the country, but by no means in seclusion, for the letters, written to Joseph Hill, her man of business, with whose family she had a close and friendly relationship, reveal a constant stream of visitors to Warwickshire, including Lady Radnor for two weeks in August 1790. In September 1791 she wrote: 'I have been wonderfully engaged in receiving and paying visits which will end I believe with the Dolbens who come ... for a few days'. A few weeks in October, before the start of the Season, were passed at Bath or, more usually, Cheltenham, often in the company of either a Mrs Hales or a Mrs Herbert, who were regular and long-term visitors. The winter months were spent, latterly, at Grove House, of which she wrote: 'it is impossible for me to have so agreeable and suitable a place as is Grove House in every particular'.

There is no evidence that her interests were as intellectual as her brother's, the only reference of any literary or musical nature in her letters being to Boswell's *Life of Johnson*, which she bought in 1791, 'and left it at Grove House for my Winter's amusement. I was very much pleased with what I had time to read in it'. A clearer picture of her social circle may be gleaned from the list of keepsakes distributed to friends and relations after her death. The list includes not only family and Warwickshire connections – Leighs, Cravens, Bagots – but also the leaders of London society, the Ladies Sefton, Ormond and Howard. A letter of December 1791 indicates a favoured activity: 'I have some money in my Card Purse', presumably a gambling fund. But, from a letter to the Hills, it is clear that her life had not been all social whirl: 'I shall ever retain a grateful remembrance of the kind friendly reception you ... gave me at Wargrave at the times I was very unhappy'.[84]

By the mid nineteenth century family legend had grown up around Mary: Agnes Leigh, the family's historian, later recorded:

> It is said that she was very short, almost a dwarf, but ... She seems to have had
> some liking for smart clothes ... We were told that she liked to go up to the
> Keeper's Lodge in the Deer Park for tea – and that there were high stools put
> about for her to sit on – Also that she did not much like to be stared at
> (because of her lack of inches) by the poor people; though she was very
> generous and charitable in her dealings.

Family tradition also recorded an unrequited *tendre* for her cousin, Lord Craven, perhaps accounting for her single state. There is, however, no evidence for this other than a close interest in his declining health evinced in her letters.

Whatever the truth of the legends, the *Annual Register* remarked in her obituary: 'the worthy lady ... was not unmarked by some eccentricities, but of the most harmless nature. Her munificence was immense and her loss will be long felt in the Circle in which she moved'. One of those eccentricities may perhaps be identified in her payment, in July 1794, to William Penn for 'consenting to have his children innoculated'.[85] She died at Grove House on 2 July 1806 and was buried, according to her instructions, at Stoneleigh. With her the direct line from Sir Thomas, the first baronet, came to an end.

Both Edward and his grandfather, the third lord, had been anxious that the estates should remain in the Leigh family, the elder man even providing for a female branch to take the name if necessary. At the time of Edward's death, the senior Leigh line, descended from Sir Thomas of London's eldest son, Rowland, was thriving and active in Gloucestershire. There should have been no problems over the transfer of the estates but matters were to prove far from simple. Despite her brother leaving her only a life interest in the estates, Mary had made her own dispositions of the real estate in several wills, drawn up between 1786 and 1803. In 1786 she had devised the freehold and copyhold lands in trust to the use of the eldest representative of the senior line, the Reverend Thomas Leigh of Adlestrop, for his life, then to James Leigh Perrott of Scarlets for life, a further life tenancy to James Henry Leigh of Adlestrop (Thomas's nephew) and then to his heirs.[86] A condition was included that all these life tenants were to join together within six months of her death to agree to the uses of her will, 'It being my wish and intent that the devises made ... may tend to prevent any Contests concerning the property hereby devised'. The leasehold property was later devised to the tenant for life, who was also entitled to appoint a rent charge not exceeding £1,000 for the jointure of any wife.[87]

These provisions made it clear that Mary Leigh regarded the Adlestrop Leighs as her heirs, but the implication in her brother's will that she was only a life tenant herself brought other claimants, mainly descended through the female line (who had providentially taken the name Leigh in the years after 1786), clamouring for their rights. Her obituary in the *Annual Register* makes it clear that Stoneleigh was a prize worth fighting for 'one of the finest estates in England comes to the Heirs at Law, not less at the present rents than £17,000 p.a. ... But what makes this estate of immense value is that the rents have not been raised these 50 years and ... if relet ... annual revenue would not be less than £30,000'. This is both an underestimate and an exaggeration: the annual rental in 1806 for all the Leigh estates came to £19,000, but this was in fact two and a half times what it had been in 1749 and an increase of more than £5,000 on the rental in 1786.[88]

A few claimants were bought off, whilst close family negotiations resolved other problems. In 1806, James Leigh Perrott, the second tenant for life and cousin of the Reverend Thomas, was seventy and had earlier changed his name on succeeding, in 1751, to the Oxfordshire estates of his great-uncle, Thomas Perrott. He therefore agreed to sell his interest in Stoneleigh in return for lump sum of £20,000 and an annuity of £2,000 for the lives of himself and his wife. He died in 1817 but his wife continued to receive the annuity until her death in 1836 at the age of ninety-two.[89]

These arrangements left the estates in the life tenancy of the Reverend Thomas Leigh, the oldest surviving son of William of Adlestrop. Born in 1734, he was a widower without children and had been rector of Adlestrop since 1763, where he lived with his unmarried sister, Elizabeth. Caroline Austen later wrote that 'the change came too late in their lives to be pleasant to them' and they spent as much time as possible at Adlestrop. Whilst he may have preferred Gloucestershire, this did not mean that he neglected the running of the large estates for which he was responsible: within two years the annual rental value had increased to £25,675. It is clear, however, that much of the increase went out again in effecting repairs and improvements: in 1812, the year before his death, a balance of only £3,339 remained after estate expenditure.[90]

Thomas Leigh died at Stoneleigh on 26 June 1813 and was succeeded at Stoneleigh by his nephew, James Henry Leigh, the only son of his elder brother James, by Lady Caroline Brydges. James Henry had inherited the Gloucestershire estates in 1774 at the age of nine and in December 1786 married his cousin, Julia Judith Twistleton, eldest daughter of Lord Say and Sele.[91] The couple divided their time between Adlestrop and London, where their only son, Chandos, was born in 1791. The 'mischievous wicked eyes' which captivated James Henry reflect a character which in adulthood became autocratic and strong-willed. Two weeks before Thomas's death in 1813 Thomas Hill Mortimer, the family lawyer, had sent Julia sketches of the rooms and windows at Stoneleigh so that she could order curtains and carpets, and had provided her with general details as to what landscaping and building work had been undertaken. The major changes during Thomas's tenancy had been the work in the grounds by Humphry Repton in 1809 and this was to provide a setting for substantial expenditure on the interior over the ensuing years. Between 1813 and 1823, when James Henry died, the Abbey was totally refurbished and the Riding School, stables and picturesque lodges erected.[92] That much of this was under the direct control of Julia Judith is apparent from the majority of surviving letters for this period being addressed 'Dear Madam' with a multitude of answers, memoranda and instructions issued in her spiky handwriting. It is also clear that she maintained a firm control over the running of the estates in general, James Henry featuring in correspondence only infrequently.[93]

The arrival of James Henry and family at Stoneleigh opened a new era in the history of Stoneleigh Abbey. During the eighteenth century, although much major and important work had been undertaken, the fortunes of the family with regard to family size, untimely death and incapacity, allied to a low political profile, meant that the house never functioned as a social centre worthy of its grandeur. During the nineteenth century, however, the house was to flourish both as home to large families and as a centre of county life, reaching its apogee with the visit in

1858 of Queen Victoria. Between 1813 and 1823 nearly £11,000 was spent on furniture and furnishings, £7,000 before 1817, when a house was bought in Portman Square, London. There was plenty of money: James Henry had, of course, also inherited the substantial Gloucestershire estates, but even without these, improving revenues meant that in 1822, the year before his death, the rental value of the remaining estates was £31,000.[94]

This income was not of course, free from encumbrance. Payments had to be made to various annuitants, the most expensive of whom was Jane Leigh Perrott at £2,000. An 1812 settlement of the estates between Thomas and James Henry, had also provided for fortunes of £20,000 to each of the latter's four daughters, £10,000 with interest at the age of twenty-one or marriage, and the remaining £10,000 on the death of their father. These sums were to be paid at the annual rate of £500 each until James Henry's death and £1,000 each thereafter. By 1823 three of the four girls were married and the money found from the estates.[95]

Chandos (Fig. 93), the only son and heir of James Henry, was educated at Harrow, where he was sent in 1799, aged eight. Among his schoolfellows were Robert Peel and the future Lords Aberdeen, Palmerston and Byron, whose fag he allegedly was. According to his grand-daughter's account 'he was of a very literary turn & wrote poetry - He was very delicate in health and quiet and retired in his habits ...We were told that Byron dined in company with Chandos the night before he left England for the last time'.[96] Chandos's health and literary inclinations may account for the fact that, even after his marriage and succession to the estates, it was his mother, Julia Judith, who remained in control. Her grandson, Sir Edward Chandos Leigh, wrote of her: 'My grandmother had a striking personality. A very beautiful woman ... her strong will and powerful intellect sometimes inclined her to be too managing; but her kindness of heart never failed'. He also credits her with the transformation of Stoneleigh which, 'after she went there in 1813 became a different place. The present grand stables, the handsome stone bridge over the river Avon ... the ornamental lodges ... and the keepers' lodge in the deer park are memorials of her taste and energy'.[97]

After Harrow, Chandos went to Christchurch, Oxford, before setting up as a young man about town in bachelor apartments in the Albany, previously occupied by Byron. This was his principal address until his marriage in 1819 to Margarette Willes, daughter of the Reverend Shippen Willes of Astrop House, Northamptonshire.[98] Margarette brought with her a portion of £5,000, and was awarded a jointure of £2,000 annually. Provision was also made for the portions of younger children, of whom there were to be nine.[99]

There were, however, clouds on the horizon. The peerage had become extinct on the death of Edward, the fifth lord, in 1786. Rival claimants of the Adlestrop Leighs to be the heirs at law had come forward after the death of his sister Mary in 1806 but had been dealt with. After the death of James Henry, however, rumours began to circulate of a claimant descended from

Christopher, the third son of Thomas, the first lord. Christopher had died in 1673 leaving by his wife, Constance, a son Thomas who died, unmarried in 1698. He was buried at Stoneleigh as 'Thomas Leigh of London, gentleman'. In 1829, however, a George Leigh of Cheshire, claiming descent from the issue of an alleged previous marriage of Christopher to Penelope Cotton, claimed that until 1811 there had been a monument in Stoneleigh Church to substantiate this. Statements were produced from various workmen, tenants, and former servants of the Leighs alleging that, during work in Stoneleigh Church in 1811 this monument was removed to the Abbey for safekeeping and never seen again. Witnesses for the Leighs denied the existence of such a memorial. Those supporting the claimant placed great emphasis on the prominent part supposedly played by Julia Judith in this affair, James Henry appearing only in his wife's shadow. The claim was ultimately rejected by the House of Lords but a more sinister and distressing allegation was made in the 1840s. Largely as a result of the efforts of Julia Judith, aided by Chandos's friendship with several of the leading politicians of the day, not least Lord Melbourne, Queen Victoria was pleased, in May 1839, to create Chandos, Baron Leigh of Stoneleigh. This seems to have triggered the hopes of other alleged descendants of Christopher Leigh, and in 1844, after the death in 1843 of the redoubtable Julia Judith, the accounts of dark deeds were taken a step further. It was now asserted that during the building of the new bridge over the river in 1814, the missing memorial, together with coffins and coffin plates removed from the vault in 1811, had been concealed in the foundations of the bridge. To make matters worse, hapless workmen involved in this had been murdered to keep them quiet, their bodies also forming part of the new foundations. A crowd actually attacked the Abbey in 1844, the new claimants and several of their supporters being later charged with riot, and sentenced to terms ranging from eighteen months to three months. Charles Griffin, a Leamington solicitor who had defended several of the rioters, became so convinced of their case that in 1848 he published a booklet *Stoneleigh Abbey thirty four years ago ...* which not only outlined the alleged events from 1811 but, in essence, accused James Henry, Julia Judith and possibly Chandos, of murder.[100] This was too much for the family, who seem to have been remarkably forbearing hitherto, and Griffin was tried and imprisoned for libel.

Work at the Abbey continued throughout Julia Judith's life, largely under her supervision. Chandos spent several periods of time abroad, both for his health and possibly to recoup his finances; for, despite the size of the estates and their rental income, cash in hand was a continuing problem. In 1835 Chandos wrote to his lawyer that he thought he could only pay his sisters' fortunes by sales of land: 'My mother seems to think that ... I have been living beyond my means'. His agent had allowed arrears of rent to accumulate and Chandos was 'in terrible hot water about it'. Conversely, he wrote to her from abroad urging economy in the matter of works at the Abbey 'in consideration of his eight small children'.[101]

FIGURE 91
Francis Dudley, third Lord Leigh of the second creation (1855-1938), by Ellis Roberts, 1907

FIGURE 92
Marie Campbell (d. 1949), second wife of Francis Dudley, third Lord Leigh, in 1927

Between 1836 and 1839 the family was abroad, during which time twins James and Sophia were born. Chandos's elevation to the peerage occurred shortly after the return. In 1842 Julia, the eldest daughter, married Charles Adderley, later first Baron Norton, and 1848 saw the spousals of another daughter, Mary, to the Honourable and Reverend Henry Pitt Cholmondeley and, more importantly, of the heir, William Henry to Caroline Amelia Grosvenor, a daughter of the marquess of Westminster. The stress of these events took their toll on Chandos's health and he was forced to leave England's climate for Europe, where he died at Bonn on 27 September 1850 of apoplexy and paralysis, aged fifty-nine.[102] His widow moved to the family home at Adlestrop with her younger children and died in 1860. Two opinions of her, by a contemporary and a son, whilst differing in tone, describe the same character.[103]

William Henry Leigh, who inherited the title at the age of twenty-six, was the first of the Gloucestershire Leighs to have been born and brought up in the knowledge that he would become the master of Stoneleigh.[104] His tenure, which lasted more than fifty years, saw the family reach its apogee and then begin its long decline, a fate shared by so many landed families during the later nineteenth century. Born at Adlestrop in 1824, he was, like his father, educated at Harrow, but then proceeded to Cambridge, being admitted to Trinity College in January 1843. He had parliamentary aspirations, standing unsuccessfully as a Liberal candidate in 1847 and continuing to support Liberal policies when a regular attender in the Lords. His life took a new direction in 1848 with his marriage to Caroline Amelia, which was to last for fifty-seven years and produce ten children.[105] Stoneleigh became a family home during this time in a way it never had been before: Chandos had a large family, but had spent much time abroad and was long under his mother's influence. William Henry and Caroline were true *pater et mater familias*, loving and loved, as is apparent from the voluminous correspondence between parents and children throughout their lives.[106]

Throughout the nineteenth century, the family was consolidating; disposing of outlying estates and concentrating on the major holdings. These sales were often provoked by a need to provide a marriage portion for the numerous daughters born to Chandos and William Henry. Between 1681 and 1806 the Leighs of Stoneleigh had nineteen children between them, of whom only eight survived. The nineteenth-century owners of the Abbey (James Henry, Chandos and William Henry) produced a total of twenty-four children between 1791 and 1866, all of whom survived to adulthood and had, in some way or another, to be provided for.

William Henry (Fig. 96) became the archetypal county leader, closely associated with the local volunteer regiment and serving, among many other offices, as Lord Lieutenant from 1856 until his death in 1905. The high point of his career was no doubt the visit of Queen Victoria and the Prince Consort in June 1858, when they made Stoneleigh Abbey their base for two nights. The prestige was great but the long-term financial implications severe. By 1871 rental income had fallen from £45,000 to £27,000 and during the next twenty years decreased by a further 21.5

percent. This phenomenon was not confined to Stoneleigh: in the country as a whole, rents fell by a third between 1878 and 1900, and William Henry's paternalistic attitude made him less inclined than many to bear down hard upon his tenants for arrears. In 1883 he was in possession of the largest estate (14,891 acres) among the Warwickshire nobility, but this yielded only £23,043 a year, scarcely more than at the Reverend Thomas's accession in 1806, with a greatly increased cost of living. A report in 1890 by the family agent outlined annual expenditure of around £15,000 with estimated receipts from all sources amounting to not more than £20,500. This left only £5,500 for casual payments. [107]

By the time William Henry and Caroline Amelia celebrated their Golden Wedding in 1898 they had suffered a severe blow by the death in 1884 of their eldest son, Gilbert Henry, killed in an accident whilst on a shooting expedition in Wyoming. He had been a promising young man, educated at Harrow and Cambridge, where he was the first heir of the Leigh barony to take a degree. He then travelled extensively in America, Japan, China, Singapore, Java, Ceylon and India, and was at the time of his death, Member of Parliament for the southern division of Warwickshire.[108] The heir to the title was now his brother, Francis Dudley, born in 1855.

William Henry, Lord Leigh died in October 1905, aged eighty-one, beloved and respected: 'The handsomest, most good-natured, least assuming, person possible who had lived in the highest respect among men of both parties'.[109] With him the great days of Stoneleigh came to an end. Francis Dudley (Fig. 91), who succeeded to the title, had earlier taken the route followed by so many of his contemporaries faced with declining revenues and increasing responsibilities by marrying in 1890 an American heiress, Helene Beckwith. She died in 1909 without issue. He served as an ambulance driver during the Great War and, in the following years, sold the Cheshire estates and large tracts of those in Staffordshire and Gloucestershire, together with outlying portions of the Warwickshire holdings at Cubbington, Weston-under-Wetherley, Hunningham and Long Itchington. By his direct order, the various lots were offered first to the tenants before going on the open market.[110]

In 1923 he married again, another American, Marie Campbell (Fig. 92). Although there was a disparity in age, the marriage 'achieved perfect happiness. They were, what is so important in married life, good companions'. After his death in 1938 it was Lady Leigh who was credited in most obituaries with the conservation of the estates, 'in spite of the huge taxation'. She too was acclaimed for bringing the Abbey back into full use after the retrenchment of the period 1910-1925 when 'Lord Leigh lived in only half a dozen of Stoneleigh Abbey's 240 rooms'.

This was but a brief upturn, and the underlying story of the twentieth century was of constant retrenchment and adaptation to the rapidly changing economic and social climate. As an obituary of Francis Dudley in 1938 remarked: 'His death breaks another link with the past, when income tax was negligible and country houses had dozens of footmen'.[111]

C H A P T E R   S I X

THE JANE AUSTEN CONNECTION

Gaye King

There has always been something elusive about Jane Austen, 'difficult to catch her in the act of greatness', difficult indeed to trace much of the detail of her life. The Leigh papers at the Shakespeare Birthplace Trust have helped fill the gap of a few short weeks between her residence in Bath and the home she took with her brother in Southampton. The fact of her being at Stoneleigh was known, her journey further north to her cousin at Hamstall Ridware was uncertain. This can now be clarified. There has also been some surprise expressed at the shock to both Jane Austen and her cousin at the outcome of the negotiations over the settlement of the Stoneleigh estate when it passed to the Gloucestershire branch of the Leigh family in 1806. The papers shed some light on this. With flesh put on the bones of her experience on her Midlands tour, extraordinary in her life, we begin to see how important it was. This crucial period in the history of the Abbey coincided with a turning point in the life of the novelist. Retracing her steps, armed with new information, we can now see what it meant to her, and with what skill she used this experience, weaving into her novels much that she gleaned from her Leigh inheritance.

Jane Austen was related to the Gloucestershire Leighs through her mother, who descended from the senior branch the Leighs, settled at Longborough in the late sixteenth century, and then Adlestrop from the mid-seventeenth. Her father, Thomas, was one of six sons of Theophilus Leigh (c. 1643-1725) and Mary Brydges. He was born at Adlestrop, educated at Oxford, and became rector of Harpsden in Berkshire. He married Jane Walker, whose mother was Jane Perrot. Through the Perrot connection Thomas and Jane Leigh's son, James (Mrs Austen's brother), inherited the Northleigh estate and fortune, adding Perrot to his name. They also had two daughters: Cassandra, who married George Austen, and Jane, who married Dr Edward Cooper. The families of two of Thomas's brothers, William, the eldest, and the younger Theophilus,

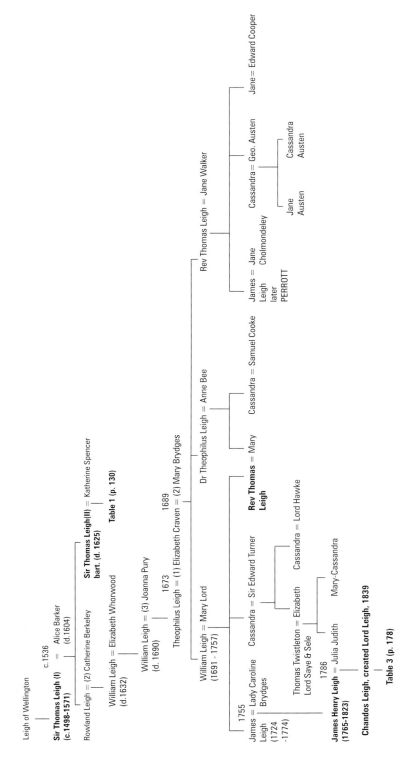

T A B L E   2

The Leighs of Adlestrop

(owners/occupiers of Stoneleigh in bold)

appear most frequently in Austen biography. Theophilus became Master of Balliol College, Oxford. He had two daughters, Cassandra, who married Samuel Cooke, rector of Great Bookham, who became Jane Austen's godfather, and Mary, who married her cousin, Thomas, son of William of Adlestrop and his wife Mary Lord. The eldest son of William and Mary, James, married his cousin, Lady Caroline Brydges, sister of the second duke of Chandos. James inherited Adlestrop and, with his brother Thomas, rector of Broadwell and Adlestrop, started the grand alterations to the house and estate, which culminated in the landscaping project there under the guidance of Humphry Repton. One of the sisters of James and Thomas, Elizabeth, was godmother to Jane Austen's sister, Cassandra Elizabeth. The other daughter, Cassandra, married Sir Edward Turner of Ambroseden and had daughters: Elizabeth, who married Thomas Twistleton, Lord Saye and Sele of Broughton Castle; and Cassandra, who married Martin Bladen, second Lord Hawke. Elizabeth and Thomas Twistleton had two daughters: Julia Judith, who married James Henry Leigh, son of James Leigh of Adlestrop, and Mary-Cassandra, the adulteress of Jane Austen's letter.

James Leigh died in 1774, a year before Jane Austen was born. His son, James Henry, was only nine years of age. James's younger brother, the Reverend Thomas, already resident at the parsonage at Adlestrop, was one of the boy's guardians, becoming *paterfamilias* for the period of James junior's minority. The other guardian was James's maternal uncle, James Brydges, third duke of Chandos. By this time, the insanity of Edward Lord Leigh had drawn attention to the Adlestrop Leighs' interest in the future of the Stoneleigh estates. By the time of Edward's death, in 1786, the Austens were aware that the male relatives most closely connected to the Stoneleigh branch included Mrs Austen's brother James Leigh Perrot, her cousin the Reverend Thomas Leigh, and her second cousin, James Henry Leigh. Under Edward's will, the Stoneleigh estate was to pass to his sister, Mary, for life, with reversion to their nearest male relative. Negotiations for a settlement on the Adlestrop Leighs were underway as early as December of that year.[1]

At the start of these negotiations involving her uncle, James Leigh Perrott, Jane Austen was in her eleventh year. She grew up with an understanding of the importance of kinship. Like most clerics of the period, her father owed his living to wealthy relatives. Her eldest brother, James, was able to trace his relationship to Sir Thomas White, founder of St John's College, Oxford. As Founder's Kin he was entitled to a scholarship.[2] A few years later, his brother Henry was able to use this genealogy for the same purpose. Through family and friends, Jane Austen's clerical brothers were to find their livings, and her sailor brothers promotion in their naval careers. Her sister Cassandra's fiancée, Tom Fowle, also had expectations of one or more of the livings in the gift of his relative, Lord Craven.[3] It was to the Stoneleigh branch of the family that James Austen turned when he sought an increase in his income to enable him to marry. Mary Leigh's agent and friend, Joseph Hill, was a neighbour of the Austens' uncle, James Leigh Perrot. He put in a good word for James,[4] who was subsequently presented to the livings of Cubbington and Hunningham in Warwickshire.[5] Jane Austen's cousin, Edward Cooper, was equally resourceful, rushing up to present his young bride to the Honourable Mary Leigh at Little Bookham. Mary Leigh became godmother to his first daughter, Isabella Mary. In time she would present Edward to the living at Hamstall Ridware.[6] It was Edward Cooper's invitation to visit him at Hamstall which brought his aunt, Cassandra Austen, and his cousins, Cassandra and Jane, unexpectedly to Stoneleigh Abbey.

On 2 July 1806, Jane Austen, and her mother and sister had closed the door on their last home in Bath. Their five-year residence had not been entirely happy for Jane Austen. It worsened after the death of her father in January 1804 when Mrs Austen and her unmarried daughters went from one lodging house to another moving steadily down the social scale. Their income was limited, leaving them embarrassingly dependent on whatever donations the Austen brothers could afford. Mrs Austen had the annual interest on her jointure, small as it was, and Cassandra a similar amount left by her fiancée. Jane Austen herself had no financial independence. None of her novels had yet been published. Now, her brother Francis Austen invited them to share a home with him when he returned from honeymoon. Meantime, they were to accept the invitation to visit Mrs Austen's nephew, Edward Cooper, in Staffordshire. They would spend some time at Clifton and then with their Leigh relatives at Adlestrop, *en route* to Hamstall Ridware.[7]

When they arrived at Adlestrop, it was abuzz with news of Stoneleigh, for the Honourable Mary Leigh had died at her London home the very day the Austens left Bath. Some letters among the Austen papers of this period give an idea of the stir the death caused among those concerned, and dovetail well with those in the Leigh family archive. Mrs Austen's brother, James Perrot, wrote in great detail to his wife from Hatchett's, in London. Commencing precisely at 4 o'clock, on Friday, 4 July 1806, he wrote to 'My Dearest Jenny', told her of his arrival in London, his dining with Joseph Hill, and of letters sent to himself, Thomas Leigh and James Leigh as 'those materially interested in the Landed Property'. 'Lord Craven and his brothers and Miss Minshull, and Col. Dalrymple, who married Mrs Johnson's Daughter', were all expected, but all awaited the arrival of Thomas Leigh. Thomas received Mr Hill's letter, James Leigh Perrot writes,

> which By the bye he never answer'd, but instead of coming directly to London went to Stoneleigh to take possession I suppose of the Estate: This Behaviour has greatly offended Mr James Leigh and not a little nettled Mr Hill. By this delay he will hardly be in London till late tonight. Till he comes I am in an uncertain situation: you may be sure my thoughts and wishes are at Scarlets, and I will be there as soon as I can … I have seen Mr Hill this morning, but he was going out on very particular Business; he wishes to have a good deal of Conversation with me, and has forced me to dine quietly with Mrs Hill and himself at Six o'Clock today that we may not have any Interruption.[8]

It seems clear that poor Joseph Hill was having some trouble with this fractious man who was anxious to get his share of the spoils. He goes on to talk of details of Mary Leigh's death at which Hill was present, of Hill and the apothecary sealing the drawers, which would be opened and the will and codicil read after Thomas Leigh's arrival. He ends with fond and lengthy declarations of his love. This letter reveals the agitation of the man. The detail he gives of his every movement, every dish of the food he eats, even his climbing and counting the stairs at Hatchett's, suggest not so much a man devoted to his wife, but one who has been completely dominated by her.

Still awaiting the arrival of Thomas Leigh the next day, James Perrot met Joseph Hill, James Leigh, and Colonel Dalrymple at 'Mr Child's Bankers' to open and read Mrs Leigh's will. It was then discovered that Mary Leigh had made Joseph Hill and Thomas Leigh joint executors and residuary legatees. He goes on to say:

> Mr James Leigh was particularly attentive to me and uncommonly civil in his
> enquiries after you; from which I infer that he is apprehensive that I may make
> use of the Power I have and give his Uncle and him some trouble … Mr Hill
> tells me the Uncle and Nephew must and will act handsomely towards me.
> When Mr Thomas Leigh thinks proper to make his appearance, some
> Proposals and Steps must be made and taken towards an accommodation: I
> hope and flatter myself they will be satisfactory to you and me. To the Uncle
> and Nephew any accommodation must be highly advantageous.

In these letters James Leigh Perrot gives a poor impression of Thomas Leigh, in not having the politeness to answer Joseph Hill's letter, but rushing up instead to claim his estate in an effort to throw difficulties in the way of a settlement that would favour the Perrots. In fact, his letter sets the scene for long months of negotiations and letters which were to show Thomas in a more favourable light. Thomas Leigh had long proved himself a capable and caring man. For years he had taken on the mantle of responsibility for the senior Leighs. After the early death of Sir Edward Turner in 1766, Thomas's brother, James, had been guardian to the Turner children. Thomas took over the management of their affairs when James died in 1774. He also managed the affairs of his cousin, Lady Reade of Oddington, and those of his maternal aunt, Mrs Wentworth. On this occasion he probably saw it as his duty to attend to practical matters at the Abbey. He was perfectly familiar with Stoneleigh. For years he and his brother, William, had been accustomed to riding over every summer to wait upon Lord Leigh. The warm friendship and trust that existed between Thomas and Mary Leigh is evident in the responsibility devolved on him. Now the staff would need to be informed, and appropriate preparations made for mourning and for the body to be interred in the family vault at Stoneleigh Church. He also quite properly notified the local paper of the event. The entry in the *Warwick and Warwickshire*

Advertiser for Saturday 5 July 1806, records the death, and acknowledges the charitable life, of 'the Honourable Mrs Leigh at Stoneleigh', whose benevolence would be much missed.

The same paper could enlarge on this information a fortnight later when it gave lengthy details of the magnificent funeral, which took place at Stoneleigh Church on 14 July. Included for general interest were elements of the settlement:

> The Revd Thomas Leigh, James Leigh Perrot, and James Henry Leigh, Esq, of
> Adlestrop, and his issue male; and in failure of such issue, on Thomas Charles
> Lord Viscount Tracy, Dr John Tracy, and Henry Tracy Esq; in tail male
> successively; and in failure of their issue male, on Sir Justinian Isham, Bart, and
> his issue male, and in failure thereof, on her male heirs forever.

The Traceys and Ishams had married daughters of Thomas, first Lord Leigh. Two Traceys of a subsequent generation married into the Leigh family, one to a daughter of Sir Robert Dudley, husband of Alice Leigh. Descendants of these families were still in touch in 1806. Thomas Leigh asked that 'the Revd Ferdinando Tracy Travell, M.A, Rector of Upper Slaughter be inserted in the Commission from Doctor's Commons for proving the will'. Jane Austen was also acquainted with the Reverend Dr Edmund Isham (1745-1817), Warden of All Souls, Oxford, a distant collateral relative.[9] Dr Isham was evidently on intimate terms with the Coopers as well, becoming godfather of Edward Cooper's third child, Cassandra Louisa.

After the funeral Thomas Leigh went back to Adlestrop, where his unmarried sister, Elizabeth, awaited his return. From then, 17 July, until they returned to Stoneleigh there was a daily exchange of letters with Joseph Hill. This correspondence reveals the significance of the negotiations to Jane Austen and her family. The letters commence the day after their return to their homes, on 18 July, with Joseph Hill's to Thomas Leigh concerning Perrot's negotiations. Leigh's reply reveals a more charitable response than Perrot appeared to expect. Perrot had calculated that he could expect £3,000 a year from James Henry Leigh as compensation for relinquishing his claim on Stoneleigh. Thomas Leigh found this excessive – 'a small excess one wd not regard' – but suggested that his nephew should agree to pay the interest on £20,000 and an annuity of £2,000 during the lives of Perrot and his wife. The principle would be paid only when James Henry succeeded to the estate. Knowing that his nephew would not be able to meet this demand, Thomas planned to raise the sum himself from the Stoneleigh rents. His own considerations were based on his desire that his nephew should succeed him immediately upon his own demise. The amount he decided on was also 'from my regard to Mr Leigh Perrot and for the Cooper & the Austen families, & to assure to Mr L.P. the means of better providing for them who are so very numerous'.[10]

No doubt the Austens' visit to Adlestrop, which chanced to coincide with this period of negotiations, reminded Thomas Leigh of their difficult circumstances. An outcome in their favour could have saved them many privations and much embarrassment. It also becomes evident that they were given to believe that James Leigh Perrot would do well by them. In one of his letters he tells his wife that 'Mr Hill privately whisper'd to me that he thought my seeing Mr Thomas Leigh at this time would be of consequence and advantage to me'.[11] The same message could have been conveyed to Mrs Austen.

However, when Joseph Hill spent just three days of this very busy time at his home in Wargrave on purpose to clarify matters with his neighbour and one-time friend, James Leigh Perrot, the meeting had not gone smoothly. Instead of coming away with an agreement they could put to the other parties, James Leigh Perrot had taken the papers away to consult his wife. He wrote a rather acrimonious letter to James Henry Leigh insisting that the settlement he proposed would be advantageous to his Adlestrop relations, that he, James Perrot, lived very comfortably, and any increase in fortune would merely add to 'show and Parade, but make no addition to his happiness'. Yet he threatened that this was his last offer. Should it be refused, the Adlestrop relations should take the consequences whatever they may be.[12] Joseph Hill soon saw the hand of Perrot's wife in the action. To Thomas Leigh, he wrote: 'Mrs Leigh Perrot was not present at the conversation but I believe her influence has great weight with his determination …'. Hill was trying to persuade James Leigh Perrot that £8,000 of the £20,000 he wanted immediately 'should be settled on Mrs Austen's family and Mr Cooper's … but Mr Leigh Perrot would not agree to this plan. He sayd that he would make such provision himself, as he thought proper'.[13]

To James Leigh Perrot, Joseph Hill wrote:

> it appears to me you are not aware of the necessary outgoings of the expensive
> establishment inseparable from such a Property. I have had many
> opportunities of seeing such establishments – & if ever you find yourself in
> Possession of Stoneleigh Abbey believe me you will have yr own experience of
> the heavy expense attending it, even on the most frugal management possible
> – you will however use your own discretion. [14]

Jane Austen never liked her Aunt Leigh Perrot. To the end of her days Jane Perrot would torment the more needy Austens with the power she exercised over the inheritance. In November 1808, Jane Austen wrote to her sister. 'Yes, the Stoneleigh Business is concluded, but it was not till yesterday that my Mother was regularly informed of it, tho' the news had reached us on Monday Eveng by way of Steventon. My Aunt [Perrott] says as little as may be on the subject by way of information, & nothing at all by way of satisfaction. She reflects on Mr T. Leigh's dilatoriness, & looks about with great diligence & success for Inconvenience & Evil'. [15]

When Thomas Leigh died in July 1813 Jane Austen referred to him as 'the respectable, worthy, clever, agreable Mr Tho Leigh, who has just closed a good life at the age of 79, & must have died the possessor of one of the finest Estates in England & of more worthless nephews and Nieces than any other private man in the United Kingdom'. She fears for the elderly Elizabeth Leigh who had been so wrapped up in the care of her brother. She then adds. 'There is another female sufferer on the occasion to be pitied. Poor Mrs L.P. – who would now have been mistress of Stonleigh [*sic*] had there been none of that vile compromise, which in good truth has never been allowed to be of much use to them. – It will be a hard trial.' [16]

Meantime, however, there was still much business to be done at the Abbey. Thomas Leigh was probably planning his arrangements to suit his Austen cousin and her daughters when he finally decided on an appropriate time to revisit Stoneleigh. He replied to Joseph Hill's letter, writing from Adlestrop on 1 August 1806:

> It will be equally, if not more, convenient to me to accompany you next week to Stoneleigh, as it wd have been abt the 20th. We will therefore expect the pleasure of seeing you & Mrs Hill here before dinner on Monday next, & proceed ye next day to ye Abbey. Mrs & Miss Austens will be of ye party, & will then be so far on their road to Mr Cooper's whom they are going to visit at Hamstall. I wrote yesterday to Mr West to say yt we shd come to ye Abbey to dinner by 5 o'clock on Tuesday next, & desir'd him to have beds & every thing ready.
>
> You will be so good as to do what you think advisable respecting ye sale of Grove House, as likewise respecting ye discharge of ye Servants there, wch may now very properly take place. I shall continue a pair of Mr Smith's job horses till I can match my own. [17]

The tone and warm welcome in this letter is in striking contrast to the exchanges between James Leigh Perrot and Joseph Hill.

With two coaches, the Hills' and the Leighs', it would be possible to accommodate Mrs Hill, Thomas's elderly sister, Elizabeth, who had lived with him at Adlestrop for some years, and the three Austen women. The men often rode on horseback between the two estates, but the women would travel by coach. There would be time enough for the women to converse and get to know one another at Stoneleigh while the men were shut away 'busy a great part of the mornings', according to Mrs Austen's letter. Much writing was done. One of the visitors gave them all franks so they could send off their letters. Mrs Austen famously wrote to her daughter-in-law describing the Abbey as she found it. [18] Like Catherine Morland, in *Northanger Abbey*, she appears to have anticipated a gothic setting. 'I had figured to myself long Avenues dark Rookeries and dismal Yew Trees, but here are no such melancholy things.' She contrasts that vision with a brighter scene. 'The Avon runs near the house amidst Green Meadows bounded by large and beautiful Woods, full of delightful Walks.' Yet it could not have escaped her notice that only a fortnight before a storm had raged across many parts of the country uprooting trees and doing a great amount of damage. In the same issue which gave details of the funeral of Mary Leigh, the *Warwick and Warwickshire Advertiser* recorded the 'tremendous storm of thunder and lightening [which] lashed across different parts of the country' that week. Edward Cooper's mother-in-law was at Hamstall Ridware when Edward returned from the funeral at Stoneleigh. On 18 July she records 'a violent storm of rain, thunder and lightening had done great mischief'. Again on 21 July there was 'uncommon rain, thunder and lightening'. Two days later 'most violent rains forced [them] to take shelter under a shed where they stayed for an hour'. This was far more appropriate for a gothic tale, as also is the meeting every morning at nine, 'to say our prayers in a handsome chapel, the pulpit &c now being hung with Black'.

Mrs Austen's description of the grounds is also of interest. 'We walk a great deal, for the Woods are impenetrable to the sun, even in the middle of an August day.' The letter reminds us that, at Steventon, Mrs Austen had been proud of her own dairy, poultry and garden.

> I do not fail to spend some time every day in the Kitchen Garden where the quantities of small fruits exceed anything you can form an idea of. This large family with the assistance of a great many Blackbirds and Thrushes cannot prevent its rotting on the Trees. The Garden contains 5 acres and a half. The ponds supply excellent Fish the Park excellent Venison; there is also great plenty of Pigeons, Rabbits, & all sort of Poultry, a delightful Dairy where is made Butter good Warwickshire Cheese & Cream ditto. One Man servant is called the Baker, He does nothing but Brew and Bake. The quantity of Casks in the Strong Beer Cellar is beyond imagination: Those in the *small Beer* Cellar bear no proportion, tho' by the bye the small Beer may be called Ale without misnomer.

There is also a fullsome account of the large breakfasts. Like her brother, she seems to have liked her food.

There have been few fundamental changes in the west wing since her description of it in 1806. She was impressed with its vast size, the '45 windows in front, 15 in a row', the 'considerable flight of steps (some offices are under the house) into a large Hall: on the right hand the dining parlour, within that the Breakfast room, where we generally sit, and reason good 'tis the only room (except the Chapel) that looks towards the River. On the left hand of the hall is the best drawing room, within that a smaller; these rooms are rather gloomy Brown wainscoat and dark Crimson furniture; so we never use them but to walk thro' them to the old picture gallery. Behind the smaller drawing Room is the state Bed Chamber, with a high crimson Velvet Bed: an *alarming* apartment just fit for a Heroine ; the old gallery opens into it.' There are '26 Bed Chambers in the new part of the house & a great many (some very good ones) in the old'.

The gregarious Thomas Leigh would need many beds. His relatives and friends were soon descending on Stoneleigh to marvel at his good fortune. 'We all seem in good humour', writes Mrs Austen, 'disposed to be pleased and endeavouring to be agreeable, and I hope we succeed.' Of Thomas Leigh's niece, the mother-in-law of James Henry Leigh, she says: 'Poor Lady Saye & Sele is rather tormenting, tho' sometimes amusing, and affords Jane many a good laugh – but she fatigues me sadly on the whole.' There can be little doubt that, like her own Elizabeth Bennet, Jane Austen found diverting the 'Follies and nonsense, whims and inconsistencies' of others and laughed at them whenever she could. Elizabeth Twistleton, the dowager Lady Saye and Sele, was the daughter of Thomas Leigh's older sister, Cassandra, and Sir Edward Turner. At Stoneleigh the lady chattered away about her eating habits professing herself an epicure. She refused to eat chicken because 'after her lord had destroyed himself she had eaten nicely boiled chicken for a fortnight in her chamber … and had not been able to eat it since'. The *Hampshire Chronicle* had published details of her husband's grizzly suicide. He had attempted drowning, then cut his throat with a razor, and stabbed himself with a sword – not the things one would wish to be reminded of, nor associate with food. At one evening meal she improperly addressed the Clerk of the Kitchen, standing very correctly and silently behind her chair, asking him 'if the macaroni was made with Parmesan'. There was a hush before he answered gravely: 'Yes, my lady'.[19] She was also inclined to boast of her sister's novel-writing. This exasperated Fanny Burney, once a neighbour and friend of the Cookes at Bookham. Burney described Cassandra Hawke's gothic novel, *Julia de Gramont* (1788), as 'love, love, love, unmixed and unadulterated with any more worldly materials'.[20] Jane Austen missed the visit of Lord and Lady Hawke, the Dowager Lady Hawke and Miss Hawke, whose arrival at Stoneleigh was annouced ten days after the Austens had left.

However, she would have been pleased to see George Cooke, son of her godfather. In Bath the previous year, they were both at a party in which she says 'there was a monstrous deal of stupid quizzing, & common-place nonsense talked, but scarcely any Wit'. However, 'My Cousin George was very kind & talked sense to me every now & then'.[21] Mary Leigh appears to have found the company of George Cooke equally pleasurable, and was obliged to him for doing duty in the chapel at Stoneleigh. When the living of Cubbington became vacant in 1792, she wrote to Joseph Hill:

> The living of Cubbington given to Dr Dodson and he put in his Brother, if now vacant and in my gift I shall be much obliged of yr assistance to find out a proper person to fill it. Would it be suitable to Mr Cooke? He has not had any preferment from my gift, and I do not wish to give him anything that should remove him from his attendance at the Abbey and yet wish to show him that regard I think his due. [22]

In response to Joseph Hill's reply, she wrote: 'I am very much obliged by your reminding me of Mr [James] Austen & I think I am inclined to offer him the living'.[23]

Now, at Stoneleigh, Mrs Austen mentions George Cooke arriving once Robert Holt-Leigh had left. Holt-Leigh she describes as 'A great friend of young Mr Leigh's, a very distant Relation, a single man, the wrong side of forty; chatty and well bred, and has a large estate'. Robert Holt Leigh, Member of Parliament for Wigan in Lancashire, had interests in coal mining and canal maintenance. He was a benefactor of the church and school and the establishment of a dispensary for the sick and poor in his area. He had also attended to the education of his younger brother, Alexander, at Dr Charles Burney's school at Greenwich.[24]

Caroline Austen wrote later to her niece, Emma Austen-Leigh: 'Aunt Cassandra told me, [that Mr Holt Leigh] was a great admirer … of her sister [Jane Austen]. They were all passing guests at Stoneleigh Abbey – & all passed away, & never met again … & I … mention this … only as showing that her pretty face did not pass through the world without receiving some tributes of admiration'.[25] Holt-Leigh was forty-three at the time, Jane Austen thirty.

Perhaps she would not have been taken in by this amiable, chatty man who already had more than one illegitimate child. He was a close friend of James and Julia Leigh, and godfather to their daughter. They visited one another's homes in the country and in London from time to time. James Leigh invited Holt-Leigh to private theatricals, such as the one he wrote of as having 'recitations by myself & a few others. The whole concludes with a little farce'. He became entangled in Holt-Leigh's intrigues, arranging secret trysts with women, including 'the lady with the Black tresses' whom he was to meet in Lady Temple's box at the opera. The flirtations with many women had commenced when Holt-Leigh was very young and continued well into old age.[26]

Jane Austen may well have recognised the glint in his eye. Once, after watching Julia's sister, Mary-Cassandra Twistleton, at a ball, she boasted of having 'a very good eye at an Adultress, for tho' repeatedly assured that another in the same party was the *She*, I picked on the right one from the first. – A resemblance to Mrs Leigh was my guide. She is not so pretty as I expected; her face has the same defect of baldness as her sister's, & her features not so handsome; – she was highly rouged, & looked rather quietly & contentedly silly than anything else.'[27]

When Joseph Hill left, Thomas Leigh was able to take his guests on outings to places with family connections. This included Combe Abbey, the home of Mary Leigh's mother, Maria Rebecca Craven, and Warwick Castle, once home of Ambrose Dudley, earl of Warwick, and Anne Whorwood – this would have called to mind the splendid tomb at Longborough of William Leigh and his wife Elizabeth Whorwood of Sandwell Castle, Staffordshire. They also enjoyed the picturesque ruin of Kenilworth Castle, associated forever in their minds with Sir Robert Dudley and Alice Leigh. *The Italian Biography of Sir Robert Dudley, knt*, written by the vicar of Stoneleigh, the Reverend Vaughan Thomas, was published that year, and would have made interesting reading for the party at the Abbey.

There was plenty of material here for a novelist to work on. An abbey of great antiquity, with a gothic façade to one side, grand modernity on the other; a death; intrigue over an inheritance; winding paths in a dark wood; adultery and illegitimacy. Jane Austen's pen must have been quite as busy as her mother's.

Then it was time to depart for Hamstall, once in the honour of Tutbury, in possession of Robert Ferrers. The road book shows that they would pass Middleton Hall, the home of Sir Francis Willoughby, Lord Middleton, brother of the Cassandra so loved by the Leighs that several generations had chosen the name for their daughters. From this point not much is known of the movements of the party until the letter to Thomas Leigh on 23 August 1806, in which Edward Cooper speaks of the 'good health of all at Hamstall. Mrs C[ooper] with Mrs Austen and her Daughters unite with me in kind regards to yourself and Mrs E[lizabeth] Leigh'.[28] We glimpse them again when Cooper writes to Joseph Hill on 26 September 1806, wishing to be affectionately remembered to Mr Leigh Perrot, and saying that 'Mrs Austen and her daughters after staying with us about five weeks, have left us for Southampton. They spoke with much pleasure of having met you & Mrs Hill at Stoneleigh'.[29]

It was at Chawton that Jane Austen finally settled to revise the three novels she had already written, and to write another three. The first to be published was *Sense and Sensibility* (1811), where we find the Ferrars and Middleton families and John Willoughby. The relationship between the objectionable John Dashwood and his wife Fanny is much like that of James and Jane Leigh Perrot. The reduction scene in Chapter 2, where, step by step, Fanny Dashwood disabuses her husband of any financial responsibility he should feel towards his mother and sisters, mirrors Jane Leigh Perrot's influence over her husband and his responsibility towards the Austens and Coopers. There is also the scene where Colonel Brandon has to rush off unexpectedly and Mrs Jennings gossips about his 'natural daughter' (Chapter 13), 'a little love-child' (Chapter 30).

Jane Austen would have been pleased enough to acknowledge, as did Thomas Leigh's wife, Mary, in her 'History of the Leigh Family, Adlestrop', that, on her mother's side at least, she was 'descended from a long race of plain independent Country Gentlemen'.[30] We recall, in *Pride and Prejudice*, the arrogant Lady Catherine de Bourgh declaring Elizabeth Bennet an upstart without family connections or fortune, and Lizzy claiming that her father was a gentleman, and she a gentleman's daughter.

Jane Austen never sought proof of a grand lineage. It is with typical irony that, in *Persuasion*, she introduces Sir Walter Elliot, 'a man who, for his own amusement, never took up any book but the Baronetage'. His favourite volume always fell open at 'Elliot of Kellynch-Hall', where Sir Walter 'could read his own history with an interest that never failed'. However, it is clear that at Stoneleigh the novelist viewed with interest the portraits of of her forebears. Here she would find the portrait of the children of the earl of Strafford. One of his daughters, Anne Wentworth, married Sir Edward Watson, the second Lord Rockingham. Her eldest daughter, Eleanor, married Lord Leigh of Stoneleigh. Their third son inherited the Wentworth-Woodhouse estate in Yorkshire and assumed the additional name Wentworth. On the adjacent wall hung the portrait of a plain Mrs Wentworth. This was Elizabeth, the much loved and respected 'Betty' of the letters in the Leigh papers. We are reminded again of *Persuasion*, and of the conversation about the new tenants who were to occupy Kellynch Hall. In an endeavour to impress on Sir Walter the gentility of his new tenants his steward referred to Admiral Croft's wife as sister to a gentleman who lived at Monkford. Sir Walter could recall no gentleman. A little discussion soon brought him to mind, but with some objection. 'Wentworth? Oh, ay, – Mr Wentworth, the curate of Monkford. You misled me by the term *gentleman*. I thought you were speaking of some man of property; Mr Wentworth was nobody, I remember; quite unconnected; nothing to do with the Strafford family. One wonders how the names of many of our nobility become so common'.

Unlike the children in the opposite portrait, Elizabeth Wentworth had nothing to do with the Strafford family. But she had a romantic story all of her own. She was the sister of Mary Lord, who married William Leigh of Adlestrop. Not unlike Mrs Leigh Perrot, the widowed Mrs Robert Lord held power over the inheritance of her two daughters. She insisted that Elizabeth marry a man that pleased *her*, rejecting the man Elizabeth really loved, an impecunious Lieutenant Wentworth. The determined lovers married in secret and parted at the church door, he going off with the troops to France. Soon enough Mrs Lord learned why it was her daughter refused all the eligible men who came her way. She was greatly indignant and swore that the entire fortune would go to Mary. When he returned a very successful, gentlemanly, pleasing Lieutenant- General, William and Mary Leigh introduced their brother-in-law under a false name. Mrs Lord was enchanted with him and all was forgiven. There are elements here of the story of the enduring love Anne Elliot holds for Captain Wentworth, despite the disapproval of Lady Russell, and the many years the lovers spent apart.

We come closer to home, however, when we read of Catherine Morland and the description of Northanger Abbey. 'With all the chances against her of house, hall, place, park, court, and cottage, Northanger turned up an abbey, and she was to be its inhabitant.' Catherine's mind runs over the detail of what she could find there. Its 'long, damp passages, its narrow cells and ruined chapel', and so on. She thrills to find herself at one time walking along the cloister where the feet of ancient monks had trod. Henry Tilney puts thoughts of the dreadful possibilities she might find to match her imagination, stirred as it was by the gothic novels she had been reading. She decides that the cruel General Tilney had done something dreadful to his wife. As soon as she could steal away on her own, she went in search of Mrs Tilney's bedchamber, which had been left as it was when she died. Following her route as set out in the novel, we find it coincides nicely with Mrs Austen's description of the 'alarming apartment'. No sooner there than Catherine hears footsteps from an unexpected direction. Looking for an escape, she finds herself at the head of some stairs which lead to a long gallery. Here Henry Tilney catches the guilty Catherine and immediately understands her quest. He can more easily explain his own presence at that spot. This was the easiest route to his quarters. According to old drawings, we can locate the stables at Stoneleigh, where, in Jane's imagination, he would have left his horse, and the old steps leading from the north front into the gallery. Had he come through the ground floor entrance, he would have came up a flight of stairs at the end of the connecting passage, now marked by a narrow, ornate door, up to the gallery outside the door of the 'alarming apartment'. Stoneleigh having turned up an abbey, the lively mind of the novelist was entertained by placing there a delightful set of characters she had created for an earlier novel.

Finally, we come to the tour from Mansfield Park to Sotherton undertaken by the young Bertrams, the Crawfords, the dreadful Mrs Norris and poor Fanny. The church at Sotherton, like that in the village of Stoneleigh, is situated far enough from the great house for the bells not to cause annoyance to the family. The similarity between the factual village and the fictional includes the almshouses built by some of the family of an earlier generation. The original route from the village was through Stareton where we find, as Catherine did, 'some fine timber'. And it is half a mile downhill from the park entrance to the abbey. Finally they reach 'the spacious stone steps before the principal entrance' (Chapter 9). Mrs Rushworth shows them through one or two rooms to the dining-room. After a cold collation, she shows them 'a number of rooms, all lofty, and many large, and amply furnished in the taste of fifty years back, with shining floors, solid mahogany, rich damask, marble, gilding and carving, each handsome in its way. Of the pictures there were abundance, and some few good, but a larger part were family portraits, no longer any thing to any body but Mrs Rushworth … Mrs Rushworth could relate of the family in former times, its rise and grandeur, regal visits and loyal efforts. … Having visited more rooms than could be supposed to be of any other use than to contribute to the window tax, and find employment for housemaids ... "Now", said Mrs Rushworth, "we are coming to the chapel, which properly we ought to enter from above, and look down upon; but as we are quite among friends, I will take you in this way, if you will excuse me" … Fanny's imagination had prepared her for something grander than a mere, spacious, oblong room, fitted up for the purpose of devotion – with nothing more striking or more solemn than a profusion of mahogany, and the crimson velvet cushions appearing over the ledge of the family gallery above'. The setting, so delightfully plucked from her knowledge of Stoneleigh, Jane Austen uses as an opportunity to introduce a discussion on religious observance, and undercurrents of flirtations and reactions to them, thereby exposing the character of each of those present. There is a wonderful exchange with Mary Crawford about daily prayers in the chapel, which was 'now left off'. 'Every generation has its improvements,' says Mary Crawford. The chapel has set the scene for as delightful a piece of comedy as ever was written.

It is symbolic of Jane Austen's approach to life and writing. Places need no more description than is pertinent to narrative and character and the ideas they illustrate. People were her preference. After attending a museum and art gallery in London, she wrote: 'I had some amusement at each, tho' my preference for Men & Women, always inclines me to attend more to the company than the sight'.

Yet there is sufficient in *Mansfield Park* to take us through the grounds with her characters, meandering through the wilderness. Mrs Norris, reminiscent of Mrs Austen, makes the best of the abundance in the garden, the poultry house, the dairy, and the wine cellar. There is mention of Repton and the detail of his charging five guineas a day. A quotation from Cowper supports Fanny's regret at felling trees merely to afford a view. This cannot but remind us of the novelist's period at Stoneleigh, where Repton's improvements were contemplated and Cowper's great friend, Joseph Hill, was of the party. We must be pleased that Jane Austen was sufficiently observant of Stoneleigh, its environs, and its inhabitants in that summer of 1806 to draw our attention to the Leigh papers and all they tell us about her Leigh inheritance. She gained nothing from James Leigh Perrot's will but spent the last years of her life happily weaving threads gathered from Stoneleigh into rich tapestries to delight generations of grateful readers.

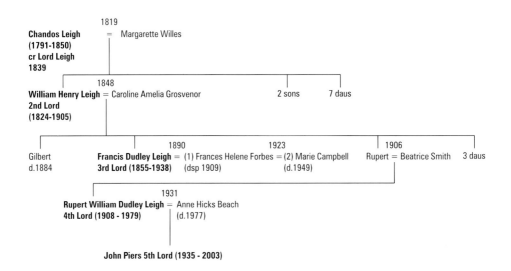

T A B L E 3
The Leighs of Stoneleigh, from 1806
(owners of Stoneleigh in bold)

CHAPTER SEVEN

THE POET AND THE PATERNALIST

Norma Hampson

This chapter examines the careers of the two barons Leigh of the second creation whose lives encompassed the whole of Queen Victoria's reign. The two men were not only very different in character but had very different attitudes towards their role. As befitted men of their social standing, both Chandos Leigh and his son, William Henry Leigh, had lengthy annual subscription lists. Promoters of charitable institutions sought aristocratic names to add prestige to their appeals and the annual accounts show many examples of the Leighs' munificence, though Chandos, unlike his son, did not appear to involve himself on a personal level. William Henry, as the first-born son and heir of a Lord Leigh, was secure in the knowledge of his succession to the title and estates and the concomitant responsibilities; Chandos, on the other hand never possessed that unquestionable assurance and had made a life for himself in the literary sphere more suited to his temperament.

Chandos Leigh was born in London in 1791, the only son of James Henry Leigh and Julia Judith Twistleton, daughter of the thirteenth lord Saye and Sele of Broughton Castle. The family came to Stoneleigh in 1813 when James Henry became tenant for life following the death of his uncle, the Reverend Thomas Leigh. Having been occupied by elderly relatives since the death of Edward the fifth Lord Leigh in 1786, Stoneleigh Abbey was in need of refurbishment and this was carried out, over a period of years, and at great expense, under the direction of Julia Judith. New riding stables were built and picturesque lodges constructed at all entrances to the park. All the correspondence from the architect, the agent and the clerk of works was addressed to her. James Henry, although footing the bills, seems to have taken a back seat during the decision making.

Meanwhile, Chandos, who had received his early education at Harrow, where he was one of Byron's fags, had matriculated from Christchurch, Oxford. He went to live in London, gaining something of a reputation as a poet. His first published work, *The Island of Love*, appeared in 1812 and was followed, at regular intervals, by other publications. Some of his earlier works were, however, 'through the prudence of friends suppressed'.[1] Both Byron and he were members of the Holland House group, a well-known literary and artistic coterie. When Byron married, in 1815, and moved to 13 Piccadilly, Chandos took over his bachelor quarters at 5 Albany and had them refitted at a cost of £600, this sum including a valuation 'of furniture and fittings from Lord Byron to you'.[2] The two men are reported to have dined together on Byron's last evening in England and a constant reminder of their friendship, the portrait of Byron, by Thomas Phillips, hung in the Library at Stoneleigh Abbey for many years.[3]

During this period Chandos was certainly a 'young man of fashion', spending, in one month alone, 'over £100 on boots and shoes and over £700 at his tailors'.[4] He also ran up huge bills at various booksellers. Some of these, particularly an account with Wilkes, led to acrimonious correspondence in later years. It was during these heady days in London that he made the acquaintance of Miss Jane Rhodes. Jane, orphaned in early childhood, had been brought up by her godfather, Sir James de Bathe, but, following his accidental death in a shooting incident, she had been sent to London to be with her elder sister. In her own words 'she was not ignobly born and had been carefully nurtured and brought up to within a few weeks of that period'.[5]

The meeting between Chandos and Jane took place in 1814 at a house in Berkeley Steet, Piccadilly, which she believed belonged to a relation of his, but which was, according to him, 'no better than a bawdy house' run by the infamous Mrs Porter and the establishment where Harriette Wilson, 'the darling of the dandies', carried on her affairs, including one with the duke of Wellington.[6] Three years later Chandos admitted, in a statement to his solicitor, that in 1814 he had received an 'application' informing him that

> he might be acquainted for a certain annual income with a young lady who was supposed to have her 'Virtue'. He was curious enough to see her and although having had no intercourse with her, in a foolish fit of generosity settled an annuity upon her.

An attorney had been called in to Mrs Porter's house and a deed drawn up to provide for Jane's education and maintenance.[7] The bond, dated July 1814, secured to Jane Rhodes (not fifteen years old) an annuity of £60, during the joint lives of Chandos Leigh, Jane Rhodes and James Henry Leigh, payable half yearly on 8 January and 8 July, with a clause to the effect that if James Henry Leigh should pre-decease either Chandos or Jane she would receive an annuity of £300 thereafter.[8]

As a result of her meeting with Chandos, Jane was placed at Miss Child's school in South Street, Finsbury Square, and was for the next three years his constant companion, paying frequent visits to his rooms at the Albany, and having the use of his box at the Theatre Royal Drury Lane and of his *vis-à-vis* whenever she chose. The account books for the Theatre Royal show that, on the evening of 13 May 1814, 'Mrs Chandos Leigh' was removed from Mr Leigh's box, on the King's Side, to the lower proscenium on the same day as 'Mr Leigh' was occupying Lord Byron's box on the Prince's Side. As Chandos did not marry until 1819 we may assume that this lady was Jane masquerading as his wife.[9]

In the early twentieth century an undated letter, written by Chandos, was discovered behind the old panelling at a house in Stow-in-the-Wold near Adlestrop where Chandos was then living. Its contents suggest a date of about 1813. Addressed to 'My dear Girl', it requests an interview at which Chandos would unfold his proposals.

> As for marriage with any being under the sun I can never think of it at present but our union will perchance be as lasting as that of marriage ... all the enjoyments of the town are insipid unless I have a kind friend to participate in them with me ... Be not angry at my proposal. Pray be silent and burn this note whatever your answer may be.[10]

Perhaps this young lady's rejection of his proposal led Chandos to seek a companion in London and to his subsequent relationship with Jane. According to Jane, Chandos, on meeting her, was 'very struck with her appearance and straightforward tone of mind'. His feelings at that time were of a 'more moral tendency' towards her but changed later when

> he attempted to do that which I resisted and our acquaintance was for sometime broken off. He then spread a report that I was not formed properly and could not either be the wife or the mistress of any man in the general sense of the term.[11]

This report was to jeopardise a future marriage proposal and was, in later years, used by her to strengthen her claim for financial assistance from the second Baron Leigh. Chandos, for his part admitted 'after she visited me I was not proof against temptation and I own that I had for once and once only a casual connection with her; this was after the money was settled upon her'.[12]

Whether this dalliance with the demi-monde had been to gain first-hand experience for his writings or whether it was just part of the hedonistic lifestyle of the upper strata of society, it was to prove a costly exercise. Jane Rhodes haunted him for the rest of his life, and the Leigh family until the end of the century, with threats of exposure and the publication of her diaries. Unlike Wellington, who, when faced with a similar threat from Harriette Wilson, told her 'to publish and be damned', Chandos panicked and paid whatever Jane Rhodes demanded in order to keep the affair out of the newspapers.[13]

FIGURE 93
Chandos Leigh (1791-1850),
later first Lord Leigh of the
second creation, *c.* 1819

FIGURE 94
Margarette Willes,
wife of Chandos Leigh,
with her daughters,
Mary and Louisa:
drawing by John Hayter, 1843

In 1818 Chandos set off on the Grand Tour, accompanied by his tutor Dr Shuttleworth. From Paris, their first European stop, he wrote to the family solicitor requesting more money as

> restaurants, spectacles and other things have run away with a great deal not to
> mention the purchase of a handsome new carriage which has made a big hole
> in my £100. Pray take care that I have a sufficient supply as otherwise I shall
> indeed be in status quo.[14]

£300 was sent to Geneva in time for his arrival there.[15] During the tour he wrote regularly to his mother and to his sister, Julia, from the many cities he visited. Every letter expressed his shortage of funds. He even had to borrow £60 from his tutor but this did not prevent him from placing orders for busts and statues, from Canova's studio, to be despatched to Stoneleigh Abbey.

On his return from Europe Jane Rhodes tried to re-establish contact. In a letter addressed 'to my dearest Chandos' she asked him to accept two little work boxes which she had brought back from Paris for his sisters and to please oblige her by paying the thirty pounds due the previous month, 8 July, as she was very poor. This epistle prompted Chandos to put the whole business into the hands of the family solicitor, Thomas Hill Mortimer, to whom he wrote:

> Will you be good enough to notice a young lady Miss Rhodes who will call on
> you. She is the Lady to whom the annuity is said to be due. She is very clever
> and cunning and will baffle examination ... I do not know what to say about the
> Annuity deed, I see by *Blackstone's*, that any Bond, the subject of which is
> improper, is cancelled, or rather I should say void. Is that a fact? ... at all events
> it would be better to conceal from her any hostile intentions unless we are
> certain the law is on our side: as her sister is a most determined fire-brand,
> and will play the devil if she conceives that I intend not to pay the regular
> income to her ... both her sisters are whores in the true sense of the word. The
> eldest, Lady Langford, has ruined a young man. The second, Mrs Valpoise, was
> guilty of some swindling tricks. Now you can see I am in a ticklish situation, if it
> is tried the Notoriety of the business might prevent a Marriage, which I fondly
> anticipate at some future date.[16]

The following year Chandos married Margarette Willes, daughter of the Reverend William Shippen Willes of Astrop House, Northamptonshire, and related to the Willes family of Newbold Comyn, Leamington. They had met in Leamington, a town which, as Chandos wrote to Margarette:

> I certainly do not like ... yet I shall always look at its red houses with
> satisfaction as were it not for that amphibious place I should never have met
> with her whom the more I see the more I admire ... [17]

A letter addressed to Miss Willes just a month before their marriage requests that they will 'use first names when they are man and wife'. As his sisters and their friends all called him Chandos, it would seem odd for her to address him as Mr Leigh.[18] Jane Rhodes, in contrast, by addressing her letter to 'my dearest Chandos', had displayed a degree of familiarity frowned upon in polite circles. Chandos and Margarette married, by licence, at Marylebone.[19] After a honeymoon at Minchenden House, Southgate, a London property of the duke of Chandos, they went to live at Adlestrop, the Leigh family's Gloucestershire home. It is from an entry, dated September 1823, in the Reverend F.E. Witts's diary, that we learn a little about Chandos.

> Chandos Leigh is an eccentric mortal, possessed of talent and studious in an
> odd way. He has been an admirer of theatrical performances and performers,
> male and female, a poet in a small way ... He resides much at Adlestrop but
> without taking a share in the public business of the county and
> neighbourhood.[20]

In October 1823, when his father died, Chandos and family moved to Stoneleigh Abbey. Any major event in the life of the Leighs acted as a catalyst for Jane Rhodes to renew her demands and claims. In this instance, the death of James Henry brought her hot foot from Paris to establish her rights. Until then Julia Judith, now the dowager Lady Leigh, had been unaware of this 'impudent and ... iniquitous transaction' and thought that 'the person might have been prevented from coming to England'.[21] However, she contributed £1,000 towards the sum necessary to persuade Jane Rhodes to give up the bond. Great care had to be taken during these negotiations to prevent the affair reaching Margarette's ears as she was near her time for confinement. Their son and heir, William Henry, was born on 17 January 1824.

Although 'having his house full for the races', Chandos found time to suggest to Mr Mortimer that the sum of £1,500 should be the initial offer to Jane Rhodes although, rather than it reach the newspapers, a larger sum might be paid. In the event, she agreed to accept the £1,500 plus interest on the arrears of the annuity, making a total of £1,785.[22] Nothing more was heard from Jane for a number of years, much to the relief of both Chandos and Mortimer who had come to regard her as 'a permanent blister'.

Apart from the spectre of Jane Rhodes, Chandos had other causes of anxiety, not least the sporadic claims to the estate by other Leigh descendants. In 1820 a certain George Leigh had made an unsuccessful attempt to claim the title based on his descent from the fourth son of the first lord. The first wife of this son, Christopher, was purported to be Penelope Cotton, daughter of Sir George Cotton of Combermere Abbey.[23] Although no record of this marriage was ever found, the stories and claims rumbled on for over twenty years. Eventually Chandos enlisted the help of Lord Redesdale in trying to persuade Viscount Combermere, whose name was being used by the claimant, to produce his family pedigree. He would only state that it had been stolen.

In 1835 another contender, James Leigh, caused a stir amongst the tenantry in Cheshire with his claims and declarations, and in 1844 a mob, on behalf of a John Leigh, seized Stoneleigh Abbey, during the family's absence. As a result twenty-eight persons were arrested and convicted at Warwick Assizes. Even though Chandos was assured by his agent that everything was under control, his anxiety remained because

> two blackguards, from Kenilworth, were insulting his people at the Abbey and alarming the servants ... there is no security against them coming at any time, to find them hovering about when my children are walking is not very pleasant. If they can get nothing from one they may, out of revenge, do something desperate.[24]

In 1848 Chandos was charged with the murder, in 1814, of four workmen then employed on the estate. At that time repair work was being carried out at Stoneleigh Church and it was said that his mother, Julia Judith, had engineered the removal of particular monuments which might have helped other Leighs to prove their claim to the estate. These monuments were purported to have been put in wheelbarrows, covered with sacking and removed to the Abbey whence, under cover of darkness, they were trundled to a site on the estate where a bridge was being constructed. They were then buried beneath the foundations under the watchful eye of the Leighs who gave the signal to lower the heavy slab which killed the men. At the time rumours were rife and tales of bribery abounded. There were almost as many witnesses who saw the monuments in the church as there were to testify against their existence. However, under cross-examination the thirty-four-year-old charge was found to be a complete fabrication and Chandos was acquitted. Demands to have the bridge excavated were refused on the grounds that, if nothing were found, the accusers would not be satisfied until the entire Abbey was excavated. The trial, no doubt, took its toll for Chandos died two years later at Bonn on the Rhine where he had gone to receive medical treatment for the partial paralysis from which he suffered,[25] a complaint which, according to Jane Rhodes, was caused by his 'past excesses'.[26]

Ill health had dogged Chandos throughout his life. In 1836 he took his wife and children to live in Europe for two years leaving his mother to oversee the alterations taking place at the Abbey. Although writing to his mother urging economy 'in consideration of his eight small children',[27] another letter to his nephew, written from Nice, stated that 'he had rented a palace for the season, engaged two governesses and a dancing master for the children and obtained the services of a capital cook'.[28]

In his autobiography, his son, Edward, recalls the journey: 'it was usual for the gentry to travel in their own coaches lashed to the railway trucks' and on this occasion they had travelled in three carriages, two for the family and one for the servants.[29] On the return journey Margarette gave birth to twins in Paris prompting their solicitor to write: 'I am happy to learn that Mrs Chandos has been safely confined though with an addition to your family more than might have been expected'.[30]

On his return from Europe, Chandos was raised to the peerage by Lord Melbourne, on 11 May 1839, becoming the first Baron Leigh of Stoneleigh of the second creation. According to his son, Edward, he never went into Parliament as 'his want of health and retiring disposition unfitted him for a poltical career'. He did, however, write papers outlining policies on economic and agricultural questions which were considered 'to be in advance of the age'. One pamphlet, printed in 1840 for private circulation only, suggested that farmers and squires need not be ruined by the abolition of protection if they improved their methods of agriculture.[31] His son, Edward, was of the opinion that Chandos's prose writing was far superior to his poetry but Dr Samuel Parr, the vicar of Hatton, with whom Chandos often dined, considered him 'an ingenious Poet and an elegant Scholar'.[32]

Another constant anxiety for Chandos was his financial situation. Apart from his personal expenses, he had three sisters and seven daughters for whom provision had to be made. As a landowner, he was dependent on rentals as his main source of income. When, in the 1830s, the agent had allowed the arrears of rent to mount up, he found himself in 'terrible hot water about it' with his mother who also accused him of 'living beyond his means'. Anxious to set himself right in his mother's opinion, he urged the family solicitor to 'make out a satisfactory calculation ... and show it to my mother ... I think it would prove I have not been extravagant'.[33]

Although only in his forties he was beginning to feel the strain of his responsibilities. A letter, written to his mother in 1838 from the Hôtel du Rhine, expresses his concerns.

> I must become much less busy than I have been and do what I think I ought
> very quietly, otherwise I fear I must quit these shores again and perhaps never
> return. The great point is not to be anxious about anything but to do what one
> thinks best and discipline one's mind so as not to be put out by anything, but
> this, for a nervous person is not an easy matter but ought to be trained by
> quiet habits, it is hard work for a single man to regulate a large property but
> much harder for one with a large family with large encumbrances. After all
> who should be fussed about a few fleeting things of this brief existence?[34]

His mother's death in 1843 at least relieved him of the anxiety of trying to please her. She had always been 'inclined to be too managing' and the men in her life appeared to be in awe of her.[35] The following year he published two more volumes of verse, *A Walk in the Country* and *A Walk in Summer*. This was in spite of the fact that he had been struggling to create a demand for a previous volume written in 1840 which, despite laudatory reviews, 'hung heavy' upon the publisher's hands.[36]

Not unexpectedly, that year too Jane Rhodes, now Mrs Charles Egan, re-appeared on the scene, calling at the Leighs' London house in Portman Square and writing to Chandos at the Abbey, in a hand so like his own that his wife almost opened the letter. Jane had kept a low profile since receiving the lump sum in exchange for her annuity and in the interim, on a visit to her sister, Lady Langford in Ireland, she had met and married Charles Egan, a barrister from Dublin who was several years her junior. They had returned to London and were living in Chester Street, Eaton Square, where she had run up debts for repairs and was threatened with eviction. Although her husband practised at the Chancery Bar and published several learned tracts, he seemed to be as inept as Jane at managing their financial affairs and never managed to keep himself or his wife out of debt.

Jane renewed her applications for financial assistance, through Mr Mortimer, asking him to intercede on her behalf and attributing to him, following the death of James Henry, the arrangement for the redemption of her annuity at much less a figure than it was actually worth. One does not need to be a mathematician to agree with her that a one-off payment of £1,785 would barely cover six years at £300 per annum. After repeated letters and visits to his chambers Mortimer suggested that she should let him have particulars of her immediate debts which he would attempt to show to Chandos. After a perusal of the debts, Chandos asked Mortimer to arrange a meeting at his chambers to finalise this business once and for all for

> if not stopped she will become another Wilkes [the irate bookseller], or a Griffin, [author of the libellous *Stoneleigh : 34 years after*] and for certain reasons more annoying personally than either. As for money I declare I can give no more. I never met with such monstrous ingratitude in my life ... am I always to give money to these people when they are in distress because I paid some years ago to keep a young person out of harm's way ... she afterwards came to me in the Albany voluntarily and in a weak moment I was once acquainted with her had she not come I never should have had any further knowledge of her.[37]

The debts, however, were paid to prevent further proceedings and in an attempt to put an end to her threats. This was, however, all in vain: immediately after Chandos died, in 1850, she renewed her application through Mortimer, to William Henry second Baron Leigh.

> I now beseech you ... to see Lord Leigh on my part and to prevail on him to do something for me ... had his Father been spared a little longer he would have done ten times over more than expect from the young Lord ... if he will authorize you to give me £1500 I will undertake never to refer to the matter again or ever write to Lord Leigh ... and all matters with reference to his father and myself will be buried in oblivion.

As on previous occasions, however, it did not end there. She repeated her threats to publish her diaries which would be 'a favourite dish of fireside chit-chat for there will be food for the young as well as the old'.[38]

FIGURE 95
William Henry Leigh (1824-1906),
later second Lord Leigh (centre),
with his siblings, Edward Chandos
and Julia:
drawing by John Hayter, 1843

FIGURE 96
William Henry Leigh,
second Lord Leigh, as Provincial
Grand Master, presented to him by
the Freemasons: oil painting by Sir
John Watson Gordon, 1862

From 1852 Charles Egan, too, began to request financial help. Firstly, he was arrested for a debt of £33 owed to his tailor, then he had his law books seized and sold, and finally was in need of £250 to rent new chambers without which he could not follow his profession. By 1855 the Egans had 'reason to believe the worst would happen'. Jane's letters became even more hysterical and frenzied as she beseeched Lord Leigh to help her out of respect for his father's memory. Eventually, after dealing with her debts and out of compassion, an annuity was settled upon her for life and references supplied to enable Charles Egan to obtain a position.

There are regular entries for both Mr and Mrs Egan in the *Leamington Courier's* list of resident nobility, clergy and gentry during the 1860s. Jane's signature also appears in the 1862 visitors' book at the Lord Leycester Hospital, Warwick.[39] Charles Egan died at Oakley House, Beauchamp Road, Leamington on 8 July 1869, having returned from the local magistrates' court where he had been defending a youth charged with embezzlement.[40] From 7 August 1869 to 18 December 1869 his widow's name appears in the Leamington residents' list after which the trail runs cold. Her solicitor, Mr Frere, informed Lord Leigh of her death at the turn of the century.[41] As for the poet, Chandos, who questioned being 'fussed about a few fleeting things of this brief existence',[42] perhaps he yearned for the irresponsible and unorthodox lifestyles of his friends in the literary world – Leigh Hunt, for example, whom he was happy to assist by paying half the rent of his Kensington home in the 1840s, the other half being paid by Mary Shelley.[43] Like Byron, with whom he had shared a love of poetry, he died abroad. Although Jane Rhodes declared that Chandos was an atheist, who laughed and scoffed at the mere mention of religion, he was remembered by his family as 'rather a religious and serious minded man ... a man of high ideals, happily married and generally respected'.[44]

The British Library has a copy of *The Island of Love*, published in 1812, which had belonged to a Captain Thomas Bonner in 1837. On the title page, along side the author's name Chandos Leigh, Bonner has written: 'later Lord Leigh and what a thorough Scamp he was'.[45]

When, in 1835, Chandos had written to his mother regarding his concerns and anxieties, he had also remarked on William Henry's progress at Harrow and expressed the hope that

> he will not be an idler as his father was when he came of age ... and will be a far
> more useful and active member of society whether in public or private life.
> What we might have at last is a Leigh in the family who can act with energy in
> all aspects of society.[46]

His hope was to be realized: William Henry not only devoted his attention to the improvement of the estate and the welfare of his tenantry, but 'threw himself heart and soul into the public work of the county'.[47]

William Henry Leigh was born 17 January 1824, at Adlestrop in Gloucestershire. He received his education, firstly, at Harrow and then at Trinity College, Cambridge. In August 1848, he married Caroline Amelia Grosvenor, fourth daughter of the marquess of Westminster. The letters which she wrote to him during their courtship reveal a true love-match, although the contents of one letter in particular show that it was not William Henry's first experience of love. 'I have been thinking over what you told me yesterday, you know what I mean, when you came of age etc. etc. but I quite believe you love me many times the best, darling for I think you do'. It seems almost an invasion of privacy to read the terms of endearment and affection, which characterize her correspondence, interspersed with delightful sketches and watercolours. In a letter dated a few weeks before their marriage, she refers to her pleasure at an invitation to dinner: 'Dearest Henry, a thousand kisses to you and I think it will be very nice meeting your father then we can talk so sensibly and eloquently in favour of simultaneous marriage and prosecutions'.[48]

Was this a reference to the murder trial earlier that year in which Chandos openly faced his accusers or to William Henry's own recent 'brush with the law'? For he was on the point of being arrested as a result of responding to an impassioned plea from a young relative, Edward Willes, who had asked him to sign bonds, in order to raise money to pay his debts. Edward, with tears in his eyes had explained that his own father was too ill to be approached and, as he was the heir to an entailed estate, he would easily settle the debts on his father's death. However, his expectations had not materialized as his mother was the sole beneficiary of his father's will. Edward immediately fled to Brussels, leaving William Henry to pay debts totalling £8,000. To avoid arrest, William Henry had instructed a solicitor to raise the money by means of a life insurance. The solicitor initially advised him to seek help from Chandos but William Henry felt that his father had enough to contend with – the trial at Warwick, his daughter Mary's wedding and the payment of William Henry's election expenses following his unsuccessful attempt to gain the North Warwickshire seat for the Liberal party, the previous year. He felt, however, that he had to confess 'his secret' before embarking on marriage to the charming girl he had chosen for his wife. His bank books for the early years of his married life show regular payments to service Edward Willes's debts, as it was quite some time before the Willes family were able to make any contribution: the estate had been left in trust for Mrs Willes but she was unable under the terms of the will to release a large capital sum.[49]

As the eldest son in a family of ten children, including two sets of twins, William Henry was no doubt imbued with a sense of responsibility towards his younger siblings from an early age. This matured into a paternalism which encompassed the household at Stoneleigh Abbey and the tenantry of the estates. A survey carried out in 1883 shows that Lord Leigh, with 14,891 acres, was in possession of the largest estate amongst the Warwickshire nobility. As such, he would have been the biggest, if not the only, employer in the immediate vicinity of Stoneleigh.[50] He is reported to have referred to Kenilworth as 'the capital of his kingdom'.[51] This acceptance of the role of ruler of his estate carried with it responsibility for the protection and welfare of his workers and tenants, 'knowing what was best' for them and acting accordingly.[52] He was determined to involve himself in the workings of the estate and thus avoid some of the problems encountered by his father. He examined every account book personally, noting any discrepancy in the margin prior to initialling each page and appending his signature to the half-yearly statements. He made a point of visiting the tenants, on an annual basis, as he felt in his paternalistic fashion that it was

> not only desirable to see what they require, but I think it very important to see that the cottages are not overcrowded with grown-up children, and kept clean and that cheap papers which many cottagers like to have on their walls is not allowed being dangerous to health.[53]

A collection of notebooks from 1853 to 1896, written in his own hand, record the nature of repairs required at every farm and cottage plus the number and gender of children at each abode.[54] Although his concern ensured that the tenants' living conditions were clean and reasonably comfortable, it also allowed him to exercise a certain degree of control over their lives. There were many rules to be adhered to, as one would expect in a well-run 'kingdom', firstly, the annual internal white-washing of all cottages in spring. This work was carried out by estate workmen for the aged and infirm but the able-bodied were expected to do the work themselves with materials supplied by the landlord. Secondly, drains had to be kept clean to maintain their effectiveness. Other rules concerned overcrowding. After the age of sixteen an offspring was considered to be a lodger, and lodgers were not allowed on the estate. Girls were expected to go into service and boys to find work with accommodation provided. Lady Leigh shared his view in this matter, remarking:

> how horrified people would be if they happened to read in a newspaper that Lord Leigh who is supposed to be so attentive to poor people ... has a cottage in which he allows a father of three grown sons and two girls of a wide awake age viz. fourteen and ten together with a mother and several young children all herding together in a three room cottage. How can the commonest proprieties of life be observed in that house ...[55]

The village school was included in his annual inspection with notes made about its state of repair, staff changes and the standard of education. Although subsequent Education Acts diminished the need for such paternalistic interest in schools, Lord Leigh continued his annual subscription and his supply of coal as he considered that provided by the Local Education Authority to be of a much inferior quality.

Lord Leigh took a particular interest in education. He was chairman of the Masonic Boys' School where he was instrumental in setting up the 'Leigh Perpetuity Fund' to raise money for appointing one Warwickshire boy annually to the school. He was a Governor and Trustee of Rugby School and extended his interest in the education and welfare of the young into his work as a magistrate. In 1856 the County Reformatory for Boys was erected on a site at Weston-under-Wetherley, given by Lord Leigh at a nominal rent for ninety-nine years. It catered for ninety boys who were either taught various trades or were employed in the cultivation of the adjacent eighty acres of ground. This agricultural experience proved useful, when, as part of an emigration scheme, three boys, used to farm work, sailed to Canada aboard the *S.S. Polynesian* on 3 July 1884.

Conditions in gaols were also a concern for William Henry. The two existing ones in Warwick and Coventry were seriously overcrowded and 'little better than schools of vice and depravity'.[56] He introduced a motion for the establishment of a new single county gaol and this was accepted at the July 1853 Sessions. As a member of the Visiting Committee for Prisons, he continued to concern himself with prison environment and regime and many reforms, such as an improvement in diet, were brought about as a result of his intervention.

He was also very active in the rehabilitation of prisoners on their release from gaol. He liked to be notified in advance of their release so that he could visit them, in many instances offering them employment on his estates. On one occasion he secured the early release of a prisoner to enable him to take up an opportunity to emigrate to Canada.[57]

His paternalistic concern was not, however, confined to the young. Charles Booth, in his 1895 report on the condition of the aged poor, noted that Stoneleigh, Ashow and Westwood were among the parishes where the old were either kept on at light work or pensioned by the landowner. Only one family had been removed to the workhouse in the last twenty years and that through its own fault.[58] A Friendly Society had been set up at Stoneleigh in 1845, when William Henry had come of age, and this had successfully resolved the question of old-age pensions.

Correspondence in the Leigh collection reveals countless instances of compassion shown towards the elderly and poor, especially those who had been employed on the estate. Even when travelling abroad, William Henry kept in constant communication with Stoneleigh and, on hearing of any sickness, would instruct his housekeeper to ensure that food was made available to the sufferer and occasionally, as in the case of 'poor old William Knight', a bottle of port wine. Regular annual payments, too, were made to a tenant who had an imbecile daughter, and a recently widowed woman with four children was given four shillings a week. In instructing his agent to write, on her behalf, to the parish to apply for poor relief for the children, he said 'but you need not mention the four shillings ... as that is for her and not the children'.[59]

He obviously considered it to be his role in life to take care of 'these poor people' on the estate, ensuring that they did not go without food if unable to work, had reasonable living conditions and were kept occupied. In the case of a 'dirty slovenly fellow' who had seriously neglected his land and accrued a backlog of arrears, Lord Leigh was adamant that, even if he had to give up the holding, he should have a good garden for 'he must have something to work'.[60]

His paternalism extended beyond his tenantry. Individuals from all walks of life, some barely literate, wrote requesting help and he seemed to have a ready supply of five shilling postal orders which he sent by return of post. If, when absent from Stoneleigh, he heard of cottagers in distress, he would ask his agent to give them a pound coin which he would repay when they next met. The ribbon weavers of Coventry, who had been, in 1860, badly affected by the French Treaty, which reduced and eliminated all tariffs between the two countries, and by a very bleak winter, were one of the groups to be taken under his wing. By public appeal he raised over £40,000 and was instrumental in setting up Leigh Mills in Coventry to provide alternative employment during this period of industrial distress. In his capacity as chairman of the Coventry Emigration Committee, he assisted many of the unemployed workers to obtain passages from Liverpool to Canada. Help was also available on a personal level. A letter of 1862, addressed to Lord Leigh from William Court, contained a request for financial help to enable him to take his sister and her five children with him to Canada. A second letter, from Liverpool, stating that he had to sail the next day, or lose his deposit, and that he was only allowed to take two children with him on board the *John St. Bride*, elicited a swift response from Lord Leigh who sent a cheque for five pounds and an assurance of assistance for the remaining three children and their mother at a later date.[61]

If Kenilworth was the 'capital of his kingdom', then Stoneleigh Abbey was the heart of his family. In her autobiography his niece, Violet, recalls her childhood visits to Stoneleigh Abbey where family prayers were conducted each morning in the chapel within the house.

> We sat up in the gallery … the small army of domestics below was divided into
> males one side and females the other. Dear old Mrs. Wallace led the
> procession of maids, and Mr. Stenton, the large and pompous major domo,
> was in charge of the men servants. Uncle Leigh would appear and proceed to
> read prayers in a loud, impressive voice and dramatic manner.[62]

In her *Reminiscences* Cordelia Leigh, the youngest daughter of William Henry, recalled that her father's birthday was always celebrated by a servants' ball, held in the steward's room with supper in the servants' hall. 'My father opened the ball dancing with Mrs Wallace my mother with the butler'.[63]

The esteem in which Lord and Lady Leigh were held by their household staff was evident in the gifts made to them on the occasion of their Golden Wedding. A silver reading candlestick and silver salad bowl were presented, on behalf of the servants, by the house steward. The bowl was engraved with the Leigh crest and coronet together with the names of the house steward, the housekeeper and thirty-eight other household servants. The housekeeper, when showing

FIGURE 97
William Henry, second Lord Leigh, with his wife, Caroline Amelia, *c.* 1870

visitors around the Abbey, which was open without charge, would, after pointing out several portraits announce: 'Now I'll show you the best man in England'; and sweeping the cover aside would reveal that of William Henry second Baron Leigh.[64] This portrait had been presented to Lord and Lady Leigh at the County Hall, Warwick, to mark the occasion of their Golden Wedding. In his presentation speech the chairman, J.S. Dugdale, mentioned the numerous charities of which Lord Leigh was a trustee and commented on the fact that 'no man sent fewer excuses for non-attendance'.[65]

On top of all his other commitments, William Henry was Colonel of the third battalion of the Warwickshire Regiment, High Steward of Sutton Coldfield from 1859 to 1882 and, from 1856 until his death in 1905, Lord Lieutenant of the County. In that capacity it was his duty to act as host to Queen Victoria, when she came to open the 'Peoples' Park' in Aston, Birmingham, in June 1858. The cost of fitting and furnishing a suite of rooms for her personal use was in the region of £6,000, not to mention the sumptuous banquets prepared on each of the two nights she spent at Stoneleigh and the exhorbitant cost of illuminating the whole façade of the Abbey and gatehouse with 20,000 variegated coloured lamps. As this was half a century before the installation of electricity at the Abbey, the task of lighting the lamps was carried out by estate workers whilst the guests were at dinner.[66]

The Leigh family motto – 'Tout vient de Dieu' (All comes from God) – is appropriate for a paternalist, a man who

> never doubted that God had created a hierarchical society and that such a
> society was necessary and beneficial ... Just as children are dependent on
> those above them in the hierarchy of the family, so are agricultural labourers,
> servants, tenant farmers, and curates dependent on those of a higher rank.[67]

The *ideal* rural society was one in which a chain of hierarchical relationships existed, paternalistic in one direction and deferential in the other, with each individual 'knowing his place'.[68] Paradoxically, William Henry, as a Liberal, supported a government whose legislation gradually undermined this traditional relationship. The widening of the franchise, together with the elevation to the peerage of people with wealth accrued from sources other than land ownership, led to a more democratic system but one which gradually came to transfer dependency to the state. Following the great agricultural depression of the late nineteenth century, the pattern of land ownership also began to change. Many large estates either dwindled, through sales of small parcels of land, or sold outright to the *nouveaux riches*. Lord Leigh saw it as part of his duty to protect his tenants, as well as he could, from the severe effects of bad harvests, loss of markets and the general decline in agriculture. This he did by return of rent over a substantial period, which, of course, meant for him a fall in rentals and available income to spend on further improvements. This not uncommon predicament for landowners in the late nineteenth century was summed up by Oscar Wilde through Lady Bracknell's comment

> that between the duties expected of one during one's lifetime and the Duties exacted after one's death, land has ceased to be either a profit or a pleasure. It gives one position and prevents one keeping it up. That's all that can be said about land.[69]

William Henry's paternalistic attitude, in fact, hampered any attempt by his family or his agent to make reductions in expenditure. A suggestion, by Francis Dudley, his son and heir, to prune the labour force on the estate was rejected on the grounds that it would have meant the loss of jobs to 'old faithful employees'. Nor would he agree to his agent's proposal for charging the public a fee for driving through Stoneleigh Park, even though the maintenance of the road kept 'three men constantly at work' and, as was pointed out to him, other members of the aristocracy, such as the dukes of Portland and Newcastle and Earl Manvers, were already pursuing that source of income. The letting of shooting rights was also rejected on the grounds that tenants would not like strangers walking on their land. Any reduction in his contributions towards almshouses, annuities or subscriptions, which his agent thought to be of a 'very liberal scale', was flatly refused. As Lady Leigh commented: 'You cannot expect him to change at his time of life'. However, following his death, in 1905, his son reduced these sums considerably.

As a young man William Henry was described as 'the handsomest, most good-natured, least assuming person possible' and in old age delightful and easy going.[70] A letter of condolence to Caroline Amelia after his death supplies a fitting epitaph for a paternalist. 'I am sure there is no one to whom we all would sooner have been grandchildren ... he was to us a very real hero ... kind beyond the ordinary'.[71] To a sympathiser Caroline wrote: 'As a humble servant of God we love to think of him as at rest. The parting is bitter, but can be, for me, but a short time if God gives me grace'.

PART THREE

LANDS

CHAPTER EIGHT

The Medieval Abbey:

ITS LANDS AND ITS TENANTS

Andrew Watkins

Stoneleigh Abbey is one of the best documented religious houses in later medieval Warwickshire, and is particularly well served with material from the mid-twelfth to the late fourteenth centuries. Here pride of place must go to the Leger Book. Compiled in 1392 from the house's archive, it records all that the abbey as a landlord felt was important for posterity, such as details of its foundation, royal grants, its original property and possessions, the obligations of its tenants, purchases of further lands, the history of particular holdings. It also records some national events and gives brief biographies of the abbots up to the time of its compilation. Published by the Dugdale Society, with a characteristically scholarly and innovative introduction by Rodney Hilton, it forms the basis of much of our knowledge of the topography and society of the Forest of Arden in this period, supplemented by an extensive collection of deeds, some court rolls from the late fourteenth and fifteenth centuries, the rolls of the court of bedripe, and a few rentals and surveys.[1]

The monks of Stoneleigh Abbey could read the story of the origin of their house in the Leger Book in their library. They would have known that, had it not been for the aggressive behaviour of the bishop of Lichfield's foresters in the twelfth century, the abbey would never have been located at Stoneleigh. The story in the Leger Book tells of two devout hermits, Clement and Hervey, and their followers, who were granted land at Radmore, or Red Moor, near Beaudesert on Cannock Chase by King Stephen. Roger de Clinton, bishop of Chester, confirmed this grant and allowed them to follow whatever regular life they desired. From the time of their foundation the hermits complained that they were disturbed from their devotions by the bishop's foresters, and they appealed to the Empress Matilda to change their site. She agreed, provided that they would agree to adopt the Cistercian rule. They accepted this condition and Radmore became an abbey, and William, who had ruled over the hermits, its first abbot in

1140. Henry, duke of Normandy, the future Henry II, confirmed to them Radmore, with Mellsho and Wryley for tillage, and Hednesford for pasture. He allowed them to build a suitable church with a conventual house, and granted them Cannock. Other donors made gifts, such as Ranulph earl of Chester, Osbert de Arden, William Croc, Roger de Clinton and his kinsman, Geoffrey de Clinton, the chamberlain. The abbot and his monks appealed to Hamon, the abbot of another Cistercian house at Bordesley in Worcestershire, to send two of his convent to instruct them in Cistercian ways. However, in spite of this consolidation, its generous endowment, and powerful and influential benefactors, all was not well. The community continued to be inconvenienced by the foresters and Henry II was petitioned on the day of his accession in 1154 to exchange Radmore for his manor of Stoneleigh in Warwickshire. He agreed and the monks initially tried, but failed, to establish their new home near what subsequently became Cryfield grange. Then, on 11 April 1155, the abbey's foundation stone was laid, and its churchyard consecrated by the bishop of Coventry, on a site near the confluence of the Rivers Sowe and Avon.[2]

Originating in 1098 with the foundation of the 'New Monastery' at Citeaux by a group of Cluniac monks, the Cistercians were one of the new monastic orders of the twelfth century. Their aim was to return to the original ideals of the rule of St Benedict, which they modified, however, in a number of ways. For example, they spent less time attending the liturgical services and instead undertook private prayer, reading and manual labour. In contrast with other orders, they sought to distance themselves in worship from the laity and reduced the amount of ritual in their services. To further spiritual simplicity, the Cistercians used iron for their candlesticks rather than gold or silver, did not have elaborate vestments and wore linen rather than silk. They were an order with strict discipline and scorned the comfortable life by locating their houses in remote, sparsely populated places. They believed in the spiritual benefits of hard labour and, to aid this, developed a new class of monks called the lay brethren. These men were generally drawn from the ranks of the uneducated peasantry and undertook the manual work of the house. The Cistercians were strict vegetarians and were often called the White Monks by contemporaries because of their undyed habits, in contrast to the lay brethren's which were brown. Another symbol of their austerity was the order's insistence on a lack of underwear and breeches, while the use of combs and bedspreads and cooking with lard was also forbidden. They deliberately avoided feudal obligations and, because they believed in generating their income through hard work rather than through tithe, they did not have any appropriated churches. Therefore each abbey was meant to be self-sufficient. The Cistercians were innovative farmers and throughout England they brought marginal land into cultivation, developing a mixed economy of cereals and livestock. Their granges often specialised in cattle and sheep ranching and they encouraged industry on their lands, with many Cistercian abbeys being active in metallurgy and coal-mining.

FIGURE 98-99
The Stoneleigh Leger Book
(SBTRO, DR 18/31/1)

FIGURE 100
Cistercian monk, as illustrated in W. Dugdale,
Monasticon Anglicanum, 1817-30 edn, v, 219

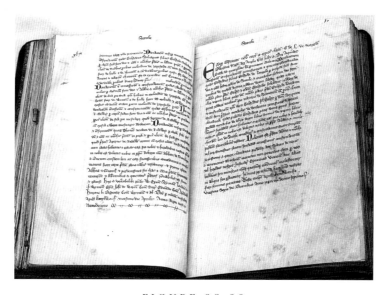

FIGURE 98-99
The Stoneleigh Leger Book (SBTRO, DR 18/31/1)

These beliefs and ideals evidently struck a chord in contemporary society and the movement enjoyed rapid growth. The Cistercians established their first house in England at Waverley in Surrey in 1128. They soon became very popular and received great patronage, with the peak of their foundations coming during Stephen's reign (1135-1154). The decision to locate a Cistercian house at Stoneleigh in the mid-twelfth century, along with others at Merevale in 1148 and Combe in 1150, tells us much about the area at the time, given the order's association with uncultivated, untamed lands, where their monks and lay brethren could help to fulfil their ideals through austerity and hard travail.[3]

The Leger Book tells us that Stoneleigh had been ancient demesne of the crown at the time of Edward the Confessor. The estate was then much larger. Besides Stoneleigh, it included Kenilworth, Baginton, Ryton-on-Dunsmore and Stareton, which were later granted to loyal supporters by Henry I. The endowment given to the monks of Radmore was therefore smaller than Edward the Confessor's royal manor. The abbey was always well aware that Stoneleigh had once been ancient demesne of the Crown, and, following the grant of rights in the second charter of King John, which clearly defined their special jurisdiction, the monks reinforced this with the self-conscious concept of their jurisdictional rights within the manor as a 'soke', a term common enough in eastern counties at this time, but unique in Warwickshire.[4]

The abbey enjoyed royal patronage. In his foundation charter Henry II had given the monks twelve ploughlands, a mill worth forty shillings, easement in his woods, firewood and timber for the building of the house, and granges at Radway and Merston. He also granted them twenty-five *summa* of salt, which later charters suggest was a relic of some earlier arrangements involving the ancient salt-producing borough of Droitwich and the previously royal hundred centre of Stoneleigh. In a subsequent grant Henry II exempted the monks from passage, pontage and all customs. Richard I confirmed this as did King John in 1204. In a second charter, John gave Stoneleigh the status of a soke and made reference to the waste of Wetherle and the assart of Hurst. All these grants were confirmed by the Lateran Council of 1215.[5] The abbey continued to receive royal patronage: in 1241, following a fire which badly damaged the monastic buildings, the sheriff of Warwickshire had to deliver forty oaks from of the king's wood at Kenilworth to help with the repairs.[6] The abbey attracted other benefactors. Richard, bishop of Coventry, granted the abbey two hides in Radway, Osbert de Arden gave his lands in Merston, and Geoffrey de Clinton three yardlands.[7] The abbey also received many gifts from the less exalted in the first few years after its foundation, such as the four selions from William le Harper, a peasant from Canley, the two roods in Ashow from William Tysoe, the furlong in Bericote from William Fromund, and lands and rents in Loxley and Cubbington.[8] The abbey received a number of small gifts at Radway on Edgehill, sometimes known as Edge Grange, or the grange of Radway. The monks were also given land in the neighbouring parish of Ratley by Waleran, earl of Warwick, between 1184 and 1204, and by various members of the Arden family. The abbey's endowment was further increased in 1286 when Thomas de Ardern granted the church of Ratley, together with four carucates of demesne arable there, and John de Mercote lands in Ratley and Radway. By the 1390s some of these gifts were for specific purposes – to pay for tapers burning at the abbey's high altar, for example – while gifts of lands and rents continued into the fifteenth century, including Sir Thomas Cokesey's extensive gift in 1497 of a messuage and lands.[9] The extent of the abbey's lands at the end of the thirteenth century is reflected in a papal bull of Nicholas IV of 1290 which confirmed to the monks land in Stoneleigh, Home Grange, Bericote, Radway, Stareton, Cryfield, Dalle Wood, Westwood, Crackley, Loxley, Hill Wootton, Ashow, Ullenhall, Wetherley Wood, Radford Semele and Langley.[10]

Although Stoneleigh may have been on the very edge of the Arden woodlands and the champion lands of the Avon valley, the monks considered themselves to be part of the former. In the Leger Book they often refer to the place as 'Stonley-in-Arden'. The broad features of the historic development of the Arden are well known. Much of its landscape lies over 400 feet and, before modern agricultural techniques and fertilisers, its cold, damp soils were fit only for rough pasture. The Domesday Book shows it to have been an under-developed area compared to the Feldon in the south of the county. There were fewer inhabitants, the estates were worth less, and a great deal was still covered by woodland. The pressure of population expansion and economic development of the twelfth and thirteenth centuries saw the major colonisation of the Arden, during which time the landscape was transformed through the clearance of the woodland. Villages and hamlets grew in size, while new settlements and homesteads were carved out of the woodland and waste.[11]

At the time of the abbey's foundation, Stoneleigh was a populous manor, with sixty-eight villeins, four bordars and two priests holding thirty carucates of land. There were also four bondmen, or servants, who each held a messuage and one quarter of a yardland, by services of making the gallows and the hanging of thieves. They were to wear a red clout between their shoulders upon their upper garments, to plough twice a year and reap as often (in other words, the two bedripes), to give aid to the lord at the feast of St Michael, and to make the lord's malt and do other servile work.[12] By the mid-twelfth century six settlements existed within the soke. There was Stoneleigh itself, Stareton, a mile to the south-east on the River Avon, Finham to the north-east on the River Sowe, Cryfield three miles to the north-west of the abbey, Canley about a mile to the north-east of Cryfield, and Fletchamstead in the north-west of the parish lying adjacent to the parishes of Allesley and Berkswell.[13] In the tallage of 1305 Stoneleigh was the largest settlement with thirty-two taxed persons. Finham had seven, Kingshill (or Helen Hill), ten, Fletchamstead thirteen, Canley eleven, Stareton eleven, Cryfield sixteen, Hurst, a mile to the west of Cryfield, seventeen, and Milburn eleven. The 1327 lay subsidy confirms these relative sizes. A late fourteenth-century rental shows that these were still the divisions of the soke at the time, while the predominantly late fifteenth-century court rolls reveal that Stoneleigh, Finham,

Canley, Fletchamstead and Hurst were the tithings of the view of frankpledge.[14] The evidence of non-hereditary locative surnames recorded in the 1280 Hundred Rolls, the 1305 tallage and the 1327 lay subsidy suggests an influx of new colonists into the Stoneleigh area during this time. Although some of the abbey's tenants, from the evidence of their surnames, had come from settlements within the Arden, such as Alpsath, Pinley and Chilvers Coton, many others had migrated from places outside the woodlands, such as Withybrook, Stretton, Offchurch, Hampton, Halford, Wroxton and Chesterton, all in Warwickshire, and Shackerstone in Leicestershire. Non-hereditary surnames also show us that many of the peasants were involved in wood and metal crafts, as well as agricultural activities.[15]

As in other parts of the Forest of Arden, there was much assarting (woodland clearance) in Stoneleigh. In 1086 it was a well-wooded manor, with pasture for 2,000 swine. By the second half of the twelfth century the cultivated fields are recorded in the valleys of the Rivers Avon and Sowe, around Cryfield, and on a smaller scale at Canley and Fletchamstead. Hilton has estimated that by this time only about a fifth of the area of Stoneleigh parish had been brought under cultivation while the remainder was pasture, marsh, heath and woodland.[16] The Leger Book tells us that throughout the late twelfth and thirteenth centuries the abbey was actively clearing woodland and buying up the land of free peasants to extend and consolidate its demesne. There was some assarting around the abbey itself, to the south-east at Echills, and four open fields were brought into cultivation from Waverley Woods. Much greater assarting was undertaken in the north of the parish, at Hurst and to the north of Finham Brook. Much of this cleared land was in closes in severalty, small enclosed fields that lay outside the communal system of agrarian regulation.[17] By the later middle ages Stoneleigh had a landscape typical of many other Arden parishes with some open fields divided into furlongs – Brook Field, Little Field and Wood Field, along the Avon and Sowe valleys – and many hedged and ditched closes in severalty lying to the north of the parish.[18] Despite the assarting, much woodland remained in the later medieval Arden, in carefully managed, enclosed seignorial woodland. By the fifteenth century Westwood was the largest surviving tract of woodland in Stoneleigh, lying to the north of the soke and merging into the woods of neighbouring Allesley and Berkswell. By the time of the Hundred Rolls of 1279, when the assarting movement within the Arden was largely abating, the abbot of Stoneleigh still had 1,000 acres of common woods and waste in Dalle, Westwood and Crackley.[19] The Arden peasants enjoyed many common rights in woodlands, but this evidently caused some social tension at Stoneleigh. Many peasants felt that the abbot was trying to deny them such rights: in 1290 there was a petition to Parliament in which the peasants, as men of the king's ancient demesne, claimed rights of estovers in the woods, which would have included the rights to be able to collect nuts and pannage for pigs and other animals, to be able to build pigsties, and to use roads and paths to the church, market and vills of the abbot.[20]

As well as trying to assert his rights at the expense of his tenants, there were other ways in which the abbot behaved as a typical landlord of the period. In 1284 he obtained a grant of free warren in Stoneleigh, Echills, Home Grange, Stareton, Waverley, Milburn, Cryfield, Bockendon, Horwell, King's Hill, Hurst, Finham and Canley. This would have allowed him to enjoy privileged hunting rights over small game, such as hares, rabbits and game birds. The *Quo Warranto* returns, an inquiry ordered by Edward I into the jurisdictional rights of landlords, reveals that the abbot had strong and extensive rights of jurisdiction in his soke, including the view of frankpledge, the assize of bread and ale, infangtheof (the right to hang thieves caught red-handed), the right to distrain the goods of felons, the tumbrel (the right to parade those who infringe the court) and pillory. These are almost certainly a reflection of Stoneleigh's late Saxon status as a royal hundred centre, a place where royal justice would have been administered. The abbot sought to exploit the upsurge in marketing of the period, obtaining a charter in 1284 for a Thursday market and a lengthy eight-day fair around the eve of the feast of the nativity of St John the Baptist. However, when compared to other towns and village markets in the Arden, these are comparatively late foundations and do not appear to have met with any long-term success.[21]

The early economic history of the house is poorly documented. It owned the almost 10,000-acre manor of Stoneleigh, properties in the Avon Valley at Hill Wootton and Loxley, and the lands on Edgehill, on the fringe of the Cotswold Hills, in the adjoining parishes of Ratley and Radway. Compared to other Warwickshire houses, such as Coventry Cathedral Priory and Kenilworth Priory, its land endowment was never great. By the thirteenth century Stoneleigh's agriculture was based upon the system of granges, a characteristic feature of Cistercian foundations. These were farms within an integrated estate system and were usually composed of a complex of agricultural buildings staffed by the monks and the lay brethren, producing foodstuffs and wool for the consumption of the house and for the market. Often these granges specialised in production, either in cereals, sheep farming or cattle ranching.[22] The Cistercians have earned themselves a generally bad reputation in their creation of granges, as often, and notoriously, they were established through the enclosure, eviction and depopulation of existing settlements. However, although the initial relocation of Stoneleigh Abbey from Red Moor involved the removal of tenants from Cryfield to Hurst, the creation of its granges does not seem to have caused the sort of social tension and ill will that occurred at Moorbarn on Merevale Abbey's estate, or as the result of the actions of the abbot of Combe at Smite.[23] Stoneleigh Abbey had eight granges within the soke: the home grange, Stoneleigh, Bockendon, Cryfield, Milburn, King's Hill, Stareton and Horwell, as well as a grange at Radway. During this time it probably practised cereal and legume cultivation, and the keeping of beef and dairy cattle herds. In 1291 the home grange consisted of five ploughlands, a mill and stock worth two pounds, while Cryfield supported animals to the value of three pounds.[24] As with other Cistercian houses, wool production was important, although it may be that the sheep were grazed on the abbey's lands in the Feldon which were better suited to a regime of sheep and corn farming. The grange at Radway was said to have pasture for 300 sheep, while a list compiled by Pegolotti, the agent of the Florentine Bardi house, shows that Stoneleigh Abbey, along with the other Cistercian houses in the Arden – Merevale and Combe – was maintaining a large sheep flock in the early fourteenth century, with Stoneleigh Abbey selling Pegolotti up to ten sacks of wool a year. A later reference of 1324 reveals that the abbot was in debt to two Italians, Gilebaldi and Malocello, in the sum of £150, and this should most likely be seen in the same context.[25]

Social controls and servile obligations were never heavy in the Arden. In their eagerness to attract settlers to develop their woodland resources, many lords were prepared to overlook their new tenants' original status. The 1279-80 Hundred Rolls show that in Stoneleigh Hundred fifty per cent of the landholding population were free tenants, twenty-three per cent were cottagers or small holders, and the remainder unfree. In contrast, in Kineton Hundred in the south of the county, almost fifty per cent were unfree. Between 1086 and 1279 there was a decline in the number of villein tenants in the Arden, whilst the number of freeholders increased, particularly in those areas of greatest population growth. The undeveloped Arden therefore offered the opportunity to escape from servile status.[26] On the Stoneleigh Abbey estates such obligations were light, with reaping services of a few days, commuted to small cash payments. The Leger Book contains detailed customs of the manor. Many of these are concerned with the grazing of animals. The abbot was not allowed to put his cattle onto the commons, while the tenants could pasture cattle, sheep and their cows there. Pigs were banned from the commons because they would destroy the pasture by breaking up the ground. Peasants were forbidden to cut down trees from the commons or to take away thorns, broom and ferns. They were allowed the estovers of husbote, haybote, and firebote, that is, the rights to enter the abbey's woodlands and take underwood to repair their houses, their fences and enclosures, and for firewood. They also had the right to pasture swine in the Out Wood. Some of the Stoneleigh woods were inter-commoned with peasants from Canley, Stivichall and Kenilworth, but no such arrangements existed with the men from the Templar manor at Fletchamstead, nor with those from Berkswell and Allesley. There were also more general customs which can be found on many other manors. The tenants were obliged to grind their corn at the abbot's mill, they could not give hospitality to any stranger or foreigner, they could not sell their property without the lord's permission, they could not fish in the small brooks of the manor and they had to pay a halfpenny per pig for pannage at the feast of St Martin.[27]

The same customal gives details of the court of bedripe. All tenants were required to come into the fields to reap the abbot's corn. The sokemen were to ride to the fields carrying a white wand, presumably a symbol of their status. All were to be there before sunrise and to

OUTLINE MAP OF STONELEIGH PARISH AND SOKE

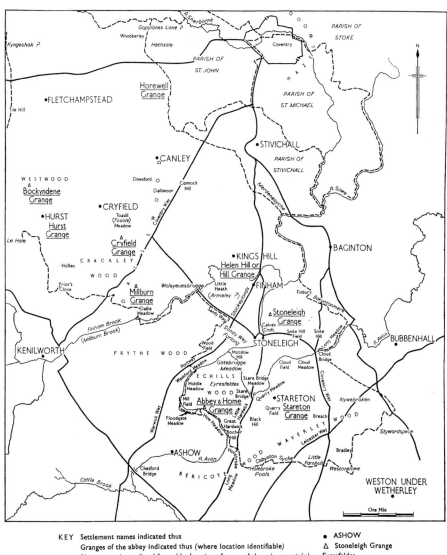

KEY Settlement names indicated thus
      Granges of the abbey indicated thus (where location identifiable)
      Place names in medieval form (the location of some of these is uncertain)
      Place names in post-medieval form
      Boundaries of Stoneleigh and Coventry extra-mural parishes indicated thus

• ASHOW
△ Stoneleigh Grange
Eyresfeldes
Cloud Field
- - - - - - - -

FIGURE 101

Map to illustrate the principal places mentioned in the text: reproduced, with permission, from *The Stoneleigh Leger Book*, ed. R.H. Hilton, Dugdale Society, xxiv, 1960

work until sunset. They were not allowed to sit down before breakfast, nor to eat during the lord's time, nor to expect the lord to provide food for this meal. After breakfast they were allowed to rest once before dinner, when the abbot supplied drink. At nine o'clock the abbot was supposed to give meat, food and drink to the sokemen, while the other reapers were to sit and presumably feed themselves. The sokemen were to be given a small white loaf, four eggs and a pottage made without meat (which the Leger Book calls 'Gruwel'), along with cheese and sufficient drink. Even into the 1490s, bedripe courts were maintained at Stoneleigh, still held in the fields, and, although largely an anachronism, fines levied on defaulters there still generated some benefit to the abbot.[28]

Although the plague was in England by the late summer of 1348 it probably did not reach Warwickshire until 1349. It is difficult to appreciate or quantify the high mortality rates the disease caused, but it is believed that about forty per cent of the Warwickshire peasantry died from the epidemic. On the Stoneleigh Abbey estates whole families, such as that of John le Heyr, were wiped out. Robert Bedull and Geoffrey Doore both lost all their heirs. The death rate was also high among the religious communities, such as at Henwood Priory, where only three survived out of a prioress and fifteen nuns, while the death of the sixteenth abbot of Stoneleigh, Robert de Hockley in 1349, may well be attributable to the plague.[29] Bubonic plague remained in England until the late seventeenth century, but with national epidemics becoming less frequent and outbreaks more localised. However, before 1485 there were at least another eleven national outbreaks. This heavy mortality led to a restructuring of rural society in the fifteenth and sixteenth centuries, most obviously in the relaxation and eventual abandonment of social controls and servile status, and the conversion of arable land into pasture.[30]

The prevailing economic condition of the fifteenth century encouraged many landlords throughout England to abandon the direct farming of their estates, and instead to lease out their manors for a regular cash income.[31] However, within the Arden a number of religious houses, such as Maxstoke Priory, Nuneaton Priory and Merevale Abbey, continued to manage some of their lands directly. They all maintained home farms and judiciously used their tithe grains either to feed their households or to sell in the market. They grazed large cattle herds and Maxstoke Priory made some money from sales of dairy produce. Others maintained the monastic tradition of sheep farming. Merevale Abbey had large sheep flocks on its Derbyshire and Leicestershire granges and Coventry Cathedral Priory continued to keep large sheep flocks in pastures around Coventry. Some of these houses made money from shrewd use of their woodlands and mineral resources, such as making charcoal, selling off underwood and timber, mining coal, quarrying stone and manufacturing tiles and bricks.[32] Much of the information for Stoneleigh Abbey's economic activity during this time is incidental, occasional terse references scribbled on rentals and court rolls. There are a number of late fifteenth-century rentals which show that most of the estate, including grain and fulling mills, fisheries, pastures and the granges at Milburn and King's

Hill, were at farm.[33] However, as with other landlords, the monks often retained some lands to provision their household with foodstuffs. It appears that the home grange was maintained for this purpose. There are also references in 1466 to the abbey selling off wheat and barley, while a Coventry butcher bought from the monks fourteen ewes, nineteen calves and fourteen bullocks.[34] However, the most detailed information about the house's economy comes during the 1530s during the final few years of its existence. After the end of the rule of Abbot Robert Sutton in 1532 it was felt necessary to hold an inquiry into the abbey's assets, conducted by the abbot of Mary Graces in London and the abbot of Bordesley. Interestingly, they interpreted this to include not only listing the silverware of the house, such as the crosses, chalices, pyxes, crewets and ampulas, but also all the abbey's livestock. This operation must have been based upon the home grange outside the abbey's walls. It would appear that, as with other Arden landlords, the emphasis had moved from sheep husbandry to cattle grazing by the end of the medieval period. There was a large dairy herd of forty cows with five bulls, along with thirty-four calves, while the house grazed a further forty steers. There were thirty horses, a very large number for the use of a comparatively small household, and it may be that, as with Maxstoke Priory, there was a horse stud within the abbey. There were thirty pigs and a sheep flock of 226, whose clip no doubt went through entrepreneurial merchants into the Coventry wool industry. These livestock numbers seem far too large just to feed the abbot and the twelve monks in the abbey in 1536.[35] Therefore the abbey was generating income, along with many other Arden landlords, by selling the profitable products of animal husbandry – meat, dairy produce and wool — to the large urban market of Coventry. The abbey was probably also cultivating cereals and legumes at this time, but the two abbots in 1532 did not deem these of sufficient value to record. When the abbey site was leased after the Dissolution in 1536 it included gardens, orchards, stables, ponds and fisheries, a water mill, thirteen acres of pasture and nineteen shillings-worth of meadow and their herbage. The home grange lay adjacent to the abbey. In 1539 this consisted of 177 acres of pasture and 102 acres of arable land. In contrast to many other Arden home farms of the period, it had not been converted entirely to pasture and a significant acreage was still given over to arable cultivation.[36] A list of debts of the abbot drawn up in 1536 reveals the abbey was still active in cattle grazing. Most of its beasts were bought from local peasants, such as the three kine and ten beasts bought from Thomas Nelson of Stoneleigh. In the months covered by the list of debts, the abbey bought thirty-three cows, eleven steers, ten heifers, two bulls, and 'four fate bease' ready for slaughter. At the same time the monks were buying up malt to brew ale. They owed Roger Palmer, a fishmonger of Coventry, £2 17s. 6d. for 'lenten stuff', presumably for fish to eat during this time of dietary restriction. They also made visits to the great fair at Stourbridge and were still directly exploiting their woods, as shown by their debt of nine pounds to Richard Hill for carriage of faggots made on the abbey's estate to Coventry.[37]

The abbey's court rolls, which survive from the 1470s until the first decade of the next century, give something of the flavour of rural life in Stoneleigh at this time.[38] Errant peasants were fined for failing to keep their ditches in good repair, others were instructed to ring their pigs to try and restrict the damage their rooting could do, whilst any stray animals coming into the lordship were impounded.[39] As on other Arden manors, there are obvious signs of rural decay, with property apparently often in poor condition. Seignorial assets, such as mills and fisheries, were in need of repair, abandoned servile holdings give hints of vagabondage, while references to tofts and land falling out of arable cultivation show property and land surplus to requirements.[40] Well-known adjustments in land ownership which occurred on other Arden manors are also apparent on the Stoneleigh lands. There was a gradual abandonment of unfree status and the evolution of copyhold, while tenants and lessees were committed to longer leases.[41] Another well-known feature was the ability of certain peasant families to build up large holdings composed of both free and unfree land, such as the well-established Bacon family who, by the end of the fifteenth century, had amassed a holding of two messuages, three yardlands, two acres of wood and twelve acres of meadow in Finham. On an even larger scale, Oliver Burdet, a rising peasant from Kinghill, was able to build up a holding composed of the grange of Kinghill, along with seven messuages, four curtileges, six and a half yardlands, three tofts, three crofts, 14½ acres, a cottage, three butts, 65½ acres and eighty selions.[42]

Cereal cultivation was important in the later medieval Arden, although the acreage under communal control was significantly less than in the Feldon. The irregular nature of the Arden field systems has long been appreciated and the typical arrangements of a champion village of two fields planted with winter and spring crops, whilst a third lay fallow, was very unusual in the Arden.[43] At Stoneleigh, as with other Arden settlements, there were many cropping units, and many tenants owned their land in a mixture of open fields, crofts and enclosures in severalty, such as John Shuckbourgh, whose holding of thirty-eight acres lay in open fields and enclosed lands. Many Stoneleigh tenants defied the manor courts and made their own enclosures. This had the advantage of increasing the value of the land and also gave the peasant greater freedom of choice over what use the land was put to, whether to graze, plant the crop of his choice or to deny fallow, which would have kept it in almost constant cultivation.[44] At Fletchamstead a number of men were enclosing land from the abbot's waste and from Westwood. This piecemeal enclosing continued well into the sixteenth century and beyond, and the open fields at King's Hill and Stareton were enclosed by agreement among the cultivators in about 1580 and 1598 respectively, while Canley was also enclosed sometime in the sixteenth century.[45]

Enclosing land and then converting it to pasture was not only widespread among the peasantry. The Domesday of Inclosures, a survey resulting from concerns in Henry VIII's reign over the harmful effects of enclosure, reported that the abbot had enclosed some lands in 1486, putting two ploughs out of use and making sixteen homeless. The survey of monastic estates made in 1540-1 shows that most of the abbey's more profitable leases were pastures. Many, such as at Griggs Pool in Stoneleigh and Juyngs, Sloberds and Horewell in Fletchamstead, were also described as waste, implying land which had fallen out of cultivation.[46] The Smyths, a family of lawyers from Coventry actively seeking the status of gentry, acquired many leaseholds in Fletchamsted, including the Catesby's small estate of Nether Fletchamsted. In 1497 John Smyth was amerced in the manor court for enclosing 12½ acres from Westwood. The depopulation commission of 1517 reported that John Smyth had emparked over 100 acres in Fletchamsted in 1493, while his son, Henry, had converted another 160 acres of arable into pasture at Fletchamsted in 1497, making four ploughs idle and twenty-six persons homeless. The family also enclosed lands in Grafton, and continued its consolidation of its lands in Fletchamsted until the 1640s.[47] The number of tenants was falling in the settlements of the soke of Stoneleigh in the fifteenth and early sixteenth centuries, reflecting a combination of the low level of population at this time, the greater social mobility among the peasantry and the desire of landowners to create large, more profitable enclosed pastures. The situation in Stoneleigh was evidently so well known locally that it came to the attention of John Rous, who was able to record that by the beginning of Henry VII's reign there was depopulation on the abbey's lands. He understood that at Hurst, out of nineteen houses, only one was left; at Cryfield, out of twelve, only the Grange remained; at Finham eight out of twelve houses had gone; and that Milburn, the site, significantly, of another of the abbey's granges, had been completely depopulated.[48]

On a number of other Arden manors at the turn of the sixteenth century there was an apparent shortage of land for cereals and this renewed demand for arable land was partly accommodated by ploughing up land which had either lapsed out of cultivation or had never been used. In 1501, at Finham, Richard Kyng was amerced for ploughing up a meer in le Churchway and a common croft called Henscroft, while John Clerke of Coventry was reported as having ploughed a common 'balk' (a grassy bank which lay between the strips of an open field) in the abbot's waste. This suggests that Clerke was bringing back into use land which had lapsed from arable cultivation into waste.[49] Sixteenth-century inventories show that in Stoneleigh rye was sown as the main winter crop and oats for spring, while evidence dating from other fifteenth-century Arden settlements shows that peasants typically grew wheat, barley, oats, and peas and beans, while John Kent from the neighbouring manor of Stivichall had rye, oats, drage and barley harvested from his holding in 1481. Although not recorded in Stoneleigh until much later, it is well known that other Arden peasants grew industrial crops on their lands, often in special plots – for example, flax to make linen, and hemp to make canvas.[50]

One of the main features of Arden agriculture in the later Middle Ages was the movement away from arable to pastoral farming. Birmingham and Coventry were particularly large centres of the cattle trade and many acres of land in those manors immediately surrounding Birmingham were given over to pasture for this purpose, many of the animals originating in north and mid Wales. Sheep were of much greater importance to the economy of Coventry and lands to the south and east of the city than to that of Birmingham. By the late fifteenth century many sheep were pastured immediately around the city, at times causing considerable social discord. Much of the larger scale enclosure recorded by John Rous in these manors should probably be seen in this context. Stoneleigh's position on the southern fringe of the Arden in the Avon valley meant that sheep were more important there than in many other Arden manors.[51]

Before the detailed probate inventories of the mid sixteenth century it is difficult to quantify livestock numbers among the peasantry. The evidence of strays from the Stoneleigh court rolls suggests strongly that there were more cattle than sheep, even though the latter were notoriously more prone to straying. Probate inventories from the later sixteenth century suggest that a model farm economy supported a dozen cattle and between twenty and forty sheep, a likely reflection of the situation earlier in the century, while stints from the sixteenth century reveal that each yardlander could graze up to sixty sheep, twelve cattle, and three horses on Stoneleigh's commons.[52] The large numbers of animals grazing in the Arden pastures supported arable cultivation through the creation of large quantities of manure. 'Mukkehilloks' are well recorded in the court roll of 1477, while Richard Stonley and William Stockton were in dispute in 1431 over the sale of manure which was to have been used for the improvement of the former's land. A hint of the complex nature of the sub-leasing of animals among the peasantry is reflected in a quarrel in 1493 between Thomas Edwards, who had leased one of his cows for four years to William Morys, presumably for its milk: discord arose when the latter broke the agreement by failing to replace any male calves born to the cow with female offspring.[53]

Peasants continued to exploit the woodland resources of the manor, taking oaks and underwood from the lord's woods and waste, and lopping branches off the lord's ashes on the waste.[54] Others were involved in industrial processes. Many craftsmen migrated out of Coventry to the manors and parishes of its hinterland, partly to escape the restrictive practices of the gilds. The most obvious industry in Stoneleigh was fulling, and the abbey granted many leases of its fulling mills on the Avon. In 1535 the monks received £15 10s. 0d. from their six mills, most of which had been converted for fulling. The court rolls contain references to cloth workers, and also to a man from Chipping Warden in Northamptonshire putting out a white cloth to a Stoneleigh fuller. By 1600 there were still six fulling mills in Stoneleigh. A number of other crafts are mentioned in the court rolls and deeds, such as wire-drawers, who were also important in cloth manufacture, and others involved in metal and wood crafts, while in the Canley area there was some pottery manufacture using local clay.[55]

Very little evidence has survived about the daily life within the abbey. A sacrist's account survives from 1466. He was the official who was responsible for the maintenance of the services and the account reveals him buying large amounts of wax for the candles and tapers which burned on the altars, in the chapels, and before the statues and images within the abbey church – for example, the five pounds of wax bought for the feast of the Holy Cross. He paid for repairs to vestments and an altar frontal, and for altar cloths to be washed. He purchased silk and a veil cord, and spent 2s. 4d. on cloth to make a canopy. He paid a glazier the same to repair a window, and eight pence to a paver for work on a pavement in the church.[56] Within the abbey were the monks, their domestic servants, and also corrodians. These were usually elderly people who negotiated agreements with the house to allow them to spend their declining years in accommodation within the abbey, with a specified food allowance and often with arrangements for other incidental matters such as firewood and washing clothes. Only two corrody agreements survive for Stoneleigh. In 1391 an agreement was reached between the abbot and John de Etone, whereby the latter received a chamber in the abbey next to the porter's chamber, and a curtilege or garden, with a generous weekly allowance of twelve white loaves called 'prycked myches' and twelve other loaves called 'second dozen', presumably of inferior quality. He was also to receive meat and fish from the abbey's kitchen, which he could wash down with seven gallons of the convent's ale. A later agreement of 1477 between William Huby, a recently-retired abbot of Warden in Bedfordshire, provided him weekly with twenty-four loaves of white bread, fifteen gallons of ale and two dishes of meat and fish.[57]

The Leger Book gives some biographical details of the abbots. Some were clearly learned and worthy men, such as William of Gyldeford, the ninth abbot, made penitentiary to Pandulf, the papal legate, and who subsequently was sent to Wales with legatine authority. However, he made many enemies and, because of his countenancing of a duel fought by the abbey's shepherd and of his hanging a cattle thief, he was prosecuted and deprived in 1235. The tenth abbot, Osbert of Westwalle, presided over much laxness: in 1258 it was reported that several monks were wandering abroad. Robert of Hockley was the abbot between 1308 and 1349. He contributed much to the buildings of the abbey. The Leger Book records that he built new stalls for the choir, commissioned much carved work, including the rood screen under the tower, had a great window installed over the altar, had the gatehouse built and had it and most of the church covered with lead.[58]

Thomas Pype is generally thought to have been the compiler of the Leger Book. He became abbot in 1352 when he was still in his twenties, and it is likely that he came from a family from the Erdington area whose status lay somewhere between the gentry and the greater peasantry. Dugdale held Pype in some considerable regard for his gift to posterity of the Leger Book, but he evidently led a colourful and scandalous life. In 1364 the administration of the abbey was taken into the king's hands because of Pype's involvement in a violent attack, and his 'misrule by granting corrodies to improper persons, improvident of the demises of lands, and the excessive and unfruitful expenses of the (abbots)'. A jury of local men reported that the main beneficiary was Isabella of Beausale, his concubine with whom he had a blatant liaison, and their eldest son, John. In all, their children were said to out number the monks at mass. In October 1364 the king took the abbey into his own hands, and Pype went on the run with a group of accomplices who menaced the house. His successor, Abbot Alexander, denounced him to the king as a vagabond in secular habit and his arrest was ordered. A number of Pype's accomplices then broke into the abbey and stole the abbey's seal, deeds and muniments. In 1368 inquiries were ordered into the robbery and destruction of the abbey's property, and in the following year six more monks were reported as vagabonds in secular habit. Amazingly, in 1372, Pype was once again the abbot, although in 1380 there was a renewal of hostilities over leases made by Pype and accusations of the misuse of the abbey seal. By 1382 he had retired and was farming Cryfield grange.[59]

The great survey of the wealth of the church lands, the *Valor Ecclesiasticus* of 1535, shows that Stoneleigh Abbey had an annual income of £178 2s. 5½d. in 1536. It received £6 5s. 11d. from rents of assize from properties in Stoneleigh, Finham, Kingshill, Canley, Hurst, Fletchamsted and Cryfield, as well as from places further afield such as Warwick, Leamington Priors, Ullenhall, Horley, Ashow, Hill Wootton, Cubbington and Radway. By far the greatest income was generated from the leases of the abbey's lands, tenements, meadows and pastures within Stoneleigh, including six mills on the River Avon, and also properties at Hill Wootton, Cubbington, Radway, Nuneaton and Loxley, a garden within the city of Coventry, and meadow land at Napton-on-the-Hill, Leamington Priors and Stivichall. The abbey was also farming out to divers persons its demesne, previously reserved for the use of the household, and this brought in a further £43 6s. 8d., while sales of wood generated forty shillings.

In 1536 the Commissioners reported that the house was ruinous, but with bells and lead the site was worth £214 19s. 4¼d. The stocks, stores and chattels were worth £173 15s. 3d. and the abbey owned 548 acres of wood, with the whole abbey complex worth £208 3s. 0d. There were found to be the abbot and eleven monks, as well as the abbot's (presumably elderly) predecessor, fifteen yeomen servants, twenty-one hinds, two dairy women, five corrodians, two found of alms, and one having an annuity by the covenant seal. It owed £212 19s. 10¼d. On its dissolution in 1536 it passed, along with Maxstoke Priory, to Henry VIII's brother-in-law, Charles Brandon, duke of Suffolk.[60]

And thus after 381 years the abbey at Stoneleigh came to an end, its monks were pensioned off, its resources plundered, and the stage set for the arrival of the Leigh family.

Acknowledgements

I am very grateful to Christopher Dyer and Robert Bearman for their helpful advice in the preparation of this paper.

CHAPTER NINE

From Hermitage to Hunting Lodge:

STONELEIGH DEER PARK –
A LANDSCAPE HISTORY

George Demidowicz

In about 1640 a deer park was carved out of part of the Stoneleigh and Stareton estate. This chapter could confine itself to the process of emparkment and analyse the subsequent developments which led up to the significant extension of the park in the early nineteenth century (see Chapter Ten). The documentary record, however, is remarkably thin, particularly on the way the park was managed, perceived and appreciated after its creation. This is ironic in view of the deep and extensive nature of the Leigh collection at the Shakespeare Birthplace Trust. Amongst its riches, however, are an estate plan and survey of 1597 and the Abbey cartulary, known as the Stoneleigh Leger Book.[1] The cartulary, with other related but less well known material, allows a journey back to the medieval period, returning via the enlightened Leigh administration of the 1590s to the decision in the late 1630s to create the first park at Stoneleigh. Within this broader chronological perspective we can see how the landscape, eventually enclosed within the park, evolved through 500 years. Various units of land use, tenancy and ownership have been identified which waxed and waned until they were captured in a 'still frame' by emparkment. In effect, this is a landscape history of a particular part of the Stoneleigh estate, an area that happened to be caught up in the popular wave of deer park creation in the seventeenth century.

The ancient manor and parish of Stoneleigh was an extensive area of approximately 10,000 acres, stretching from what are now the western suburbs of Coventry in the north to the fringes of Leamington Spa at Cubbington to the south (Fig. 102). The deer park, when first created, measured about 300 acres, or three per cent of the total area of the estate. It straddles the River Avon between the villages of Stoneleigh and Stareton and for the most part its boundary is defined by roads (Fig. 103). There is only a 90-ft difference between the lowest and highest point, but this is sufficient to produce an attractive undulating landscape.

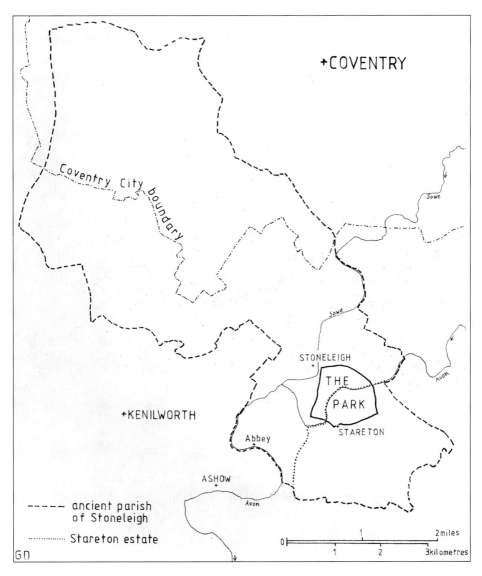

FIGURE 102
Stoneleigh Park: location plan

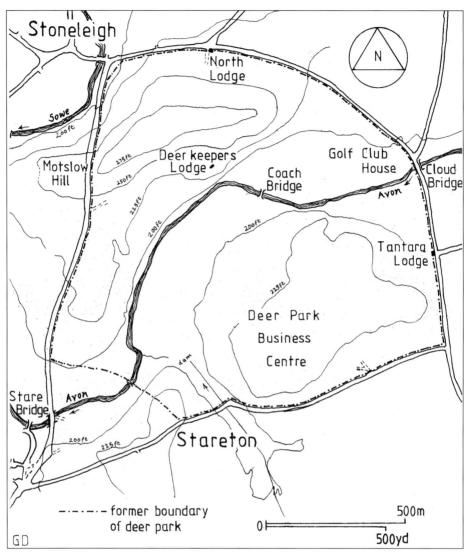

FIGURE 103
Plan of Stoneleigh Park today

Historically, the Stoneleigh estate stands in an area of landscape transition between the bosky Arden and open Feldon of Warwickshire.[2] In the medieval period it contained extensive areas of woodland and waste to the north where fields tended to be hedged and settlements small and scattered. To the south there was less woodland; settlements were larger, nucleated and associated with arable fields, most notably around Stoneleigh, Stareton and Ashow. The estate open fields did not conform, however, to the classic three-field system, operating a three-course rotation of winter, spring and fallow on three large identifiable fields. Open fields here were smaller, usually numbering more than three for each settlement. The fields were not extensive nor contiguous and were inconsistent in the allocation of strips to tenants and in the application of regular cropping rotations.[3] It is difficult, however, to generalise in an area of transition: by way of example, Ashow, which by the end of the sixteenth century had a compact and contiguous area of open fields strips immediately around the village, had beyond large areas of hedged fields and a considerable amount of woodland.[4] An additional complication in the medieval landscape structure, after the foundation of the Cistercian abbey in the mid-twelfth century, was the introduction of monastic granges, principally organised as sheep farms but also with some arable in enclosed fields.[5]

The Stoneleigh Leger Book provides the earliest information on the landscape of the future deer park. Even if this had not survived, an important division can be identified running along the River Avon between the lands that belonged to Stoneleigh village to the north and those of Stareton to the south. This territorial boundary was to cause a greater or lesser fracture in the landscape on either side of the Avon, depending on how the history of two estates of Stoneleigh and Stareton converged or diverged. In the Domesday Book both belonged to the king. In about 1150 Stoneleigh was granted by Henry II to the monks of Radmore, Cannock Chase, who established a Cistercian house, first at Cryfield (now in Coventry), but quickly transferred to the present Abbey site. About the same time Henry II granted, or re-granted, Stareton to Simon the Cook, alias Hasteler, and in the mid-thirteenth century his successors (de Arderne) conveyed this manor to the abbot of Stoneleigh. Stareton and Stoneleigh were thereby united until the dissolution of the Abbey.[6]

The Stoneleigh Arable

The author of the Leger Book, Thomas Pype, gives the names of several fields that lay in the deer park area between Stoneleigh village and the River Avon. Writing in 1392, he states that according to tradition these had formed part of the original royal grant of twelve ploughlands in the mid-twelfth century, of which six were in Stoneleigh and six in Cryfield.[7] Unfortunately the original grant does not name the ploughlands and the date of the field names, and by inference the date of the creation of the fields themselves, is therefore uncertain. The names given by Pype are 'Struttespece', 'le Conyngerfurlong', 'le Conynger', 'le Conyngerpece' and two 'cultura'. Rodney Hilton has attempted to locate some of these fields,[8] from the evidence of a lease of Stoneleigh Grange in 1528 to Thomas Dunton, which mentioned 'Conyngur pece' and 'Strutyspece' or 'Comhill'.[9] Although Hilton warned that the 'Conynger' fields were not to be confused with the 'Conygre' east of the Abbey itself, he could not suggest an alternative location for this field and none at all for 'Struttespece/Strutyspece', alias 'Comhill.' From the evidence of the 1597 estate map and survey, however, it is with some confidence that these fields can be identified with the Cunningrie (various spellings) fields and Coome Hill, which lay immediately south-east of Stoneleigh village, forming the northernmost section of the later park (Fig. 104).[10] The location of the two 'cultura' or furlongs, as described by the medieval author, can be placed in a narrow neck of land between Coome Hill to the north and Stare bridge to the south. In 1597 these two 'cultura' are given as Cole Haunch and Stare Hill.

By the late fourteenth century at the latest (the date of the Leger Book compilation) almost the whole of Stoneleigh's lands that were to become the park was covered by these ploughed fields. It is probable that these were open fields, divided into strips or selions and distributed to the tenants living in the village. The allocation of strips and the regime of crop rotation is unknown. Within these fields a 'conigrey' or rabbit warren had been created. This is somewhat surprising as rabbits and arable crops do not make good neighbours from the ploughman's point of view. Monasteries were particularly active in the establishment of warrens, but it was more usual to place them on heathland or common.[11] To protect the crops it was important to enclose the warren with fencing or even a bank and ditch. It is possible that the enclosures numbered 325 and 326, 'Cunningreie grove' and 'Cunnigre Croft' on Fig. 107, reflect the shape of the original enclosure. If so, this happens to be the steepest slope in the area, perhaps difficult to plough. The warren would not have been a peasant venture but one controlled directly by the Abbey, but there is no information on when it was created nor whether it was still operating at the time of the Leger Book. The management of the warren may have been one of the functions of Stoneleigh Grange, the early history of which is uncertain. The grange was situated to the east of the River Sow and the village, about half a mile from the suggested site of the warren.

The Stareton arable

It is likely that in the medieval period much of the land south of the River Avon also formed open fields, but cultivated from Stareton. Thomas Pype did not list the field names in the Leger Book, as they did not form part of the original royal grant to the Abbey. There is evidence, however, that most of the area formed a single large field called Cloud field and this is confirmed by the 1597 map. The issue is complicated by the fact that there was another extensive Cloud field to the north-east of Cloud bridge and in Stoneleigh territory rather than Stareton.

Cloud

The occurrence of the name Cloud on two separate estates suggests that a tract of land bearing this name had been created before Stoneleigh and Stareton were divided in the mid-twelfth century. On the other hand, it is possible that the Stareton Cloud was the first in existence and, as new land was cleared on the edge of Stoneleigh, it acquired the name Cloud from just across the boundary. A small estate known as Cloud with an intriguing history grew up close

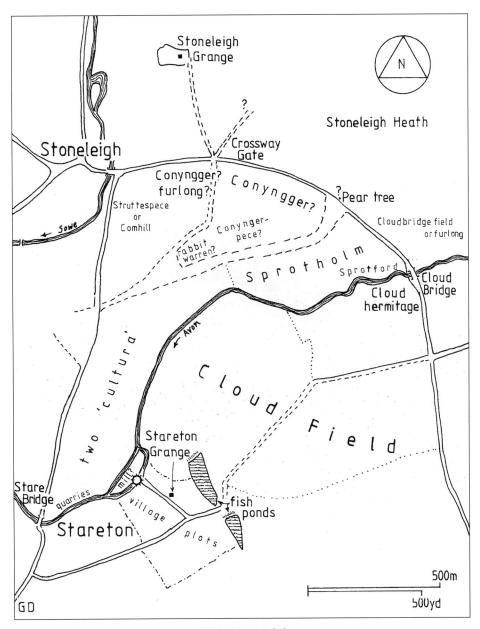

FIGURE 104
Plan of the Stoneleigh Park area in the medieval period

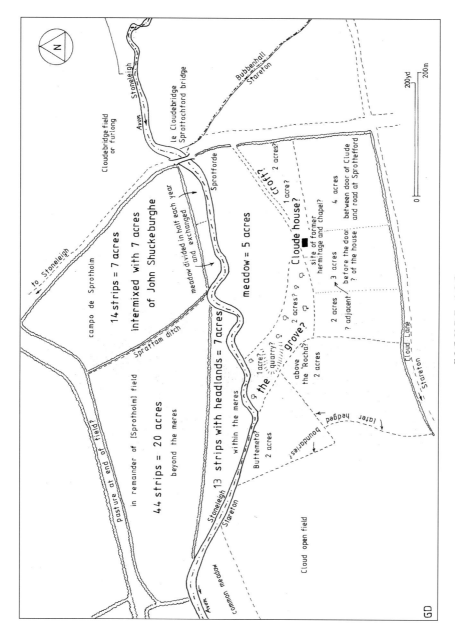

FIGURE 105

Plan of the Cloud estate in the medieval period

to the bridge of the same name and formed the third medieval building block of the later park (Fig 105). According to the Leger Book, before the foundation of the Abbey (and hence before the division of Stoneleigh and Stareton), there was a chantry chapel 'apud le Cloude iuxta Startone'.[12] William Hasteler had succeeded his brother, Simon Hasteler, to whom Stareton was granted by the Crown in the mid-twelfth century. At an unknown time, but before 1224, William gave to Edmund, a hermit and priest 'de Clouda', certain lands in Stareton.[13] Edmund was buried in the chantry chapel and subsequently no priest was presented to the chantry. Presumably abandoned, the building was then burnt down by thieves. The prior of Kenilworth, as rector of the parish, subsequently entered upon the lands of Cloud chapel without right or title. The holdings or tenements of Cloud and in Sprotholm ('tenementa de Cloude et in Sprotholm') belonging to the chantry were worth 60 shillings annually.[14]

This is the history of the Cloud chantry chapel or hermitage as given in the Leger Book. There is, however, other contemporary evidence, at once contradictory and considerably more detailed topographically, to be found in the three Kenilworth priory cartularies, two in the British Library and the third, a sixteenth-century copy in the Leigh collection in Stratford.[15] The latter two have separate sections devoted to 'Cluda'.[16] One of the earliest charters (c.1175-1224) appears to be a grant by William, lord of Stareton, to the brothers of Cloud (*fratribus de Cluda*) of four acres of land together with fourteen acres previously granted with liberty to ditch and enclose the land.[17] A more detailed charter of the same period is a renewal by William of Stareton of an earlier gift from his brother, Simon, specifically to Edmund the hermit, and the brothers of a place called 'Cluda', of a house and croft next to 'Sprottochford' bridge and a meadow that extended from a grove to the bridge.[18] In addition ten acres had been granted: three acres before the door of the house, two above the 'Rocha' (rocks?), two in 'Butumeco' (butimen - marsh? or butmedow? - see below), two in the said croft and one at the grove. To this William added another four acres: two near the existing three before the door of the house and two at the grove.

The next charter is a grant of the same land by William le Hasteler of Stareton to Kenilworth Priory and this gives yet more topographical information:[19] a place called 'Cluda' with a house and croft next to 'Sprottefford' with a meadow extending from the grove to the bridge, ten acres (three acres before the door of the house called Clude, two *supra Roch'am*, two in Buttemeto (Buttmeadow?), two in the said croft, one at the grove) and another eight acres (two near the three acres before the door of the house, two near the acre at the grove, four extending in length from the door of Clude as far as the road at Sprottefford and in width from the door of Clude which in width is as much as the length of the croft extending towards Stareton).

If this topographical information is reliable, then in the latter half of the twelfth century there was a house at Cloud near Sprotford, probably at the same place as Cloud bridge, the ford name deriving from the field called Sprotholm lying adjacent and to the north of the Avon (see below). The river crossing here could be described using both Sprotford and Cloud bridge.[20] Around the house there were at least eighteen acres in several locations, including one above the rocks (*supra Rocham'*) and another in 'Buttemeto', probably Buttmeadow. Since all this land was granted by the lord of Stareton, then it should lie south of the River Avon, the boundary between

Stareton and Stoneleigh. The most likely place is the area of relatively small enclosures on the 1597 Stareton map, in the north-east corner of the extensive open field of Cloud immediately south of the river (fields 93-96, Figs 107-8). The house itself could not have stood immediately against the ford, as four acres stretched in length from the door of the house to the road at Sprotford. It is not made clear in these charters whether the house and the hermitage were one and the same. It is probable, however, that the chapel was a separate building. The hermit, Edmund, was not alone but lived within a community of 'brothers', who would have needed living accommodation. In these circumstances it was sensible to live and worship in separate buildings, though they may have been connected.

These charters affirm that the priory of Kenilworth did not seize the land of the Cloud hermitage but received it from the lord of Stareton, presumably some time after Edmund the hermit's death. It is possible that the charters are forgeries, produced by the priory to establish title where none existed, but the affair should be seen against the background of long disputes over land between the monasteries at Stoneleigh and Kenilworth. The compilers of the Stoneleigh hundred roll of 1280 claimed that the prior had appropriated the hermitage ('prior appropriavit sibi hermitagium de Cloude') but they may have been influenced by the view of Stoneleigh Abbey.[21] It would not have been unusual for William of Stareton to have re-assigned the Cloud land to Stoneleigh rectory once the hermitage had failed, for he had originally granted the land in alms. The prior of Kenilworth was the rector of Stoneleigh and Stareton and so the land could have passed to Kenilworth Priory by these means.

Whether the claims were falsified or not, the topographical information appears to be genuine and provides an insight into the geography of the Cloud estate with its lost house, hermitage and chapel. The land does not appear to lie in selions or strips but is all listed as acres and in specific locations. This would imply hedged fields – one of the charters permitted the land to be enclosed and ditched.[22] As already suggested, such a landscape is encountered immediately south-west of Cloud bridge and it is worth attempting to locate the hermitage more precisely. It is known from the charters cited above that Cloud house stood away from the road that led to Sprotford: another charter describes a meadow between the hermitage and the river Avon.[23] Figure 105 gives a possible position for the hermitage together with its surrounding fields.

After the priory of Kenilworth took possession of the Cloud hermitage it was apparently granted to John, vicar of Stoneleigh, for life with land and a meadow which lay between the hermitage and the River Avon.[24] The hermitage had been burnt and was derelict and the vicar was expected to rebuild it, with the prior supplying timber and roof tiles. In 1280 a Gilbert or a William, vicar of Stoneleigh, held a croft from the prior, which may be another part of the rectorial glebe, the basis of Kenilworth Priory's holding in Stoneleigh and to which the Cloud estate was subsequently attached.[25] In 1276-7 Robert of Idlicote, his wife Agnes and his son Simon received 'land near Cloud with Sprotholm' from prior William.[26] Sprotholm was a field immediately north of Cloud and the River Avon and will be discussed below. In another charter relating to the same transaction the phrase used is 'all the land of Cloud with Sprotholm'.[27] It appears that this is the Cloud hermitage estate with some extra land which is being granted in exchange for land in Idlicote. This explains why a family 'de la Cloude' figures so prominently in the Leger Book, but unfortunately only in relation to their holding in Canley.[28] 'Symon del Cloude' (1295) could be the son of Robert mentioned above, and father of Richard 'de la Cloude' (1357).[29] During this time Cloud was clearly a recognisable place. The family does not appear in a 1390s list of Kenilworth tenants and it is not possible to identify which of the people named held Cloud at this time.[30] In the Cloud cartularies, three individuals quitclaim their right to land: 'lands and tenements called la Cloude,' a 'tenement in Stoneleigh called Cluda', and 'land leased next to Cloud'.[31] The dates of these quitclaims are not known.

Sprotholm

In its description of the scattered lands of the Kenilworth rectorial estate, the Leger Book also mentions the field Sprotholm, which gave its name to the ford (Sprottochford).[32] This can be identified with the three Sprattam fields on the 1597 Stoneleigh map, situated immediately west of Cloud bridge (and ford) and north of the River Avon (Figs 107-8). This well defined block of land accounts for the balance of Stoneleigh territory incorporated into the park. In Sprotholm field the prior held fourteen strips, measuring seven acres, which were intermixed with another seven acres held by John Shuckburgh, a tenant of the abbot of Stoneleigh. There was also half a meadow, exchanged with the other half on an annual basis with the same John. Significantly, the prior held the residue of the Sprotholm 'between the hedge, ditch and the Avon with meadow and pasture belonging to the chantry of Cloud'.[33] Here there were '13 strips between the meres [boundary markers] with the headlands making seven acres and beyond the meres towards the pasture at the end of the said field – 44 strips making 20 acres.' This entry is difficult to interpret but it is likely that the reference to meadow and pasture of the Cloud chantry is technically in parenthesis so that the acreages given do not include them. The areas given are not enough to cover both the residue of Sprotholm field north of the River Avon and the Cloud chantry lands to the south. The twenty-seven acres of Sprotholm were probably situated at the west end of the field (Fig. 105) and can be equated with the twenty acres and a meadow of four days math called 'Sproteholme' leased in 1570 by Thomas Dunton.[34]

The part of Sprotholm that contained the seven acres of intermixed strip lay at the east end of the field against Cloud bridge (Fig. 105). Listed in two documents, probably of early sixteenth-century date, are these very same fourteen strips equalling seven acres and the meadow adjacent divided on an annual basis. This was described as 'extendinge in lengh from Sprattam ditch unto Cloude brigge in breadth from the nether parte of the seaven Acres ... unto the River Avon'.[35] The late fourteenth-century survey of the prior of Kenilworth's holdings also lists five acres of meadow 'opposite Sprotholm belonging to the Cloud', which could be identified with Cloud Lesow (no. 94, Figs 107-8) and the meadow mentioned in the grant to John, vicar of Stoneleigh.[36]

Cloud in the sixteenth century

There is no further information on Cloud until the sixteenth century. In 1513 the abbot of Kenilworth leased the parsonage of Stoneleigh to Richard Kempsey and William Cotton of

Coventry, and in 1539 the same was leased by the abbot of Kenilworth to Thomas Rowley and Isabell his wife. This appears to have been only one holding with the tithe barn and a house called Gardner and farm of all the great tithes.[37] A year before, in 1538, the remainder of the rectory estate was leased *en bloc* to Humphrey Reynolds.[38] After the dissolution of Kenilworth Abbey in 1539 all its revenue reverted to the crown and it was not until 1562 that the rectorial lands and tithes, along with Stoneleigh Abbey and its estates, were granted to the Leigh family.[39] Three Stoneleigh rentals have been preserved from the Crown administration around the year 1550 and reveal that Cloud was rented by George Cox.[40] By 1564 'Cloude Grounde' was held equally between Thomas Holland and Thomas Deyne, confirmed by the detailed Leigh rental of 1570, which lists 'cloud house', tenanted by Thomas Deyne and being 'sometyme ... parcell of the possessions of Killingworthe Abbeie', and Cloude meadowe, held by Thomas Holland.[41] Both these holdings can be identified with the original Cloud chantry and demonstrate that there was a Cloud house still standing in the latter half of sixteenth century. It is unlikely that this was the same house mentioned in the twelfth-century charters, but it is possible that there was at least continuity of occupation of the same site. In 1597 a Thomas Deane of Stoneleigh held Cloud Lesow (field 94, Figs 106-7), but by this time there was no house in this field and Thomas was living in Stoneleigh village.[42] With the loss of the house the use of the name Cloud as a description of a tract of land or estate began to fade, surviving only in the name of the local bridge.

Cloud was recognised as being in Stareton, and Sprotholm, part of the Stoneleigh estate north of the River Avon, had originally been included in Humphrey Reynolds's lease, passing to his remarried widow, Emma Littley.[43] The field was eventually sub-let to Thomas Dunton (see below), who in the 1560s paid no rent 'for certain considerations'.[44] By 1575 Sprotholme was in the hands of James Howe and it remained with the Howe family into the seventeenth century (see below).[45]

Stoneleigh Grange

By the early part of the sixteenth century all the medieval arable of Stoneleigh village later incorporated into the deer park had been absorbed into the fields of Stoneleigh Grange. The grange buildings and its core territory lay between the River Sowe and Chantry Heath (earlier Stoneleigh Heath), immediately to the north of the road from Stoneleigh to Cloud Bridge. Before the mid-twelfth century, Stoneleigh Grange was probably a royal manor farm but nothing is known about its management either before or after its transfer to the abbey. The Leger Book unfortunately concentrates on tenant rather than demesne property. It is known, however, that 'olde land tilled at Stonley graunge' was tithe free, an indication that an area of demesne was in existence in the earliest years of the abbey's ownership.[46] In the thirteenth century it may have been developed as a sheep grange by the Cistercian monks, but by the late fourteenth century its fields were apparently small in acreage, hemmed in by the strips of Kenilworth Priory land to the north and east and the River Sowe to the west.[47]

In 1528 the abbey leased Stoneleigh Grange to Thomas Dunton.[48] Remarkably much of the Stoneleigh villagers' arable was included (see Fig. 106).

FIGURE 106 Stoneleigh Grange 1528 - future parkland

Field Name	Acreage (approx)
Connyngur croft	3
Connyngur pece	30
Struttys pece alias Comhill	16
Piece underneath Comhill	2
Pece extending down lane caled per'tre lane	5
Starhull	17
Colehaunche	<u>23</u>
Source: SBTRO, DR18/1/722	Total 96

This immediately prompts the question whether or not the villagers of Stoneleigh gave up their land voluntarily. An important source, the 1517 returns on the commission of enquiry into enclosures, suggests that the land was confiscated and not freely given up.[49] The Stoneleigh villagers claimed that the abbot of Stoneleigh had seized 300 acres of arable and evicted sixteen people from their homes, converting their land to pasture. Though only allegations, they do provide a simple explanation of how the villagers' arable came to be absorbed into Stoneleigh Grange. Depopulation was occurring elsewhere on the Stoneleigh estate, the hamlets of Finham, Hurst and Cryfield shrinking considerably and Milburn (admittedly already tiny) disappearing completely by the late 1480s.[50] By 1533, however, Finham and Hurst had partially recovered. With no single trend, the most dramatic change is in the number of tenants in Stoneleigh village itself, falling from about seventy-eight in the 1390s to forty-one in 1553.[51] The explanation for this long term decline is not obvious, although evictions to create sheep pasture seem an apparent and immediate cause. There was only a small increase in numbers of tenancies recorded by rentals and hearth tax returns in the next 130 years to 1664. It is against this demographic background that the motivation for the creation of the deer park at the end of this period should be seen. It is difficult to determine, however, whether the Stoneleigh landlords, both monastic and lay, perceived an opportunity to re-use land no longer intensively cultivated or imposed new land uses on a reluctant tenancy, precipitating population instability.

1597-1640

Stoneleigh is blessed with one of the earliest reliable estate maps in the country, surveyed by John Goodwine in 1597. With the accompanying written survey (Fig. 108), an accurate picture of the land use of the future park can be established. Since 1562 there had been a single landowner for this area, the Leighs having gathered together the lands of both Stoneleigh Abbey and Kenilworth Priory.

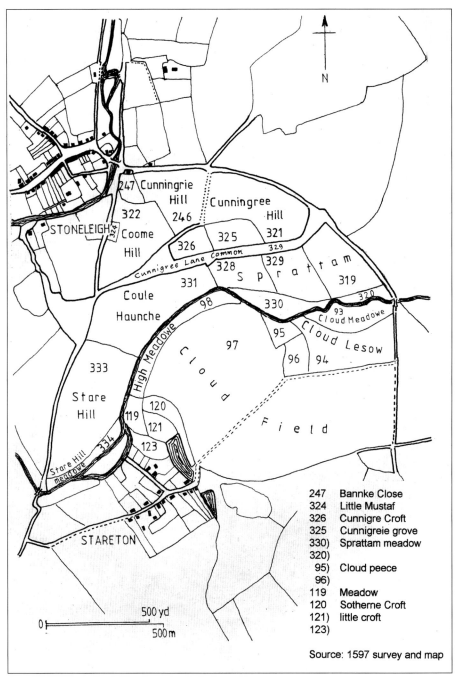

FIGURE 107
The area of the Stoneleigh deer park 1597, based on Goodwine's map

FIGURE 108 List of fields 1597 (name of tenant in brackets)

STARETON

Common Field

		A	R	P	
97	Cloude feild	105	1	08	
95	Cloude peece	3	0	00	held by 'OldNelson'
96	Cloude peece	4	0	00	
	Total	111	1	08	

Common Meadow

98	High meadowe	7	1	15	

Enclosed fields and town crofts (in severalty)

93	Cloude Meadow [Whiting]	7	2	36	
94	Cloude Leasow [Deane]	17	2	14	
120	Sothernes Croft [Sotherne]	3	3	12	
119	meadow [Whiting]	3	0	34	
121	a little croft [Whiting]	2	1	37	
123	another little croft [Whiting]	2	3	02	
127	farm house and crofte [Whiting]	1	2	26	
132	meadow (part) [Whiting]	1	2	00	
124	Croft [Nelson the elder]	0	2	20	
125	Croft [Nelson the younger]	0	1	00	
130	Croft [Nelson the younger]	0	1	20	
128	orchard [Morrie]	0	3	00	
129	house with yard [James]	1	0	00	
[126]	?croft [Shatwell]?	0	1	20	
	Total	44	0	21	
	Grand Total	162	3	04	

STONELEIGH

Common field

246	Cunningrie Hill	12	3	01	
321	Cunningree Hill	18	0	04	
326	Cunnigre Croft	3	1	20	
319	Sprattam				
320	[Sprattam] medow	14	2	38	
322	Coome Hill	16	0	32	
	Total	65	0	15	

Enclosed Fields (in severalty)

247	Bannke Close (Baker)	1	2	36	
324	Little Mustaf (Morton)	0	2	00	
331	Coule Haunch (Morrie)	23	0	10	
332	Stare Hill (Morrie)	17	3	09	
334	Stare hill meadow (Morrie)	1	2	00	
328	Sprattam (Howle)				
329	Sprattam (Howle)	14	3	10	
330	Sprattam meadow (Howle)	4	2	00	
	Total	64	0	16	

Woodland

Cunnigree grov		5	2	00	
	Grand Total	134	3	31	
GRAND TOTAL STARETON AND STONELEIGH		296	2	35	

Source: SBRTO, DR18/30/24/279a.

By 1597 the territory of Stoneleigh Grange had shrunk to perhaps its original size, confined to an area north of the road from the village to Cloud bridge. Once more the land south of the road was being leased by the Stoneleigh villagers. The Cunigrey (Cunningrie, Cunnigre) fields and Coome Hill had returned to common arable, except for just over five acres (Cunningree grove), which was woodland on the steepest slope. The east field of Sprotholm adjacent to Cloud bridge, formerly a series of strips intermixed between two tenants, one from each of the two religious houses, had also been added to common arable. The remainder of the fields between Cunigrey Lane and the Avon had been left in severalty, shared between a tenant of Stareton (William Morrie) and the Howe family of Stoneleigh mill, who had taken on the west part of Sprotholm. It is not known whether subsequently the balance between common arable and enclosed fields of this part of Stoneleigh's town lands changed before being incorporated into the park in about 1640.

The enclosure of Stareton's fields

In contrast to Stoneleigh, there is a considerable amount of information on Stareton's fields between 1597 and 1640. The 1597 map shows 'Clowde fielde' as one of Stareton's common fields, subdivided into strips without hedges. It was bounded by the River Avon to the north, the road from Stoneleigh via Cloud bridge to Cubbington to the east, Stareton village to the west and the line of the present lane running east out of Stareton to the south. Occupying the north-east corner of the common field were the enclosed fields, Cloud Leasow, Cloud Meadow and two Cloud Pieces formerly belonging to the medieval Cloud estate where the hermitage once stood (see above). Fringing the remainder of the Avon was a long strip of Stareton common meadow named High Meadow. Again without dividing hedges, the meadow was allotted to the villagers, perhaps on an annual basis.

An unhedged roadway (Cloud Lane, see below) cut Cloud Field almost in half. It led north-eastwards and then eastwards from Stareton village towards Bubbenhall. Between Stareton and Cloud Field lay a pond (Stareton Pool, see below), created by the damming of a small south bank tributary of the Avon. Another smaller pond lay not far to the south on the same stream. These were likely to have been fish ponds and were probably those listed in the 1390s in the 'lord's hand', at that time the abbot of Stoneleigh – 'duo vivaria sub villa de Startone' (two fishponds below the village of Stareton).[52] What is significant about the larger pond is that the abbot, in order to retain access, held a right of way across 'the grange', which was then in the hands of the Baker family. This grange had presumably at one time been monastic, farmed directly by the abbey, but by the 1390s was leased to Adam and Joan Baker and their son John. It is likely that the grange was located on the west side of the pond, on a site between the latter and a side lane in the village running towards the Avon.[53] In 1597 this coincided with one of the largest farms in Stareton held by Henry Whiting, who also had Cloud Meadow.

According to Goodwine's survey, Cloud Field measured 105a.1r. 8p. out of a total of 596a. 3r. 4p.of common arable. The Stareton common fields were also assessed using an ancient measure called a yardland. There were ten and a quarter yardlands of Stareton arable and these were shared in unequal portions between twelve tenants. The thirteenth tenant in the village held no common field. A yardland was traditionally about thirty acres but the survey reveals the Stareton yardland was generous – almost twice this size (596.775/10.25 = 58.2 acres). By this period the surface of Cloud Field would have been sculpted into the distinctive 'ridge and furrow', characteristic of any area that had been cultivated without interruption for centuries.

One year later, in 1598, the Stareton villagers obtained permission from their lord, Sir Thomas Leigh, 'to exchange our lands on with another amongst ourselves in Starton ... and to inclose the same so exchanged and keep one part allotted to us severall'.[54] John Goodwine was appointed to survey the consolidated holdings: those tenants with land in the open field of Cloud are listed in Fig. 109. The combined acreage of the allotments (107a.1r.13p.) is slightly larger than the figure calculated by the surveyor the year before for the field as a whole (105a.1r. 8p.).

F I G U R E   1 0 9   Cloud field enclosure, Stareton 1598

Tenant	Location	A	R	P
1 William Mory	Cloud field under Cloud hedge abutting Edward Sotherne	7	0	21
2 Edward Sothern	Cloud Field	18	2	38
3a Houmphrey How	Upon Cloud field betwixt Heming and	12	0	20
3b	in Cloud Field next Pynknell	4	0	30
4 Lenord Hemings	in Cloud Field next Howe	5	2	24
5 Georg Baker	in Cloud Field next the pond	11	0	00
6 Thomas Nelson	in Cloud Field	10	2	21
7 Edward Malym	in Cloud Field betwixt Nelson and Sharman	9	2	15
8 Robert Sharman (Shatwell)	upon Cloud Field one Mydle Forlonge	3	3	26
9 Wydow James	in Cloud Field betwixt Sharman and How	4	1	18
10 Henry Whyting	in Cloud Field	20	0	00
	TOTAL	107	1	13

Numbers refer to allotments on Fig. 110

Source: SBTRO, DR18/30/23/3.

This is an early case of enclosure by private agreement, but it did not go so far as the parliamentary enclosure of the late eighteenth and early nineteenth centuries, where the aim was to bring together in one place most, if not all, of all the lands of a scattered holding, even

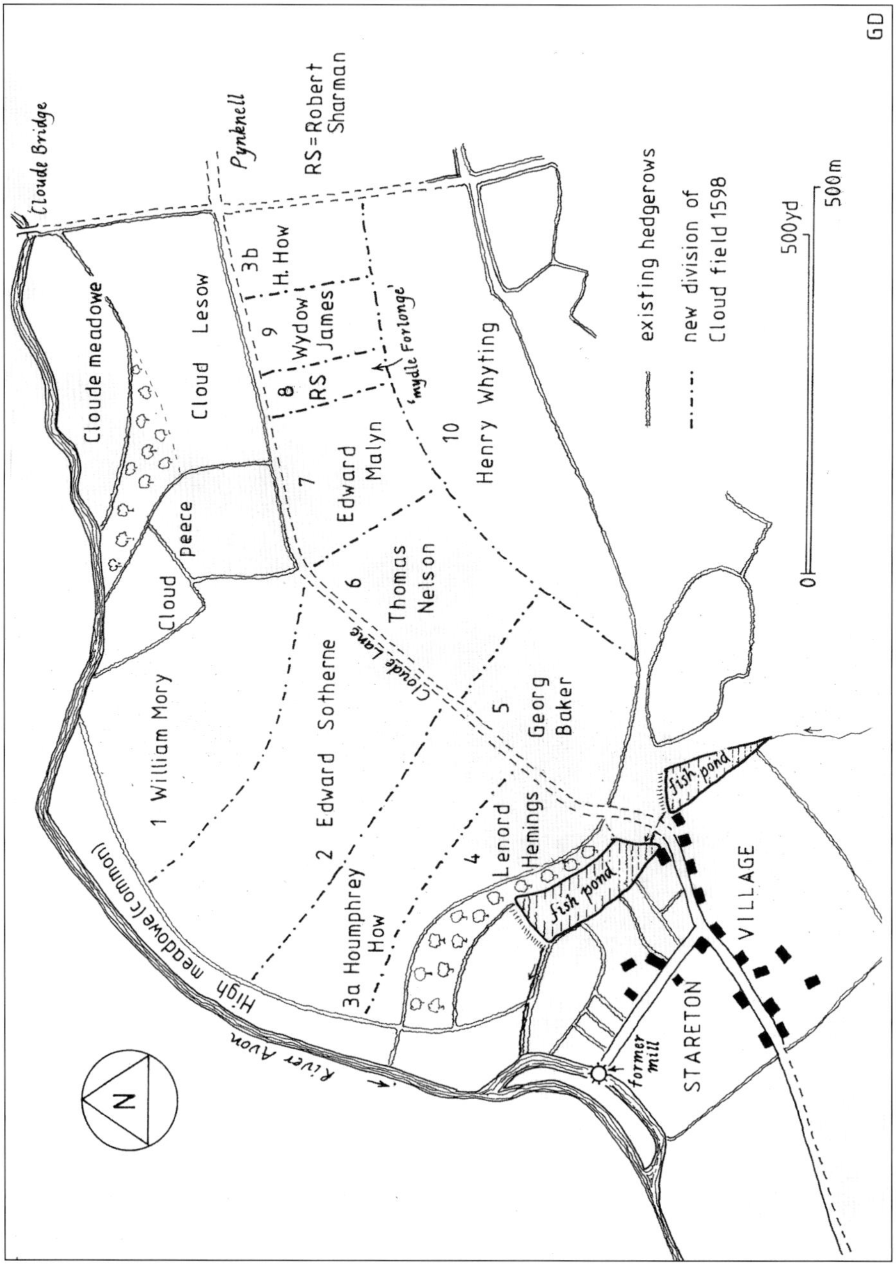

FIGURE 110
Plan of the Cloud
Field Enclosure, 1598

GD

Cloude Bridge

Pynknell

RS=Robert
Sharman

Cloude meadowe

Cloud Lesow

3b

H. How

9

Wydow
James

RS

8

myddle Fortonge

Cloud Peece

7

Edward
Malyn

10

Henry Whyting

6

Thomas
Nelson

Cloud

1 William Mory

Cloude Lane

2 Edward Sotherne

5

Georg
Baker

4

Lenord
Hemings

High meadowe (common)

3a Houmphrey
How

fish pond

fish pond

River Avon

VILLAGE

STARETON

former
mill

N

existing hedgerows

new division of
Cloud field 1598

500yd

500m

0

230

if it meant building a new farmhouse outside the village. In Stareton, holdings were consolidated only within individual fields such as Cloud field, so that a tenant's holding still lay scattered around the other village fields, but in larger compact blocks. The farmsteads remained in the old village area. Goodwine's enclosure survey provides abuttals (the names of adjacent tenants and their land) for some of the consolidated blocks (Fig. 109). An attempt has been made here to recreate the new allotments of Cloud field (Fig. 110). The reconstruction was guided by the frame of the hedgerows within Cloud field which appear on the later eighteenth-century plans of the area.[55] It is assumed that these hedgerows were created soon after the 1598 enclosure agreement. Eight trees have recently been identified in the area as dating from about 1600, six oaks and the others – a horse chestnut and a sweet chestnut. Their location seems to be closely related to the new field and Cloud Lane boundaries created at this time.[56]

Despite the reservations made above about the regularity of the crop rotations practised on the common fields of the Stoneleigh estate, it appears that some attempt was made in Stareton to operate a three-course rotation. In 1598 most of Cloud field was under winter rye and the other fields were under spring oats or fallow.

1640: The creation of the park

In 1616 Sir Thomas Leigh obtained permission to empark 700 acres 'in Stoneleigh and Fletchamstead'. He was the second son of the first Sir Thomas of Stoneleigh and, according to Dugdale, 'made a Park there [at Fletchamstead] and built a fair house within it'.[57] The letters patent, however, do not provide any details of its location. In 1640 his grandson, also named Sir Thomas, obtained a licence to empark 800 acres.[58] The document is precise about the roads that are intended to be closed and describes the alternative routes that were already in existence or were to be created. One road to be extinguished was 'Clowde Lane', which crossed the former open field of Cloud, enclosed in hedgerows since about 1598. It was described as the lane leading from Stareton to Bubbenhall, the section to be closed measuring 194 perches (1067 yards, or 975 metres) leading from Stareton Pool to Offchurch Way (now the lane from Stoneleigh to Offchurch via Cubbington). Tantara Lodge now stands at the eastern end of this extinguished road. The other lane, 'Connigray Lane', was defined as part of the road that led from Stoneleigh Abbey to Baginton, 140 perches in length (770 yards, 703 metres), ending at Crossway Gate, also situated on the lane from Stoneleigh to Cubbington, the site now better known as North Lodge, built in the nineteenth century. The other fork of 'Connigray Lane', a broad green lane, separated the north side of Sprotholm from the 'Connigray' fields on the 1597 map. This was known as Peartree lane ('pertre lane') in 1528 as it led in the late 1390s to the pear tree ('le Petreo'), situated on the lane from Stoneleigh to Cloud bridge, where the Stoneleigh

Cloud bridge field ('Cloudbruggefeld') bordered the road on the east side (Fig. 104).[59] The lane was called 'Peartree greene' in a 1639 document and so, for the purposes of the letters patent, was also considered to be common pasture rather than a highway to be closed.[60]

It is difficult to understand why in 1640 it was intended to enclose up to 800 acres to form the park. The lanes to be extinguished correspond closely to what was actually taken into the new park, which only measured about 300 acres when first created. It was not until the early nineteenth century that a park approaching the size authorised in 1640 was finally achieved when a major extension was added taking in the great meander of the River Avon and the former medieval demesne. In the intervening period the deer park remained physically separated from the main abbey buildings.

The emparking under the 1640 letters patent heralded the second major change to the use of Stareton's Cloud field in fifty years. This is documented in some detail but the corresponding material for the Stoneleigh part of the park is not extant. The Avon, which once divided the Stareton villagers' lands from those of Stoneleigh, was to become the spine of the new deer park. The survey of Stareton, dated January 1639, describes exactly which land was to be taken into the park.[61] Altogether 171a. 0r. 32p., out of a total of 679a. 2r. 36p., of Stareton tenants' land were enclosed within the pale. This land included former open-field arable, common meadow, old enclosures and part of the village itself. In the forty years since the enclosure of Cloud field many of the new hedged subdivisions had acquired separate names such as 'Well Hill' and 'Well Close', 'The Loe' and 'The Farm Piece'. These names were to prove ephemeral but it has been possible to locate them more or less precisely by comparing the surveys of 1598 and 1639 (Figs 109, 111). In 1683 the remaining lands of Stareton were reorganised, probably with the aim of ironing out any inconsistencies or inequalities that had persisted after the creation of the park.[62]

In 1639 there were thirteen holdings in Stareton and all except one smallholder lost land to the park to a greater or lesser extent. The relevant information from the 1639 survey has been tabulated in Fig. 111 in the same order as for the 1598 survey, and has been mapped in Fig. 112.

Two of the largest holdings had fallen in after the recent death of their tenants, Widow Salmon (no. 10, Fig. 111) and Widow Sotherne (nos 2, 2a, Fig. 111). Widow Sotherne's total holding was 72a. 0r. 39p., of which 23a. 1r. 37p. was set aside for the park and the remainder quickly re-tenanted by the Russell family (48a. 3r. 2p.).[63] Of a total of 147a. 2r. 32p. of Widow Salmon's grange tenement, 56a.0r.2p. were incorporated into the park, leaving just over ninety-one acres available for redistribution, not sufficient to compensate for the potential loss of the remaining tenants' land to the park. The death of Widow Salmon also released to the park the two ancient enclosures of the Cloud hermitage (Cloud Meadow and Leasow)

FIGURE 111 The 1639 Survey of Stareton

	Tenant	Location	Land use	A	R	P
1	Thomas Hurlston	The Cloud	enclosed arable	24	0	13
		Eye meadow	common meadow	1	1	18
2	late Widow Sotherne	Cloude Fielde	enclosed arable	18	1	12
2a		Poole Close	old enclosure	4	1	00
		Eye Meadow	common meadow	0	3	25
3	Humphrey How	Well Close	enclosed arable	11	3	00
3a		The Loe	enclosed arable	4	1	13
4	Widow Hemmings	Poole Close	enclosed arable	5	1	30
		Eye meadow	common meadow	0	1	34
5	Thomas Monk	Well Hill	enclosed arable	10	1	30
		Eye meadow	common meadow	0	1	35
6	William Middleton	Banke Close	common arable	1	1	25
6a		Well Hill	common arable	7	3	20
6b		The Littel Peece neere the Farme House	town land	0	0	39
		Eye meadow	common meadow	1	1	04
7	Richard Sucklin	Crabtree Close	enclosed arable	9	0	24
		Eye meadow	common meadow	0	3	20
8	Widow Shachwell	Cloude Close	enclosed arable	3	1	13
8a		The Littel Peece neere the Farme House	town land	0	1	09
		Eye meadow	common meadow	0	0	35
9	John Hands	The Loe	enclosed arable	4	2	30
9a		House and Homestead Close	town land	0	3	20
		Eye meadow	common meadow	0	0	35
10	late Mrs Salmon	The Farme Peece in 4 partes	enclosed arable	19	1	06
10a		The Farme House Yardes Orchard & Banke Close	town land	5	0	00
10b		The Grove and Grove Meadow	old enclosures	6	3	27
10c		Cloude Fielde hermitage	enclosure	16	13	01
10d		Cloude Fielde meadow	hermitage enclosure	7	3	00
		Eye meadow	common meadow	0	1	30
11	John Malin	parte of ... Meadow at Bridge Foot	old enclosure?	0	1	30
11a		Meadow joyneinge the Farme Grounde	town land	10	0	8
12	Edward Robinson	Eye meadow	common meadow	0	1	04
13	John Gibbes	no land given to the park				
			TOTAL	171	0	32
		pools lanes and waste		5	3	03
			GRAND TOTAL	176	3	35

'enclosed arable' denotes Cloud open field enclosed in 1598

Source: SBTRO, DR 18/30/23/4

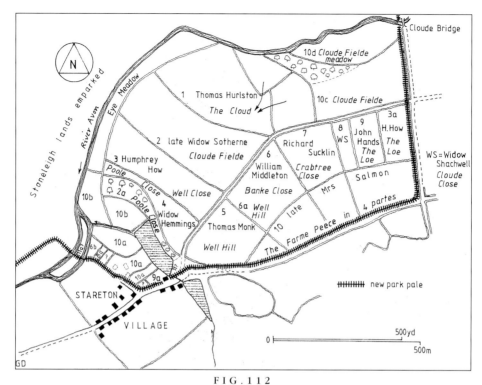

FIG. 112

Plan of the Stareton allotments making the park, 1639

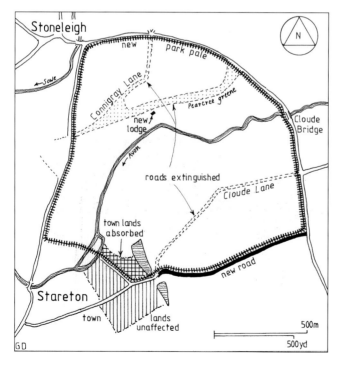

FIGURE 114

Plan of the new park

FIGURE 113 Stareton 1639 - tenancies available for redistribution (in acres, roods, perches)

Tenant	Into park			Outside park			Total		
Widow Sotherne	23	1	37	48	3	2	72	0	39
Let to Russells				48	3	2			
Widow Salmon	56	0	2	91	0	2	147	2	32
Total available to Stareton tenants				91	0	2			
Total taken from Stareton tenants	171	0	32						

It is not known if the shortfall of about eighty acres caused discontent amongst the Stareton tenants. All except one had to contribute to the new park acreage, varying between the late Widow Salmon's fifty-six acres, through the late Mrs Sotherne's twenty-three acres, to just over a quarter of an acre from Edward Robinson (Fig. 111). It appears that the matter of the shortfall was resolved by allowing tenants to retain some of their land until the leases expired.[64] If this were the case, then the emparking may have taken place with little resistance from the tenants, beyond the expected complaints and grumbles about disruption brought about by change. The sources are, however, mute on the reaction of Stareton villagers.

There is an even more profound silence on the manner in which the Stoneleigh lands were incorporated into the park and the tenants' reaction. Only the contemporary rentals are available and information as to which tenants held land destined for the park is thereore thin. In 1635 the hedged 'Starrhill' and 'Colehauch' were tenanted by Thomas Partridge and 'Sprotholme' (west side?) by Mary Hoo. In the 1640 rental, Partridge's fields had first been written in and then crossed out, and Mary Hoo's 'Sprotholme' omitted, presumably on account of these fields being taken into the park.[65] As for Coome Hill, the Cunigrey fields and the remainder of Sprotholm, if these were still common arable, then there is no indication of their loss to the park through an appropriate reduction of Stoneleigh rents.

The New Park (Fig. 114)

Although at its northernmost angle the park almost touched the Avon bridge in Stoneleigh village, the village did not lose any built-up area to the park. Stareton, on the other hand, ceded the north-east quadrant of the village, east of the side lane leading to the River Avon and the former mill site. Significantly this included the largest holding in Stareton, Grange farm, formerly held by Widow Salmon. The site was then cleared of buildings, which might have been already much decayed. The other farmhouse in this area belonged to Widow James and survived at least to 1683 when it is shown on a map but within a much smaller enclosure (Fig. 115, W.D.).[66] Dr Alcock has suggested that this house may eventually have been moved to a new site to become Yew Tree Cottage.[67] Stareton never recovered its former size and constitutes a classic shrunken village, a category of settlement less well studied than Warwickshire's deserted medieval villages. The village had been shrinking before the emparking occurred, however. There had been twenty-four tenants in the late fourteenth century but numbers had fallen to only fifteen in the 1530s.[68] The area has been relatively undisturbed since emparking and the

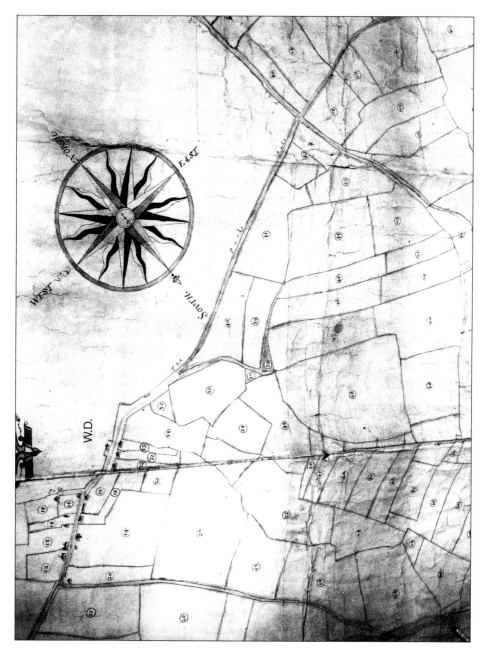

FIGURE 115
Part of the plan of
Stareton, 1683
(SBTRO, DR 671/12)

humps and bumps of the house platforms still survive. Dr Alcock observed some decayed masonry there which he interpreted as the remains of the manor house of the medieval lords of Stareton (le Hasteler, later de Arderne).[69] These are unlikely to be the remains of a motte and bailey castle, as recorded in the Warwick County Sites and Monuments Record.

As discussed above, the 1640 licence to empark defined road closures in considerable detail. The enclosed track, Cloud Lane, which crossed Cloud field, was the principal route from Stareton to Bubbenhall. This lane was incorporated into the park and an alternative route made, swinging farther southwards on an axis just east of the village of Stareton, dislocating the direct route to Bubbenhall. The new lane ran along the new southern boundary of the park and joined the old road from Cloud bridge to Cubbington, which formed the eastern boundary. Three hundred yards to the north, where the nineteenth-century Tantara Lodge now stands, the old public cross-roads was converted into a T-junction, completing the long dog-leg diversion in the route from Stareton to Bubbenhall. In contrast, a 'Y' configuration of lanes on the Stoneleigh side, Conigrey Lane and Peartree Lane, was entirely extinguished and replaced by the two existing lanes which crossed the Avon at Stare bridge and Cloud bridge, to converge at the Sowe bridge on the edge of Stoneleigh village.

Parks are repositories of ancient landscapes and it is likely that the corrugations of common field arable ('ridge and furrow') survived for the next 250 years. They were finally destroyed in the twentieth century by deep ploughing and by war-time building operations, particularly in the area of Cloud field. In the forty years between enclosure and emparking the Stareton farmers continued their arable cultivation, but it is not known how ploughing within the new enclosures would have affected the ridge and furrow earthworks. It is probable that the period was too short to flatten them entirely. After emparking, grass was the normal cover, which effectively preserved any remaining earthworks. After 1683, when the remainder of Stareton's arable was enclosed and consolidated, there was no common meadow or pasture available after the harvest and the villagers' grazing animals had to be fed within the hedged fields of each farm. During the seventeenth century, barley gradually replaced rye as the principal winter crop and this reflected a general move from arable to a more pastoral economy, using the barley as a cattle feed.[70] From the mid-seventeenth century, however, such wider changes in agriculture were largely irrelevant to the deer husbandry of Stoneleigh park.

A park pale of riven timbers was normally erected on the perimeter of a deer park. This was more effective if it could be raised upon a bank, between two ditches, the interior ditch to prevent deer escaping and the exterior to hinder entry by poachers. The 1683 map of Stareton clearly marks 'the parke pale'.[71] Observations along its route, however, have not revealed anything more than an average-sized field bank raised above the land level of the former deer park within, and in places so degraded as to be almost non-existent. The perimeter road runs well below the level of the park close to the present Stareton Lodge, but gradually rises so that at the entrance to the Business Centre the road and the park are at the same level. This gradually diminishing bank is probably caused by the natural lie of the land. It appears that the Lords Leigh did not wish to invest in expensive boundary earthworks. Along the roads which

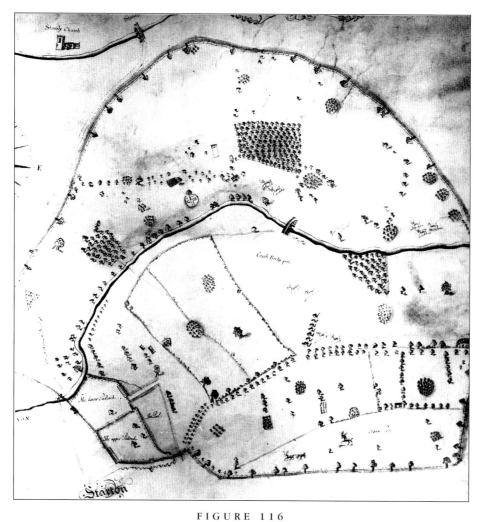

FIGURE 116
The park, as shown on Thomas Wilkes's map of Stoneleigh, 1749
(SBTRO, DR 671/24)

fringe the park north of the Avon there is again no sign of a massive bank, although the holloway and quarrying on Motslow hill has given the false impression of steep and sizeable slopes here. For the most part, however, there are only modest field banks. In 1999 a new timber fence was erected along this extensive boundary, not as a park pale but to fence the golf course.

The eighteenth century

There is no reliable evidence for the manner in which the deer park was physically arranged and managed until Thomas Wilkes mapped it in 1749 (Fig. 116).[72] The most distinctive feature of the Cloud area then shown is the avenue of trees that lines the old Cloud lane. This was probably planted between 1598 and 1640. North and south of the Cloud Lane avenue there are enclosed fields of various sizes, created in the same period. The pattern of hedgerows and tree lines probably followed the grain of the pre-existing strip and furlong boundaries of the medieval open fields. Only one of the field names recorded in 1639 is marked on Wilkes's map – 'the Farm Piece'. The only other field name marked in the park, 'Coach Bridge Piece', has finally ousted Cloud field in an area where the name had been used in the first half of the seventeenth century for smaller enclosed fields (e.g. 'The Cloud', Fig. 111, tenant 1). The bridge had been built, according to its date stone, in 1679. A significant feature, which must have followed emparking, is the scatter of square and round clumps of trees or coverts, used to shelter game, also, perhaps planted for aesthetic effect. In the Cloud area there were about ten of these tree clumps and a similar number north of the Avon.

On the Stoneleigh side of the Avon, the western end of Cunigrey lane was still discernible by a double line of trees, and Cunigrey Grove (see 1597 map, Fig. 107) was still a well-defined woodland. For the first time it is clear that part of Stare Hill and all of Stare Hill meadow had not been taken into the park; a sharp and awkward angle in the boundary was thereby avoided. Although the angle had been reduced, a footpath is shown taking an even shorter cut across the park from Stareton to Stoneleigh. This was an unexpected but seemingly legitimate breach of security in the impressive timber fence drawn in elevation around the whole of the park.

In the former village area of Stareton two fenced paddocks were created, each provided with a long narrow building, probably for the care and shelter of deer. The lower of the two medieval fish ponds still survived as a body of water to the east. A single storey building can be seen south of the Cloud avenue in 'Farm Piece'. It was probably not a dwelling, being shown in elevation without a chimney. Of considerable interest is the two-storey lodge situated on the steep slope north of the Avon, also depicted in elevation. It boasted a tall and centrally placed chimney and was probably occupied by a deer keeper. The position of the stack suggests that it was built soon after the park was created, adopting a plan new in the seventeenth century known as a 'lobby entry'.[73] The front door opened onto a small vestibule, the back wall of which was the side of the chimney stack. Doors to the left and right gave access to two rooms both heated by the same chimney. There are nineteenth-century illustrations of the lodge: one a measured elevation and the other a drawing from close by on the south-east side (Figs 117, 118).[74] The style of the chimney stack and the eyebrow-lintel mullioned windows indicate a seventeenth-century date.

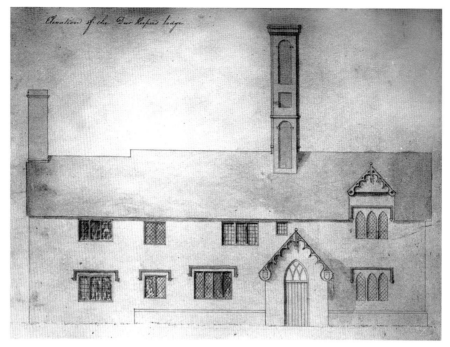

FIGURE 117
Nineteenth-century elevation of Deer Keepers Lodge (SBTRO, DR 823/19/22)

FIGURE 118
Nineteenth-century drawing of Deer Keepers Lodge (SBTRO, DR 671/381)

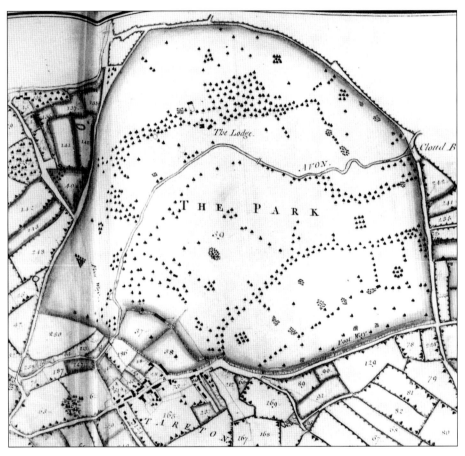

FIGURE 119

Stoneleigh Deer Park, as shown on Matthias Baker's map of the Stoneleigh estates, 1776
(SBRTO, DR 671/30a)

Some alterations to the original design, to impart a picturesque 'Gothick' look, appear to have taken place subsequently: pointed arches have been added to some of the windows and porch with a gothic-arched main door built onto the front. The barge boards to the gables are appropriately cusped. At sometime previously, a one-bay extension, in plain vernacular and with a lower roof, had been added to the left-hand side, which unbalanced the building. The lodge appears never to have been used as accommodation for sportsmen, though guests may have been provided with refreshments there, having travelled by carriage from Stoneleigh Abbey to the park. The carriages would have been able to cross the Avon from north to south over Coach Bridge.

No information has been found to date, however, on whether deer were actually hunted in the park. In an 1839 copy of directions first issued in 1776 to the keeper of the park, it appears that the slaughtering of deer was undertaken more frequently by the keeper himself under instructions from the 'House Steward'.[75] This was for the practical purpose of providing venison for the lord's table. The keeper was to send the good meat to the Abbey but could keep the skin, horns and fat. He was paid £30 per annum with an allowance of two guineas for boots, breeches and a cap.

'Expenses in keeping up and preserving Stoneleigh Park' have survived for part of 1750, 1751, 1752, 1753 and part of 1754.[76] Full year running costs varied between £151 7s.10d. and £262 6s. 5d., and confirm that the annual wage of £30 for the park-keeper had already been fixed by this time, although he could claim higher livery costs from year to year. In May 1753 some trees were planted at a cost of £2 8s.0d. and watered in September by the gardener. The deer keeper was not allowed to cut 'anything' down in the park, unless permission had been obtained; and one of his duties was to inspect 'the mounds of the Park', presumably the less than spectacular boundary banks, and report on necessary repairs to the Lord Steward.[77]

Matthias Baker's map of 1766 is more accurate than Wilkes's and his field drawings have also survived. They provide useful detail, but there is little significant change from 1749 (Fig. 119).[78] The medieval fish pond has disappeared and a channel now runs along the centre of the former pool bed. This may have been the result of a decision to drain the water, but long term neglect would have led to the silting up the pond. Again, inexplicably in terms of the security of the park, another public footway has been allowed to develop, running along the inside of the park pale along Stareton Lane rather than using the roadway itself. Relatively little was to change in the park during the remainder of the eighteenth and early part of the nineteenth century. In 1806 the Reverend Thomas Leigh inherited Stoneleigh Abbey and his employment of Humphry Repton a few years later brought about the dramatic alterations and extensions to the park, discussed by Hazel Fryer in the following chapter.

CHAPTER TEN

THE PARK AND GARDENS AT STONELEIGH ABBEY

Hazel Fryer

In the early nineteenth century, reflecting the changing taste for Picturesque ideas, Stoneleigh became the focus of improvements which were to provide an exceptional example of landscape design in this style. Humphry Repton considered the estate as one of his more important commissions and, in his Red Book for the Abbey, expressed the quality of the site: 'I look upon Stoneleigh Abbey as a place Sui generis and not to be compared to any other place.'[1] Indeed, the current landscape reflects not only Repton's work but also that of a a series of designers, includng C.S. Smith, W.A. Nesfield and Percy Cane. In the Red Book, the characteristic method Repton used to deliver his ideas to clients, he was to propose an idealised landscape created in the style of the Italian landscapes painted by artists such as Nicolas Poussin and Claude Lorraine. In presenting his designs, he chose to create a gallery of paintings, a method unique to Stoneleigh, as there are no other known commissions where he used this method. Watercolour views of before and after improvement were presented in the manner of painters, including Claude Lorraine, Ruysdael and Watteau, and the elegant series of designs presented in 1809 encapsulate the charm of Stoneleigh and its riverside landscape.

Although to review Repton's involvement at Stoneleigh it is necessary to focus on the development of the estate in the late eighteenth and early nineteenth century, the park and gardens reveal a long history of landscaping undertaken over four centuries at the behest of the Leigh family. Repton was at pains to emphasise the importance of all that was ancient and venerable, for this element lent interest and complexity of detail which as a designer he particularly appreciated. He valued the antiquity of the Abbey and in his recommendations drew upon Stoneleigh's long and interesting history, as evidenced in its unique and varied appearance.

As early as 1154 a group of hermits, recently converted to the Cistercian order, petitioned the king to allow them to transfer their home from Radmore in Staffordshire to the manor of

Stoneleigh in Arden. After a brief stay at Cryfield the monks settled in the isolated position between Echills Wood and the River Avon.[2] The community prospered and it is still possible to see fragments of the early twelfth-century stone building incorporated into later structures. The site chosen for the original abbey complex was situated on one of the meandering loops of the Avon which forms the boundary with the adjacent parish of Ashow, also part of the Stoneleigh estate.

The gatehouse, completed by Robert de Hockele in 1346 remains today, though much restored and remodelled and reflecting the many changes that have occurred in the last six hundred years. The site of the Abbey has also experienced considerable change and the estate has several sites of archaeological interest including the mill which lay close to the west front of the Abbey. The course of the river, modified in earlier centuries by the need to create weirs and level changes to feed the mill, was to change once more when it became the focus of a polite landscape. Functioning in 1789, the mill was a barometer of early nineteenth-century changes: by 1830 it had ceased to function.[3]

It was in 1640 that Thomas Lord Leigh obtained a license to empark 800 acres at Stoneleigh, the first stage in the formation of the deer park which exists today. The early park measured only 320 acres and focused on the lands between Stareton and Stoneleigh and it was not until the mid-nineteenth century that the park was to reach the size described in the 1640 license.[4]

Eighteenth-Century Improvements

In 1710, Edward, the third Lord Leigh (1683-1738) inherited the estate. Married to a wealthy heiress, Mary Holbech, and much influenced by a Grand Tour taken in 1711, Edward made plans to transform the old house. Francis Smith of Warwick was commissioned to build the great west wing, but work was not finally completed until 1726. The extensive improvements to the Abbey were not, however, matched by improvements to the grounds and the elegant accommodation was not enhanced with a park. A survey in 1749 by Thomas Wilkes provides not only a map of the Abbey's environs but also records the south-west prospect of the Abbey itself with an incongruous walled enclosure separating the imposing baroque front from the farmyard which surrounded it.[5] Stables and sheds are visible within the enclosure, together with a mill and dovecote. The approach from the south passed along the periphery of the farmyard and encircled the west front before entering the Abbey gatehouse from the north (Figs. 23B, 120).

Improvements to the gardens were not to commence until Edward the fifth Lord Leigh came of age in 1763. Educated at Oriel College, Oxford, Edward matriculated in 1761 and took his seat in the House of Lords in 1764. He had great plans for both the house and grounds and accounts for the period show vast expenditure on both the interior and environs of the Abbey.[6] There are details of planting ordered from John Whittingham's nursery at Charterhouse near Coventry as part of the restoration of the walled garden:[7] an interesting detail of this is to be seen in a plan of December 1766 illustrating the trees to be planted around the statue of Neptune.[8]

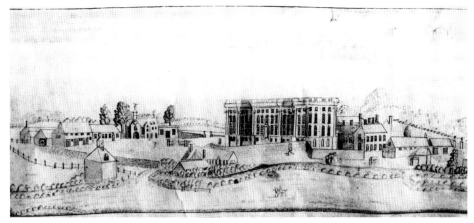

FIGURE 120
South-west prospect of Stoneleigh, by Thomas Wilkes, 1749 (SBTRO, DR 671/24)

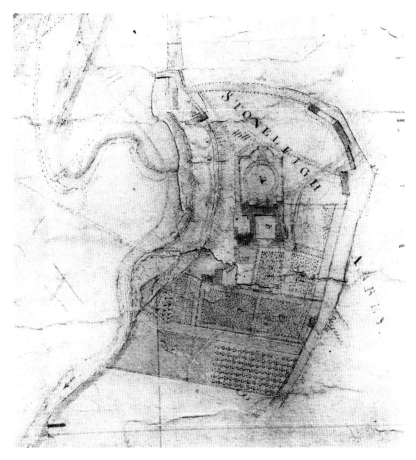

FIGURE 121
Detail from a map of *c.* 1770, based on Mathias Baker's survey of 1766/7 (SBTRO, DR 671/34)

The south front with its lawned embankments falling to the meandering river, is shown clearly in a survey of about 1770, based on Mathias Baker's map of 1766/7.[9] Also illustrated in some detail are the gardens to the north and east of the house and the walled gardens and orchards replanted by Edward. The main approach from the south can be seen passing around the south and west fronts of the Abbey (Fig. 121). It was tortuous and had to pass over two bridges across the Avon and the mill stream before winding around the perimeter of the farmyard. The landscape around the Abbey was essentially agricultural, with the only park clearly the separated deer park. Edward prepared many proposals and improvements for the Abbey, its gardens and park, but these were to remain unfulfilled after he became ill in 1763.[10]

On his death Edward was succeeded by his sister, Mary Leigh. Of a retiring nature, Mary consulted her 'man of business', Joseph Hill, on most major decisions and was to make very few changes to the Abbey. The accounts for this period do not reveal major expenditure on the estate. In 1910, Agnes Leigh, writing about Mary Leigh in her *Memoir*, describes her as leading a retired life and talks of her enjoying visits to the Deer Keeper's lodge in the park at Stoneleigh for tea in the evening. A record of such a journey is described in 1791: 'The carriage is now at the door to carry us into the park I am pleased with the new drives I found there they are judiciously made'.[11] Though this appears to be a reference to improvements being undertaken in the park, the changes seem to have been modest and Samuel Ireland in his book, *Picturesque Views of the Avon*, published in 1795, describes the full charm and unchanged quality of Stoneleigh Abbey:

> The situation of this abbey is truly beautiful: the Avon, winding before the
> house at a proper distance, supplies the corn and fulling mills, whose distant
> sound aided by the rushing waters falling from the stream, contribute in no
> small degree to render a complete landscape delicious to a reflecting and
> contemplative mind.[12]

Stoneleigh is illustrated in this volume in a view from the south west (Fig. 122). The drawing shows the approach to the Abbey and the main bridging point from the south, later to be altered as part of Repton's 'Improvements' to the River Avon. The view clearly illustrates the winding nature of the river and the boat moored in front of the Abbey suggests, surprisingly, that it was possibly navigable.

On Mary's death in 1806, the property passed to James Henry Leigh of Adlestrop, direct descendant of Rowland the eldest son of the first Sir Thomas Leigh, subsequent to a life interest of James's uncle, the Reverend Thomas Leigh of Adlestrop, who died in 1806.

FIGURE 122
Stoneleigh Abbey from the south-west; drawing by Samuel Ireland,
published in his *Picturesque Views of the Avon*, 1795

FIGURE 123
View of the gatehouse, from Humphry Repton's Red Book (SBTRO, DR 671/76a, fol.3)

The Repton Design

The Reverend Thomas Leigh of Adlestrop moved to the Abbey with his sister Elizabeth. Caroline Austen, writing in 1809, suggests 'the change came too late in their lives to be pleasant to them'.[13] This opinion was re-stated by Agnes Leigh in her *Memoir* of 1910. 'He [the Reverend Thomas Leigh] presently made arrangement with the head of the family James Henry Leigh who took possession of Stoneleigh and Thomas returned to his peaceful existence at Adlestrop!'[14] However, it is due to Thomas Leigh that Repton, who had already designed the gardens at Adlestrop, was commissioned to carry out improvements at Stoneleigh.

When he received the news of his inheritance, Thomas Leigh was staying at Adlestrop with his cousin Cassandra Leigh and her daughter Jane.[15] They undertook a journey to view the estate and it is in Cassandra's record of this visit that we have one of the clearest descriptions of the estate before Repton undertook the commission.

> I had expected to find everything about the place very fine and all that, but I
> had no idea of it being so beautiful. I had figured to myself long Avenues dark
> Rookeries and Dismal Yew Trees, but there was no such melancholy things.
> The Avon near the house amidst green meadows bounded by large and
> beautiful woods full of delightful walks.[16]

Repton, also much impressed, was delighted to undertake this commission which gave him the opportunity to advise on a landscape which had been little altered to any significant extent by previous improvers. He first visited the site in 1808 to propose the alterations that were to lead, by 1820, to a fundamental change. The separated deer park of 320 acres was extended westwards dramatically, taking in the Abbey and its surrounding lands and increasing its size to one thousand acres. A west/east ride was created through the new park, running from the Grecian Lodges on the diverted Ashow/Stoneleigh Road, past the Abbey and on to the new East Lodge on the Stoneleigh/Leamington Road. The road then passed east between the Avon and Stareton village along the old Cloud Lane, finally leaving the park via the new London Lodge (now Tantara Lodge) at the Stoneleigh/Cubbington Road.

These changes were only partially completed by Repton and it is therefore of importance to distinguish between the proposals he implemented and later improvements carried out in his style. Though Repton visited Stoneleigh in the summer of 1808, the Red Book was not completed and presented to his client until May 1809, almost a year later. It was partly prepared, as was usual, at Repton's own home at Hare Street, but also at Aylsham, possibly the home of John Adey Repton, his eldest son.[17] It is one of the few large format Red Books reserved for particularly prestigious clients and is comparable with those presented for sites such as Brighton Pavilion and Woburn Abbey. The volume has since been rebound and is now slightly smaller than it was and also lacks the characteristic red morocco binding which Repton preferred. It is likely that John Adey Repton, who was an accomplished architect, advised on the designs for the south front and possibly some of the other buildings proposed.

Not only is the Red Book for Stoneleigh unusually large, it is also particularly striking. Repton introduced his proposals as follows:

> Much has been said by Authors who have written upon Gardening concerning the necessity of making the works of great painters the models for real improvements: an assertion which I have never seen so fully justified as in the instance of this place, abounding in the most interesting subjects for the Pencil, both in the Works of Nature and of Art: yet so combined as to realize a collection of Landscapes by the best Masters.[18]

The first image that Repton chose to include was the Abbey gatehouse which he admired for 'circumstances which add much to that impression so grateful to those who delight in whatever is ancient and venerable and therefore worthy to be retained in these days of upstart innovation'.[19] As a designer Repton was at pains to emphasise the importance of all that was 'ancient and venerable' for this lent interest and complexity of detail which he so appreciated. Hence, in defining the character and situation of Stoneleigh, he turned first to this remnant of the early Abbey. It was particularly apt that this should be a focal point of the approach, always of major concern to Repton and which, at Stoneleigh, was in desperate need of attention.

> The Approach to a place is one of the first considerations in all modern Improvement, and it is impossible for any place to require it more than Stoneleigh Abbey, because from its situation, on a large peninsula, formed by the Winding of the River and the badness of the Cross Roads to Dunchurch, it is at present difficult of access from all directions.[20]

In his proposals he further observed that 'the approach must all be brought together at that one spot and therefore the roads from all quarters will obviously lead to the same object, which is not the Abbey, but the Old Gate House, through which the Abbey always has been and ought to be approached' (Fig. 123).[21] Passing through the gatehouse Repton discusses in his second view – of the west front – another of the themes he admired on this site, one of diversity. The buildings at Stoneleigh were a composition of different styles and it was this blending of various architectural elements which he considered contributed so much charm to the scene.

It would be a departure from common prudence to change this large Grecian Pile to the original Character of the Abbey; and it would be a departure from good taste in any Antiquary to destroy or alter several curious fragments of Picturesque Gothic, which serve to distinguish or preserve its former Character: I shall therefore consider how each may be preserved, restored or improved, separately, without such Strict unity of Style as I have generally recommended.[22]

In order to provide an appropriate expansive setting for the 'Grecian pile' of the west wing, Repton advocated sweeping away the existing walls in front of the elevation and opening up the view to the Avon (Fig. 124). He then went on to contrast this delightful parkland landscape, and the grove seen in the distance beyond the water meadows, with the Picturesque character of the north front of the house portrayed in the third view.

The north front intrigued Repton and he drew particular attention to the foundations and lower walls which formed part of the original Abbey. He commented on the elegantly pointed gable and the flight of steps which protected a grotto, described as similar to that at Oxmead Hall. Also discussed were the decorative balls and pointed finials which he regarded as notably Picturesque in character. His sympathy with the variety and interest of the north front is emphasised by the conjunction in his painting between the architecture and the dramatic spires of the evergreen trees (Fig. 125).

For the south front Repton proposed considerable changes and, possibly working with his son John Adey, was again to reveal his taste for the Picturesque: 'the buildings have a degree of irregularity and a play of outline producing effects of light and shadow not to be found in any symmetric Building'. Interestingly, the watercolour for the south front makes direct reference to the artist, Claude Lorraine, specifically to 'some of the palaces in Liber Veritatis held in Devonshire House'. Claude's preoccupation with the quality of light, apparent even in his engravings, clearly provided an inspiration for Repton[23] (Fig. 71). These rather magnificent proposals, however, were not to be implemented and the south front later provided the site for the construction of a conservatory, reputedly by the Victorian designer, W.A. Nesfield (Fig. 78).

In contrast to the work of Claude which inspired the paintings of the south front, Repton turned to the lively charms of Watteau when illustrating the improvements to the Avon. Doubtless he was particularly attracted to the charms of the river and his view of a sylvan scene on the banks of the Avon was enlivened by the quality of detail which owes much to the delicacy of the French artist. The watercolour before improvement is of particular interest as a figure, possibly Repton, is seen at work in the foreground pegging out the line of the improvements to the river. This self-portrait serves almost as a signature within this particular watercolour, one of the most exotic of the collection (Fig. 126).

FIGURE 124
Proposed prospect from the north-west, after improvements,
from Humphry Repton's Red Book (SBTRO, DR 671/76a, fol.9)

FIGURE 125
Stoneleigh Abbey, north from, 1809, from Humphry Repton's Red Book (SBTRO, DR 671/76a, fol.13)

Watteau was an unusual model for Repton to chose and there are few similar references to the former's work in other Red Books.

> ... without the slightest attempt to make one of his pictures my model – but the richness the amenity and the cheerfulness of his scenery, have made a very accurate dilettanti [sic] observe that as the pictures of Rembrandt, tho' crouded with Jewells and Embroidery, always present dirty old Men and Women – so the pictures of Watteau amidst Shepherds and Gardeners seem to introduce us to elegant Society.[24]

The detail of the two bridges, the central focus of the pleasure grounds, was the subject of a further view which Repton chose to present in the style of Ruysdael.

> ... the combination of two bridges of different Character which however strongly Contrasted, do not offend as a picture the old Abbey, Mill and Bridge form an interesting part of the peculiar Character of the place, and are not visible from the house, while the bridge over the new Channel will be a very material feature in the Scene and by its reflection in the Water, wilt enliven the dark reflected Shade of the opposite hanging wood.[25]

The necessity for a bridge in front of the south windows was questioned when a new bridge was built to the west. Repton emphasised its importance in gaining access to the water meadows and the wood which overhangs the river. He was, however, to experience much difficulty in achieving this detail of his design and the second bridge remains today as merely a temporary structure. Even the charm of his double view from the Grove was not to be persuasive, positioned where, with the strategic use of the axe, it was possible to open a delightful view with two points of focus, the Abbey on the right and to the left the new bridge of the west approach (Fig. 127). This watercolour he chose to contrast with all the other views and presented it as a compliment to the taste of his client. 'The Models for some other of my Sketches have been taken from the imaginary Scenes of Claude, Watteau and Ruysdale [sic], but this is taken from real Scenes at Adlestrop, where the Water is shown thro' openings, most judiciously preserved, between groupes of large trees in the foreground.'[26]

Given its richness and variety, it is perhaps not surprising that the Red Book took so long to complete. Still less surprising is the fact that in his enthusiasm to commence improvements at Stoneleigh, the Reverend Thomas Leigh, before the completion of the Red Book, sought Repton's advice over alterations to the forecourt on the west front and to the river on the south side of the house.[27] The river was, in fact, the feature to receive the greatest attention. As recommended in the painted views, the course of the water was widened to create a large, reflective surface before the south front, to show to advantage the house and garden features.

FIGURE 126

The River Avon at Stoneleigh, by Humphry Repton, 1809, with a surveyor, possibly a self portrait, overseeing improvements; from the Red Book (SBTRO, DR 671/76a, fol.21a)

FIGURE 127

Proposed double view from the Grove, from the Red Book (SBTRO, DR 671/76a, fols 25-26)

features. The confluence of the two streams also provided the contrast of calm glossy and turbulent water as a focus for the pleasure grounds. Some of the quality of this design is preserved in a view from the Grove just fifty years later, on the occasion of Queen Victoria's visit to Stoneleigh with Prince Albert for the opening of Aston People's Park (Fig. 128).

Achieving this landscape had not been easy. In January 1809, when improvements to the Avon were well under way, a sudden flood swept a large quantity of earth into a deep part of the old channel and removed the new dam which had not been secured. In a letter of 24 March 1809, Repton discussed the flood and proposed alterations to his previous layout, suggesting the bridge adjacent to the mill should be relocated further west.[28] The mill itself was not mentioned and it is not known whether the flood water, which rose several feet, damaged its mechanism. A design for a new mill, dated from about 1810 and appropriate for the site, survives in the Leigh papers but the proposal does not appear to have been implemented.[29]

Several issues concerning the river were discussed in the summer of 1809. Repton was aware that, in order to bring the approach to the Abbey from the west rather than the south, a new bridge would be required. The merits of using a cast iron bridge were discussed, but Repton recommended stone and proposed that it be of a three-arch form 'rather picturesque in outline (with) a hint from the simple, rude but celebrated bridge of Llanwrst built by Inigo Jones'.[30] This settled, it only remained necessary to appoint an engineer. John Rennie was consulted on the design and work commenced in 1812. Although the first payment was made by the Reverend Thomas Leigh, the bridge was not completed in his lifetime: it was his executors, who, after his death in 1813, were to continue the payments.

Although the approach from the west was implemented, it was not to the alignment proposed by Repton, following a straight line rather than the curve indicated in the Red Book (Fig. 129). It was not possible to complete the approach until October 1814 when agreement was finally given for the improvement of the Warwick to Coventry Road.[31] The completion of the new road, to the west of the earlier line, made it possible to commence work on the Grecian lodges. Following Thomas Leigh's death instructions for the work were given by his nephew, James Henry Leigh.

The death of the Reverend Thomas Leigh in 1813 brought Repton's work at Stoneleigh to a sudden end. This was a great disappointment to the designer who at a single blow lost one of his most important commissions. The Red Book proposals were well advanced in the summer of 1813 and a number of additional drawings suggest other improvements may have been under discussion. Unfortunately, a charming sketch, endorsed: 'Mr Repton's Green Seat', dated 1813, was, like the menagerie proposed adjacent to the west approach, never to be implemented.[32]

Repton appears to have enjoyed the commission at Stoneleigh and was intimately involved in many of the detailed decisions. James Henry Leigh, however, did not choose to recommission him, discharging his outstanding account for fifty guineas on 26 October l813.[33] Severing the connection with this commission when it was still under implementation was a considerable disappointment to Repton. Although improvements were to continue without interruption, they were sadly not to be to his design.

Reptonian Improvements

James Henry Leigh, on inheriting the estate in 1813, undertook, with the help of his wife, Julia, further extensive improvements to the landscape at Stoneleigh, at the same time completing many of the proposals commenced by his uncle. George Jones of Stareton was to record the main building and landscape work completed by James Henry Leigh and his successors in a series of detailed account books commencing on 16 April 1814.[34] One of the earliest improvements noted was in June 1814 when alterations to the terrace in front of the west wing were carried out, described in the account book as 'Abbey Gate Terraces'. The layout implemented appears to be of a different design to that indicated in the Red Book. There is, however, an early nineteenth-century pricked map of the west wing and grounds at Stoneleigh, indicating proposals for the terrace which may be the layout indicated in the 1814 accounts.[35] As the drawing indicates the approach running across the west front, it is possible that the design may have been Repton's, although this is by no means certain.

Another area of uncertainty is the appendix to the Stoneleigh Red Book in which Repton had proposed a group of cottages near the proposed bridge across the Avon. Repton advocated that the cottages should be constructed in 'Wooden Gothic', in the style of the timber-framed buildings of Coventry but also subjoined to the Red Book were several cottage designs, 'which may be varied many ways according to the Situation, Number and Circumstances of the several dwellings proposed'.[36] (Fig. 72) As the Stoneleigh Red Book was rebound in the nineteenth century, it is not clear whether or not a sheet of 'sketches of cottages at Blaise' which are of the appropriate size, were the drawings to which Repton refers.[37]

However, the 'Wooden Gothic' style for the lodges at the west gate was not chosen, the design of the buildings becoming instead the subject of much discussion. On 23 December, in reply to a letter from Julia Leigh, the architect, William Porden, sent his proposals for the lodges at Stoneleigh but these were simlilarly rejected.[38] The construction of the Grecian Lodges was to be followed by a series of Picturesque properties located throughout the estate. In the deer park alone, several lodges were built, including Bubbenhall Lodge at the Stoneleigh/Cubbington Road entrance to the park, also known as the London Lodge or Tantara Lodge (Fig. 130).

Improvements to the landscape were also being carried out. The result is very Reptonian in style and it is of interest to note that in the Red Book Repton had described in considerable detail the separated deer park which he thought to be a place of considerable beauty.

In former times the Park was very different from the Parks of the present day. It was not inhabited (exclusively) by the gentle fallow Deer, or tame Cattle; but the ancient Park was a sort of lesser forest, for the preservation of the Stag and the Wild Boar, the Bull and the Buffalo – such ferocious and dangerous animals, however formidable to the Ladies, might afford Sport for the rough hardy Lords of those days: but were removed to a proper distance from the Mansion which was placed in the midst of its Gardens, its Orchards and the part of the Estate allotted to the Farm and Grange. This will account for the situation of the mansion at Stoneleigh, and many other places, with respect to its Park, so very different from Modern houses which are generally situated in the very center of their Parks.[39]

Improvements to the existing deer park and the creation of the new park around the Abbey were to transform the estate. In the decade before his death in 1823, James Henry Leigh created a landscape with much of the charm advocated by Repton. Alterations to Dog Kennel Lane and improvements to the route from Stoneleigh village to Leamington Spa made it possible to create an improved route from the east.[40] Bubbenhall Lodge, the triumphal entrance to the park, was under construction from September 1818, as was Park Lodge, later known as Stareton Lodge (Fig. 131). A lithograph, c. 1825, of Park Lodge, situated at the Stareton entrance, illustrates the Picturesque quality of the early nineteenth-century park. Clearly shown is the ornamental planting completed at this time, including Scots pine located on both the perimeter of the park and at strategic positions within it.

C.S. Smith

A wealth of early nineteenth-century archive material details the development of both the landscape improvements and the construction of Picturesque lodges and cottages. The papers include a number of sketches by C.S. Smith, one of them a drawing of East Lodge, dated 1817.[41] It is difficult to evaluate the full extent to which Smith may also have been involved in the landscape improvement. Accounts of the work undertaken were kept faithfully by George Jones, but unfortunately he does not always record the designer. It is possible that the implementation of the Reptonian landscape was to the instruction of James Henry and Julia Leigh alone. It is likely, however, that C.S. Smith, a pupil of Wyatville, who also completed a number of Reptonian landscapes, may have been more influential in shaping the landscape at Stoneleigh than has been previously allowed.

Smith's new design for the stables was well under way in the Autumn of 1815 (Fig. 73). The bill for payments to masons and tradesmen alone, for the period October 1815 to March 1816, was £1,253.[42] James Henry appears to have favoured buildings in the Tudor Gothic style,

FIGURE 128
View from the Grove, on the occasion of Queen Victoria's visit to Stoneleigh,
from the *Illustrated London News*, June 1858

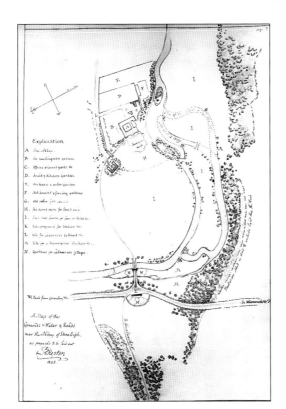

FIGURE 129
Humphry Repton's plan for
improvements at Stoneleigh, 1808;
from the Red Book
(SBTRO, DR 671/76a, fol.4)

257

not only for the stable block, but also for many of the lodges and cottages throughout the estate. The buildings were often built in local stone and have a Picturesque harmony and unity of detail. One distinctly different building is Park Lodge with its tree-trunk columns, thatch and rod work front door (Fig. 131). Constructed in brick and originally lime washed – a practice frequently advocated by Repton – the cottage appears to be of a more ornamental style than the other buildings on the estate. 'A sketch of a cottage at Woburn Abbey', endorsed Park entrance cottage, survives in the Leigh archives but there is no designer's name on the sketch which makes it difficult to validate.[43] Whether the design for this particular lodge was the work of Repton is unknown, but the delicacy of the detail would suggest his hand. The outstanding examples of Smith's work, the stable block, positioned not to the west of the house as Repton proposed but to the north, and the riding stable built nearer to the house, are both dramatically positioned within the landscape. The siting of all the buildings at this time is confident and dramatic and in all cases enhances the landscape.

The sudden death of James Henry Leigh on 27 October 1823 did not terminate C.S. Smith's work at the Abbey. Julia Leigh appears to have continued with the improvements and gave help to her son Chandos when he inherited the estate, much of the routine correspondence and bills being dealt with by her.[44] The first edition of the 1-inch Ordnance Survey map records many of the improvements which had been undertaken in the park. The new approach from the west and the improved routes through the Deer Park to the east and to Stoneleigh village can clearly be seen.

Victorian Improvements

After the dynamic period of change which had occurred in the early nineteenth century, Chandos Leigh appears to have been content to leave the landscape relatively unchanged. In many ways this period was to be particularly difficult for the Leigh family; dogged by ill health and a series of legal problems, Chandos appears to have been content to leave the guidance of much of the final improvements to his mother, Julia Leigh.

Towards the end of the 1840s, however, there is an interesting letter in the Stoneleigh papers to the designer, W.A. Nesfield. It is dated 13 January 1848 and encloses a cheque for £391 0s. 0d. drawn on the Gloucestershire Banking Company.[45] W.A. Nesfield was advising at both Adlestrop and Stoneleigh and unfortunately it is not clear whether the payment was for the terrace at Adlestrop or for designs at Stoneleigh. William Henry Leigh inherited the estate when Chandos died in September 1850 and it was not until 1858, in an article in the *Midland Florist*, that Nesfield's contribution to the remodelling of the estate was mentioned.[46] This was with reference to the conservatory which by then had been completed and was stocked with plants.

FIGURE 130
Nineteenth-century pencil sketch of London Lodge (SBTRO, DR 671/381)

FIGURE 131
Park Lodge; lithograph of *c*.1825

South Terraces

Nesfield became renowned for his parterre designs, using scroll-work displays of box and patterns of coloured gravels. It is possible that he was responsible for elaborating the terraces at Stoneleigh – and for creating the Italian garden on the west front, which provided the setting for the visit of Queen Victoria and Prince Albert on 14-16 June 1858. The Queen had come to Warwickshire to open the People's Park at Aston and her reception at Stoneleigh was a brilliant occasion. In her private journal Georgiana Leigh describes the event and the preparations that were made.[47] The rooms looking towards the south over the gardens sloping down to the Avon were chosen as the royal suite. She includes a full description of the improvements to the house and gardens in the journal and of the events which occurred during the visit, and there is also a series of delightful impressions of the entertainments by Edward Leigh who was requested by his brother to escort 'her majesty to see all the beauties of his famous Park'.

There was great festivity at Stoneleigh; a great banquet was served and the band of the Second Life Guards was in attendance all evening to entertain the great mass of people who were assembled in the home park, just outside the terrace balustrades. On this occasion not only the old Abbey Gateway was illuminated with coloured lamps, but also all the flower beds and borders in the garden. In a ceremony on the following day:

> The Queen and Prince Albert walked through the Italian Garden in front of the house where arrangements had been made that they should plant a tree, the Queen planted an oak and the Prince Consort a Wellingtonia gigantia.[48]

This delightful event was to conclude the royal visit, but the park and garden at Stoneleigh continued to be a source of delight. Like his grandparents, William Henry Leigh took a great deal of interest in the park and gardens at Stoneleigh and was to continue ornamenting it for the remainder of the nineteenth century. A series of articles published on the gardens at Stoneleigh reveal charming details of the late nineteenth-century landscape: perhaps the most illuminating was published in *Country Life Magazine* in October 1899, in an article entitled 'Old and New'. The park was said to be of great beauty, but, as Repton had observed nearly one hundred years earlier, the feature that the author particularly emphasised was 'The contrasting styles which came together to give Stoneleigh its unusual character'.[49] A *Country Life* article in 1901, titled a 'Classic Terrace', also contains a most attractive view of the pleasure grounds running down to the Avon:

> Our illustrations of this remarkably beautiful scene deserves to rank high among garden pictures. The place gains much from its surroundings, for the garden is that of Stoneleigh Abbey, the seat of Lord Leigh and the river is the classic Avon which spreads out into the river like expanse to reflect the

features of a glorious landscape and lend its supreme charm to one of die most glorious gardens in England.[50]

In the twentieth century, under the direction of Percy Cane, the landscape benefited from yet another designer of major repute. His style was characteristically simple and was always directed by a carefully studied sympathy for the individual qualities of a given site. At Stoneleigh he may have been responsible for remodelling the terraces, employing the Irish yews and enhancing them with symmetrically arranged beds of scarlet geraniums.[51] In the 1950s, however, the weir which had created the widened river, the focus of the Repton landscape, was breached and the resulting flood seems to have eroded much of Percy Cane's work. The subsequent filling in of the southern part of the channel has effected a change for the worse in the riverside landscape, transforming the relationship between the house and grounds and eliminating the reflective pool on which so many commentators had dwelt with pleasure.

With Heritage Lottery Fund support, the Abbey has now been restored and developed as a series of apartments. This offers an opportunity to reconsider the landscape and make a proper assessment of its extraordinarily rich history and quality. It is a landscape which in the last two hundred years has benefited from the attention of several of the most significant designers of their time and reflects the continuing care and attention of generations of owners. It is important that the site should be subject to measures which will recover and secure the best of its history and protect its future.

References

PART ONE: BUILDINGS

CHAPTER ONE

1. For monastic conversions, see M. Howard, *The Early Tudor Country House*, London 1987, ch. 7. Amongst the growing recent literature, see J. Hare, *The Dissolution of the Monasteries in Hampshire*, Hampshire Papers 16, 1999; N. Doggett, 'The demolition and conversion of former monastic buildings in post-dissolution Hertfordshire', in: G. Keevill, M. Aston and T. Hall, eds, *Monastic Archaeology: Papers on the Study of Medieval Monasteries*, Oxford 2001, ch.10.

2. The only authority to appreciate the significance of the surviving fabric in a Cistercian context is Peter Fergusson, *The Architecture of Solitude: Cistercian Abbeys in Twelfth-century England*, Princeton 1984, 91, 148-9.

3. For Cryfield, see most recently S. Hill, 'The archaeology of the campus of the University of Warwick', *University Newsletter*, January 1999, 6-7.

4. See *The Stoneleigh Leger Book*, ed. R.H. Hilton, Dugdale Society, xxiv, 1960, especially xii-xvi for a discussion of the foundation dates, and 'A history of the abbots', 249-54; W. Dugdale, *The Antiquities of Warwickshire*, 2nd edn, 2 vols, London 1730, i, 255-58. Also see *Victoria County History (VCH), Warwickshire*, ii, 78-81; below, chapter 8 by Andrew Watkins.

5. The gatehouse is the subject of chapter 2 by Rochelle Ramey, and therefore will not be considered in detail here, except for its earliest fabric.

6. See, for example, N. Coldstream, 'The Cistercians as builders' in: D. Robinson, ed., *The Cistercian Abbeys of Britain: Far from the Concourse of Men*, London 1998, 40-4.

7. For the Bernardine plan, see Coldstream, 'Cistercians as builders', 40-1. There is no firm evidence for the form of the twelfth-century crossing at Stoneleigh.

8. Fergusson, *Architecture of Solitude*, 149, seems mistaken in noting scalloped capitals here.

9. See further Fergusson, *Architecture of Solitude*, 46-7.

10. In the former dining room, now the drawing room of East Wing House No.1, in the east wall just above modern floor level, and belonging to the southernmost chapel; Julian Munby, Oxford Archaeology, personal communication, 1999.

11. For the Bordesley plan, see most recently J. Stopford and S. Wright, 'A group of late medieval inscribed tiles from Bordesley Abbey', *Antiquaries Journal*, 78, 1998, fig. 1; for the special relationship, see *VCH, Warws.*, ii, 79.

12. The porch in its final form, including good Romanesque-style mouldings, is probably to be attributed to C. S. Smith, *c*.1836-39; Geoffrey Tyack, personal communication, 1999. The arch mouldings seem to be copied from those of the chapter house entrance, rather than medieval ones reused, as stated in Fergusson, *Architecture of Solitude*, 149.

13. As noted in Fergusson, *Architecture of Solitude*, 93; for the Reading capitals, see G. Zarnecki *et al.*, *English Romanesque Art 1066-1200*, London 1984, 169.

14. For these sites, see Robinson, *Cistercian Abbeys*, gazeteer; Dundrennan in Scotland is an architectural derivative of Roche and Byland.

15. With the possible exception of the right edge of the right feature.

16. At Furness, Roche and Byland abbeys; see Coldstream, 'Cistercians as builders', 44-8.

17. One additional feature of the transept worth noting is an alcove space seen internally in the south-east corner at modern first- and second-floor levels (Plans 2-3F), which might be the site of a small newel stair; it is not known whether the space also exists at ground level.

18. For example, at Roche, Furness and Byland abbeys; see J. Bilson, 'The architecture of the Cistercians, with reference to some of their earlier churches in England', *Archaeological Journal*, lxvi, 1909, fig. 12. The flat-sided keels of the processional door at Augustinian Lanercost Priory, Cumbria, are especially close to those of the Stoneleigh door.

19. Illustrated in N. Pevsner, *The Buildings of England, Shropshire*, Harmondsworth 1958, pl. 10b.

20. For example, compare Buildwas (Fig. 8).

21. Specifically that bay 2 at 5 metres, and bays 3 and 4 at 4.75 metres each, produce the total distance of 14.50 metres between piers 1 and 4, centre to centre.

22. As observed in N. Pevsner and A. Wedgwood, *The Buildings of England, Warwickshire*, Harmondsworth 1966, 407.

23. 'Magna fenestra ad magnum altare', *Leger Book*, 254. It is assumed here that 'window' refers to stonework, not just to glass. The decorated tiles found recently may also belong to his abbacy; see Appendix, 2.2 and 3.2.

24. The date of the window within Hockele's long abbacy is not stated: by the 1340s, his masons were employing curvilinear tracery patterns on the gatehouse (e.g. Fig. 20), see chapter 2. It is possible that the geometrical window in the east range undercroft also belongs to his abbacy (see further below).

25. 'Selatura sub campanili', *Leger Book*, 254 ; Dugdale, *Warwickshire*, i, 257, has 'the carved work under the steeple'.

26. For room designations in the east range and for typical Cistercian monastic plans, see R. Gilyard-Beer, *Abbeys*, 2nd edn, London 1976, 31-5, 48 and figs 14, 15.

27. Following Gilyard-Beer, *Abbeys*, figs 14-15.

28. This interpretation differs from those of Silk (Fig. 2) and *VCH, Warws.*, vi, 232 plan.

29. The former existence of a staircase here might also relate to the large relieving arch in the shared wall between this room and the slype, otherwise a feature difficult to explain.

30. P. Fergusson and S. Harrison, *Rievaulx Abbey*: *Community, Architecture, Memory*, New Haven and London 1999, 146-8.

31. For more context, see S. Harrison and M. Thurlby, 'An architectural history' in: R. Shoesmith and R. Richardson, eds, *A Definitive History of Dore Abbey*, Little Logaston 1997, 50.

32. It has not been possible to check this observation with the archaeology of the building fabric. For Worcester, see most recently U. Engel, *Die Kathedrale von Worcester*, Munich and Berlin 2000, 87-8 and plates 51, 52.

33. For example, at Kirkstall, Furness and Byland abbeys; see Bilson, 'Architecture of the Cistercians', 256-7.

34. The illumination is from the *Hours of Etienne Chevalier* by Jean Fouquet in the Musée Condé, Chantilly, ms. 71, f. 36; reproduced, for example, in Robinson, *Cistercian Abbeys*, 6. For Buildwas chapter house, see Robinson, *Cistercian Abbeys*, 80.

35. There has been no opportunity to inspect the masonry of these walls at first-floor level, but their massiveness on plan (even though partly compromised by later domestic adaptation) strongly suggests that they are medieval.

36. Fergusson and Harrison, *Rievaulx Abbey*, ch. 5. The unusual aisled form of the chapter house at Rievaulx permitted a ground-floor vestibule to be incorporated, above which a passage connected the dormitory to the night stair in the transept; an arrangement which is unlikely at Stoneleigh.

37. For plans of Fountains and Kirkstall, see Robinson, *Cistercian Abbeys*, 112, 132.

38. Cistercian examples include Roche and Kirkstall Abbeys, and those of other orders include Leiston Abbey, Suffolk, and Shap Abbey, Cumbria, both houses for Premonstratensian canons: see Gilyard-Beer, *Abbeys*, figs 15 and 16 for Roche and Leiston.

39. For Margam, see Robinson, *Cistercian Abbeys*, 140.

40. I am grateful to Bryn Gethin for this observation; see further Appendix, 2.1.

41. At Cleeve, full height only in the bay east of the east range; at Kirkstall, the rebuilding of the bay east of the east range, ground floor only.

42. The weathering apparently survives now only at the east end of the wall, but its size and position imply that originally the gable shape spanned the whole width of the wall; or was intended to do so. The area in question is impossible to inspect without scaffolding.

43. See Fergusson and Harrison, *Rievaulx Abbey*, 95-9.

44. Fergusson and Harrison, *Rievaulx Abbey*, 90-94, based on a combination of documentary and structural interpretation. The central vessel of Aelred's chapter house is slightly narrower than that at Stoneleigh, but differs from it in being carried on tall arcades resulting from the unique aisled, basilican plan.

45. Examples of new-built chapter houses seen as possible rivals could include, for the twelfth century, Augustinian Kenilworth Priory, and for the thirteenth, perhaps Benedictine St. Mary's Priory, Coventry.

46. The pier is 0.685 metres in diameter, which might seem slender for a nave arcade support; however, to take two examples to hand, the columnar piers of the twelfth-century nave arcades at Chaddesley Corbett parish church (Worcestershire) are the same diameter and at Bosbury (Herefordshire) rather smaller at 0.51 metres.

47. The fourteenth-century window in the entrance facade appears to be inserted into earlier wall masonry for at least part of its height (Fig. 20).

48. See Bilson, 'Architecture of the Cistercians', for examples in the churches at Kirkstall (fig. 11, iii, iv), Roche (fig. 12, i) and Dore (fig. 12, iv).

49. Its existence would explain why the gatehouse was a free-standing structure at the beginning of Ramey's 'Period 2', 1342-5 (see Chapter 2). With regard to the discussion there of the position of the doors, the stonework of the twelfth-century entrance jambs still shows clear evidence that originally the main doors were hung from them.

50. For a preliminary survey of the field, see P. Fergusson, ' "Porta Patens Esto": notes on early Cistercian gatehouses in the north of England' in: E.C. Fernie and P. Crossley, eds, *Medieval Architecture and its Intellectual Context: Studies in Honour of Peter Kidson*, London 1990, chapter 5, esp. 47-51.

51. *VCH, Warws.*, vi, 232.

52. These are the second and fourth piers from the north: the base of the second pier is entirely renewed but that of the fourth, revealed in the recent renovations, appears original. The base of the third pier has been lost through mutilation, whilst the first pier is of a different period.

53. *Leger Book*, 252.

54. Fergusson and Harrison, *Rievaulx Abbey*, 105. For day rooms in general, see Gilyard-Beer, *Abbeys*, 34-5.

55. 'Cuius tempore sunt multa edificia', *Leger Book*, 253; though details of his building works are not given.

56. See also Appendix, 3.1, for fragments of tracery.

57. The 1749 prospect shows the main range of the structure with timber-framed walls in square panels (Fig. 120). For full references to the estate maps, see note 79.

58. In addition, the plans suggest that the southern part of the east range (the undercroft) is slightly out of alignment with the northern part. The plotting of these anomalies goes back to at least the Heating and Water Service Systems plans of 1924 Shakespeare Birthplace Trust Records Office (SBTRO, DR 18/25/59b), on which the modern plans are based.

59. With the possible exception of some masonry in the west range basement; see Appendix, 2.3.

60. For details of the Leighs in this period, see chapter 5.

61. For example, Pevsner and Wedgwood, *Warwickshire*, 408; G. Tyack, *Warwickshire Country Houses*, Chichester 1994, 178.

62. R.E. Howard, R.R. Laxton and C.D. Litton, *Tree-ring Analysis of Timber from the Buildings and Living Trees at Stoneleigh Abbey, Stoneleigh, Warwickshire*, Ancient Monuments Laboratory Report 80/2000 (unpaginated).

63. Howard, *Tree-ring Analysis*.

64. For the purchasers of the property between 1538-1561, see *VCH, Warws.*, vi, 234.

65. SBTRO, DR 18/30/24/91. I am grateful to George Demidowicz for first drawing my attention to this document, and to Mairi Macdonald for the transcription printed here. The document is undated, but Nat Alcock has reasonably suggested that it was prepared in 1545; N.W. Alcock, *People at Home: Living in a Warwickshire Village 1500-1800*, Chichester 1993, 87, note 29. The Dadleys were apparently a local family; see person index to *Leger Book*, under 'Daddele'.

66. Lichfield Record Office, B/C/11, 'The inventorie of all the goodes ... of Thomas Dadley of Stoneley Abbay ..., the xv days [sic] August anno Dni. 1558'; the rooms listed are a hall, parlour, chamber, bedchamber, servants' chamber, kitchen and buttery. I am grateful to Nat Alcock for providing me with a transcription of this document.

67. Respectively Tyack, *Warwickshire. Country Houses*, 178, and Alcock, *People at Home*, 86.

68. Howard, *Tree-ring Analysis*. It should be noted that all their eight samples from the principal trusses seem to have been taken from only the north bays of the east range roof, leaving open the possibility for other dates in the timbers elsewhere.

69. See further Howard, *Early Tudor Country House*, 151-61.

70. Hare, *Monasteries in Hampshire*, 17-21.

71. Robinson, *Cistercian Abbeys*, 125 and 168 respectively. For more detail on Rufford, see C. McGee and J. Perkins, 'A study of the Cistercian Abbey at Rufford, Nottinghamshire', in: J. Alexander, ed., *Southwell and Nottinghamshire: Medieval Art, Architecture and Industry*, British Archaeological Association Conference Transactions, xxi, Leeds 1998, 88-91. Originally the west range of a Cistercian monastery accommodated the lay brothers, but this practice fell out of use during the fourteenth century.

72. See chapter 2.

73. SBTRO, DR 18/30/24/91, is not easily interpreted in some matters of detail, but I take the relevant section to mean that all the following rooms are to the south of the core of the house, focussed on 'the fayre hawle' and 'fayre long chamber' - the buttery in an undercroft (under the 'other fayre chambre'), the kitchen, 'a great hawle hole Roofed', and a room or rooms called the 'Cloyster chamber'.

74. Major work on the refectory had been carried out in 1258-61, see above.

75. In that its floor was at approximately the same level as the south cloister walk.

76. For the list of rooms in Dadley's inventory, see note 66; for the Leigh inventories, see further below. For discussion of a structure rather like a refectory on the 1597 map (Fig. 23), see below.

77. J. G. Coad, *Hailes Abbey, Gloucestershire*, English Heritage guide, 2nd edn, 1993, especially p. 8, the engraving of 1732 by the Bucks. The refectory is shown as demolished, but part of it may have been incorporated into the earlier house (though not as hall); pp. 15, 22.

78. In contrast, apparently, to neighbouring Combe Abbey, where the cloister walks were retained on three sides and made into a feature of the new house; see Tyack, *Warwickshire Country Houses*, 56-59, especially the view from the south by the Bucks.

79. The relevant maps are: 'Map of Stoneleigh, the Estate of Sir Thomas Leigh', by John Goodwine, 1597, SBTRO, DR 671/3; 'Survey of the Desmesn Lands and the Park of the Right Honbl the Lord Leigh at Stoneleigh Abbey ... ', by Thos Wilkes, April 1749, (present whereabouts unknown, photographic reproduction in SBTRO); and 'A Map of Part of the Manor and Parish of Stoneley ... 1766' in 'Maps and Surveys of the Estate of Edward, Lord Leigh', by Matthias Baker, 1766-67, SBTRO, DR 671/30.

80. In the 1766 plan, a drive from the gatehouse past the west forecourt is clearly shown.

81. Two of them, in the plan depiction, are placed in the kitchen garden walls.

82. SBTRO, DR 18/4/1, 'Inventory of the goods ... of Sir Thomas Leigh of Stonely ... 4-5 April, 1626', the section on the 'Furniture of the Chambers and Roomes of Entertainement'. The parlour, listed first in the inventory, might have been at the service end of the hall or, if the room planning beyond the north end of the hall was double-pile, alongside one of the upper-end chambers.

83. SBTRO, DR 18/4/2, 'A true and perfect inventorie of the goodes ... of Dame Katherine Leigh ... 13-15 Feb. 1639', the section on the 'Furniture of the Chambers and Roomes of entertainment'.

84. It was converted to the library in the early nineteenth century.

85. SBTRO, DR 671/18, quoted in full in A. Gomme, 'Stoneleigh after the Grand Tour', *Antiquaries Journal*, lxviii, part ii (1988), 282, note 6.

86. Above, p. 82.

87. Measured from the west face of Smith's west range (excluding the projecting pedestals of the pilasters) in an easterly direction to the west face of the assumed medieval west wall.

88. The 1714 estimate states 'the inside to be built with the stone of the old Building', see Gomme, 'Stoneleigh after the Grand Tour', 267; and it is assumed that this procedure was carried out when work began in 1720. I am grateful to Andor Gomme for confirming that the lower interior wall facings are all likely to be in brick, as seen exposed in the Dining Room during the recent restoration work; whereas the partition walls of the upper floors are likely to be of timber.

89. There seems to be no substance in Peter Fergusson's suggestion that the hall of the post-Dissolution house was in the south aisle; Fergusson, *Architecture of Solitude*, 157.

90. Both inventories list the contents of 'The Gallery' only once, and in the same location in the sequence of rooms. In addition, the 1639 inventory provides another reference earlier in the sequence, by describing the withdrawing chamber after the great chamber as being 'next unto the Gallery': presumably the same gallery.

91. At Augustinian Newstead, there was no south aisle, but the tri-partite church facade gives the impression that one exists by overlapping one bay of the prior's lodgings, which is thus inextricably linked to the architecture of the west front; see N. Pevsner and E. Williamson, *The Buildings of England, Nottinghamshire*, 2nd edn, Harmondsworth 1979, 201-204.

92. It is not easy to cite another Cistercian precedent for this, but the abbot's lodgings at Benedictine Tewkesbury Abbey, Gloucestershire, extended into the west bay of the south aisle.

93. See chapter 10.

94. See R. Strong, *The Renaissance Garden in England*, London 1979, 138-41.

95. Not eighteenth century, as suggested in Gomme, 'Stoneleigh after the Grand Tour', 265, note 4.

96. The blocking is not necessarily all of the same period; the easternmost arch is infilled with relatively modern brick in stretcher bond, whereas the other three appear to be blocked with stone.

97. For illustrations of other examples at Hadham Hall, Hertfordshire (a painting of *c*.1639 by Cornelius Johnson), at Massey's Court, Llanerch, Clwyd (a painting of 1662), and in a garden stage set of 1633 by Inigo Jones: see Strong, *Renaissance Garden*, 107-110, 181-3.

98. Though the projection is curiously off-centre. It may be relevant that plans were afoot in the same decade for remodelling the north range, to include external stairs; see next note.

99. In addition, plans of *c*.1765-6 exist, attributed to Timothy Lightoler or William Hiorn, to build a library and music room on the site of the gallery; above, pp. 89, 97.

100. A full account of this range is beyond the scope of this chapter. I have been privileged to have had access to parts of it at various times since the late 1970s, but even so have never seen it all. It is to be hoped that the recent watching brief by Oxford Archaeology on the work carried out by Historic Houses Rescue may provide additional information and interpretation.

101. Mrs. Austen's letter of 1806, cited in G.H. Parks, 'Stoneleigh Abbey', *Transactions of the Birmingham Archaeological Society*, lxxix, 1961, 80-1.

102. The 1639 inventory speaks of 'the Space [before] going up the stairs'.

103. See further M. Girouard, *Robert Smythson and the Elizabethan Country House*, New Haven and London 1983, 115. The main difference at Stoneleigh is that the tower block terminates visually in a gabled roof, not a flat parapet.

104. See chapter 10.

105. For Wollaton, see P. Marshall, *Wollaton Hall: an Archaeological Survey*, Nottingham 1996, 94-111; for Hardwick, cf. L. Boynton, ed., *The Hardwick Hall Inventories of 1601*, London 1971, especially 6-7, and M. Girouard, *Hardwick Hall, Derbyshire*, National Trust guidebook, London 1989, 47-48 (e.g. compare the different locations each suggests for 'Lady Arabella's Chamber'). For an overview, see M. Howard, 'Inventories, surveys and the histories of great houses', *Architectural History*, 41, 1998, 14-29. The relationship of the Stoneleigh inventories to the house layout would repay close study.

106. 'Hayre' in the 1639 inventory, probably 'Hare' in 1626. The term is also applied to the bed-hangings.

107. Perhaps a common sitting room for the three previously mentioned chambers - 'hayre', blue ('inner' in 1626) and red.

108. See Howard, 'Inventories', 20-1, for this issue.

109. If 'summer chamber' implies a cool room, then the ground floor of the north-east tower would be appropriate; if a room useable in winter, then it is more likely to have been on an upper floor.

110. 1639 wording; 'In the Space and Stayres', 1626 inventory.

111. The Heating and Water Service Systems 1924 plans of the house (SBTRO, DR 18/25/59b) show this arrangement still existing in the first floor of the corner block (the chamber and the smaller south chamber have since been merged into one room). It is possible that the provision of a lobby between the gallery and the stairs might have precluded a third room in the first-floor suite. On the ground floor, the arrangement has been modified by the insertion of the east entrance porch in the early nineteenth century (Plan 1E).

112. RIBA, Smythson Drawings, II/4 and II/2, c.1590-1614, illustrated in Girouard, *Robert Smythson*, plates 105, 107.

113. Geoffrey Tyack, *The Making of the Warwickshire Country House 1500-1650*, Warwickshire Local History Society, Occasional Paper No.4, 1982, 41.

114. The fact that there is no evidence today in the east wing for the existence of a compass window, as mentioned in the 1639 inventory, suggests that the best chamber was elsewhere; though the case of oriel windows removed in the 1650s at Aston Hall, Birmingham, reminds us not to be too dogmatic. Tyack, *Making of the Country House*, 41, has 'three' state bedrooms with withdrawing and inner chambers, but it is not clear how he arrived at this figure, unless the 'withdrawing chamber to three chambers' has been included.

115. Tyack, *Warwickshire Country Houses*, 180. The brickwork still surviving in the medieval undercroft, associated with ovens and kitchen ranges, is usually dated to the eighteenth century; see *VCH, Warws.*, vi, 232. The old-fashioned looking Laundry wing, linked to the south end of the east range, is put as late as c.1760 by Gomme, 'Stoneleigh after the Grand Tour', 275; presumably based on its first appearance on the 1766 estate map.

116. For example, see the plan in *VCH, Warws.*, vi, 232.

117. Tyack, *Making of the Country House*, 39.

118. SBTRO, DR 18/30/24/91.

119. See above, discussion of Thomas Dadley's house.

120. For example, it is likely that Combe also had an abbot's lodging in the west range in the later middle ages.

121. See further Tyack, *Warwickshire Country Houses*, 56-9, especially the seventeenth-century plan on p. 56. The great hall is integrated into the north range and therefore not literally on the foundations of the refectory, which would almost certainly have been perpendicular to the range, following Cistercian practice. At Lacock, which was Augustinian, the refectory was parallel with the range and therefore easier to integrate into a courtyard house conversion.

122. Parks, 'Stoneleigh Abbey', 82-4 (he remarks that the narrow south wing is 'very difficult to date'); and Tyack, *Warwickshire Country Houses*, 185.

123. The dated timber samples are from the roofs of the north-east corner block and the northern end of the east range; Howard, *Tree-ring Analysis*, Part 2.

124. Average 85mm measured diagonally across the ovolo at Stoneleigh; 89mm throughout Leicester's Buildings at Kenilworth. For the development of ovolo-moulded windows in Elizabeth's reign, see R. K. Morris, 'Windows in early Tudor Country Houses', in: D. Williams, ed., *Early Tudor England*, Woodbridge 1989, 135-8.

125. Tyack, *Warwickshire Country Houses*, 180.

126. The closest local parallel is at Kenilworth Castle, in the early Renaissance arcades inserted into the forebuilding of the keep in about 1570 on the route to the garden.

127. See O. Fairclough, 'John Thorpe and Aston Hall', *Architectural History*, 32, 1989, 33-40.

128. See R. K. Morriss, *The Buildings of Warwick*, Stroud 1994, 101-105. The stone cross-mullioned windows towards the south end of the east range and in the kitchen block have ogee-moulded frames but non-matching roll-moulded mullions and transoms, and are difficult to understand and date (Fig. 18R). One's inclination is to date them to the second half of the seventeenth century, as in Tyack, *Warwickshire Country Houses*, 180; but Gomme, 'Stoneleigh after the Grand Tour', 267 and 275, may well be correct that they are actually of the eighteenth century. See also above, p. 52.

129. See Fairclough, 'John Thorpe and Aston Hall', 43. The ground floor section of the stair at Stoneleigh has been restored and rearranged: the strapwork panels are in the upper section.

130. Pevsner, *Warwickshire*, 410; Gomme, 'Stoneleigh after the Grand Tour', 265. I have checked the date from a ladder, and I could find no evidence for '1633' as stated in Tyack, *Warwickshire Country Houses*, 180. Of course, the dated hopper could signify no more than repairs to the house rather than more major works.

131. These are (1) an overmantel and various pieces of reused panelling in a first-floor chamber in the east range, now part of East Wing House No.2; (2) panelling in the fine first-floor chamber of the north-east block, introduced only in 1924; (3) the overmantel of the gallery fireplace, thought to have come from the Leigh house at Fletchamstead Hall, see Tyack, *Warwickshire Country Houses*, 245. The National Monuments Records Centre at Swindon has excellent photographs of all these fittings, taken in 1994: Stoneleigh Abbey Archive, 93/1192, BB95.

132. For example, Pevsner, *Warwickshire*, 408.

133. Probably executed for royal visits during James I's reign (1603-1617); T.L. Jones, *Ashby de la Zouch Castle, Leicestershire*, English Heritage guidebook, 2nd edn, London 1993, 21-3. The length of stones framing the Stoneleigh aperture suggests it could be post-medieval, but unfortunately it is too badly weathered to discern any classical mouldings or a characteristic projecting keystone at the apex of the arch.

134. Heightening is also suggested by the way in which the courtyard parapet of the gallery cuts awkwardly into one of the upper-floor windows of the north-east block (Fig. 13B).

135. The most likely improvement would be the insertion of the loggia or grotto.

136. This observation is true for at least the four bays directly south of the north-east corner block.

137. Is it possible that some of the upper parts had timber-framed walls and gables in the Elizabethan conversion? It is hoped that the final report of the watching brief from Oxford Archaeology will elucidate the archaeology of the east range further.

138. G. Chettle, P. Leach, L. McRobie, *Kirby Hall, Northamptonshire*, English Heritage guidebook, London 1993, 22-6.

139. See Girouard, *Robert Smythson*, 191-3. The consistency and crispness of detail of the Stoneleigh windows is the result of the very extensive renewal of their masonry in the early nineteenth century by C.S. Smith, but he did not invent the hoodmoulds; they are visible in Baker's painting (Fig. 25).

140. Tyack, *The Making of the Country House*, 41.

141. Gomme, 'Stoneleigh after the Grand Tour', 265-9, above, pp. 82-85.

142. I am most grateful to Cathy Coutts and Bryn Gethin of Warwick Museum Field Archaeology Section for providing the information on which this summary is based, and permitting me access to relevant materials. Where a source in an interim report (SLA) is not provided, the information is by way of personal communication. Any misconceptions in interpreting the evidence are mine, and in the meantime one awaits the publication of the full report of WMFAS's watching brief at the Abbey.

CHAPTER TWO

1. P. Fergusson, '"Porta patens esto": notes on early Cistercian gatehouses in the north of England', in: E. Fernie and P. Crossley, eds, *Medieval Architectural and its Intellectual Context: Studies in Honour of Peter Kidson*, London 1990, 47-60.

2. R. Ramey, 'Abbots' Lodgings of the Cistercian Order in the Late Fifteenth and Early Sixteenth Centuries', unpublished M.A. thesis, University of York 1996, 59-60.

3. This paper presents aspects of my research forming part of chapters 4 and 5 in R. Rowell(now Ramey), 'The Archaeology of Later Monastic Hospitality', unpublished D.Phil. thesis, University of York 2000.

4. Fergusson, *"Porta patens esto"*, 47.

5. R. Morant, *The Monastic Gatehouse and Other Types of Portal of Medieval Religious Houses*, Sussex 1995.

6. Morant, *Monastic Gatehouse*, 26-37.

7. *The Chronicle of Jocelin of Brakelond*, ed. H.E. Butler, London 1949, 39; *The Account Book of Beaulieu Abbey*, ed. S.F. Hockey, Camden Society, 4th series, xvi, 1975, 271; *Monastery and Society in the Late Middle Ages: Selected Account Rolls from Selby Abbey, Yorkshire*, 1398-1537, ed. J.H. Tillotson, Woodbridge 1988, 67.

8. *Chronica Monasterii Sancti Albani: Gesta Abbatum Monasterii Sancti Albani*, ed. H.T. Riley, London 1865, 314.

9. *The Rule of Saint Benedict*, ed. J. McCann, London 1952, chapter 53.

10. *Monastery and Society*, 253.

11. *Victoria County History (VCH), Warwickshire*, vi, 231.

12. N. Pevsner and A. Wedgwood, *The Buildings of England: Warwickshire*, Harmondsworth 1966, 408.

13. E. Carey-Hill, 'Kenilworth Abbey', *Transactions of the Birmingham Archaeological Society*, lii, 1927, 218-9.

14. Warwickshire Museum Service, report in preparation. I am grateful to WMS for permission to use this information.

15. G. Coppack and R. Gilyard-Beer, *Fountains Abbey*, London 1995, 60.

16. J. Blair, 'Hall and Chamber: English Domestic Planning 1000-1250', in: G. Meirion and M. Jones, eds, *Manorial Domestic Buildings in England and Northern France*, London 1993, 13.

17. For a photograph and discussion of the Canterbury Waterworks plan, see Patrick Greene, *Medieval Monasteries*, Leicester 1992, 109-111; Ramey, 'Abbots' Lodgings of the Cistercian Order', 30; Rowell, 'Archaeology of Later Monastic Hospitality', chapter 4.

18. R.E. Howard, R.R. Laxton and C.D. Litton, 'Tree-ring analysis of timbers from Stoneleigh Abbey, Stoneleigh, Warwickshire', unpublished, unpaginated. I am grateful to Robert Howard for a copy of this work.

19. *The Stoneleigh Leger Book*, ed. R.H. Hilton, Dugdale Society, xxiv, 1960, 254.

20. *VCH*, vi, 231.

21. W. Dugdale, *The Antiquities of Warwickshire*, 2 vols, London, 1730, i, 257.

22. Morant, *Monastic Gatehouse*, 23-24.

23. Howard, Laxton and Litton, 'Tree-ring analysis'.

24. Howard, Laxton and Litton, 'Tree-ring analysis'.

25. R. Harris, 'The grammar of carpentry', *Vernacular Architecture*, xx, 1989, 1.

26. C. Coutts, Warwickshire Museum Service, personal communication.

CHAPTER THREE

1. Shakespeare Birthplace Trust Records Office (SBTRO), DR 671/18.

2. See, for example, Christopher Hussey, *English Country Houses: Early Georgian*, 2nd edn., London 1965, 39.

3. Account book kept at Ombersley, with a copy in the Worcestershire County Record Office.

4. SBTRO, DR 671/33.

5. SBTRO, DR 18/3/47/38. The agreement gives dimensions and specifies 'parpen' walls for the staircase, but for other details refers to Smith's draft, which has not survived.

6. SBTRO, DR 18/31/447.

7. *Victoria County History, Warwickshire*, vi, 232.

8. 'The Travel Journals of Philip Yorke', ed. Joyce Godber, *Transactions of the Bedfordshire Historical Society*, xlvii, 1968, 142.

9. Above, p. 89.

10. Above, p. 87.

11. Published in Rome in three volumes (1702-21): see vol. i, plates 65, 87, 89. Rossi-inspired detail first appears in England at Heythrop (begun 1707), perhaps at the instigation of its owner, the duke of Shrewsbury, whose journal records visits to Rossi's studio in 1702 to 'lay aside plates'. See further A. Gomme, 'Smith and Rossi', *Architectural History*, xxxv, 1992, 83-91.

12. SBTRO, DR 18/1/814, 814a. For a detailed discussion of the work of Smith's team of craftsmen, see A. Gomme, *Smith of Warwick*, Stamford 2000, esp. chapter 7.

13. SBTRO, DR 671/18.

14. SBTRO, DR 18/3/47/55/6; DR/18/31/204, 457-8.

15. SBTRO, DR 18/3/47/55/6.

16. SBTRO, DR 18/3/47/55/5. For further information on John Wright, see David Whitehead, 'A Note on John Wright', *Warwickshire History*, v (2), Winter 1981-82, 59-63.

17. A knee in carpentry is 'a piece of timber naturally or artificially shaped, so as to fit into an angle' (*OED*); and to knee is to fasten with a knee or knees.

18. SBTRO, DR 18/17/4/7-8.

19. SBTRO, DR 18/3/47/55/7.

20. SBTRO, DR 671/18.

21. See Gomme, *Smith of Warwick*, chapter 12.

22. Marcus Vitruvius Pollio, *The Ten Books on Architecture*, IV.i.9-10; translated by Morris Hicky Morgan, New York, 1914/1960, 104-6.

23. William Kent, *The Designs of Inigo Jones, Consisting of Plans and Elevations for Publick and Private Buildings. Publish'd by William Kent, With some Additional Designs*, 2 vols, London 1727, i, 55-6.

24. SBTRO, DR 18/31/459, 461.

25. SBTRO, DR 671/33.

26. British Library of Architectural Drawings, R.I.B.A., London, K.10/11/19. The drawings for Platt are kept at the house (now a museum of costume). Lightoler included an even more exuberant chinoiserie overmantel in *The Modern Builder's Assistant*, published probably in 1757.

27. SBTRO, DR 18/5/4192.

28. SBTRO, DR 18/5/4192.

29. SBTRO, DR 18/5/4203.

30. SBTRO, DR 18/3/47/51/2.

31. Francis Price, *The British Carpenter*, London 1733, 8 and plate C.

32. The design resembles to some extent that of a middle-cruck frame.

33. Price, *British Carpenter*, plate N.

34. SBTRO, DR 18/17/55. I am most grateful to Geoffrey Tyack for telling me of this letter, which was unknown to me when I wrote my earlier account; and see above, p. 125.

35. SBTRO, DR 18/3/47/51/7.

36. See John Woolfe and James Gandon, *Vitruvius Britannicus*, London, v (1771), pl. 32. The ground-floor plan shows the saloon subdivided, but the annotation is clearly inaccurate, and it is uncertain how far details are otherwise reliable.

37. *Country Life*, clxxvi, 13 December 1984, 1847-8.

38. For a synopsis of information on Hercules's position and appearances in the post-classical world, see Jean Seznec, *The Survival of the Pagan Gods* (translated by Barbara F. Sessions), Princeton 1972.

39. *Acts* 14:22.

40. Samuel Redgrave, *A Dictionary of Artists of the English School*, 2nd edn, London 1878, 83.

41. SBTRO, DR 18/3/47/55/5.

42. Two of these survive, but the rest were destroyed in the fire which ravaged Stoneleigh in 1960.

43. See Joan Lane, *Country Life*, clxxv, 28 June 1984, 1913. Dr. Lane claimed all of the Stoneleigh stucco work of the 1760s for Moore, but for reasons given below, this cannot be sustained.

44. *Letters Written by the late Right Honourable Lady Luxborough to William Shenstone, Esquire*, London 1775, 79: 4 January 1749.

45. Geoffrey Beard, *Craftsmen and Interior Decoration in England 1660-1820*, Edinburgh 1981, 288.

46. 'Travel Journals of Philip Yorke'.

CHAPTER FOUR

1. W. Austen-Leigh, R.A. Austen-Leigh, D. Le Faye, *Jane Austen: a Family Record*, London 1989, 139-40.

2. Shakespeare Birthplace Trust Records Office (SBTRO), DR 671/76a. For Repton at Stoneleigh, see M. Batey & D. Lambert, *The English Garden Tour*, 1990, 247-252, and below, Chapter 10.

3. Maria Berry, *Extracts from the Journals and Correspondence of Miss Berry*, ed. Lady Theresa Lewis, 2 vols, London 1853, ii, 434.

4. R.P. Knight, *An Analytical Inquiry into the Principles of Taste*, London 1805, 225.

5. SBTRO, DR 671/76a.

6. SBTRO, DR 18/17/5. For these and later schemes for the house, see G.H. Parks, 'Stoneleigh Abbey', *Transactions of the Birmingham Archaeological Society* lxxix, 1960-1, 76-84; C. Aslet, 'Stoneleigh Abbey II', *Country Life*, 20 December 1984; above, p.251.

7. SBTRO, DR 962/1; W.A. Thorpe, 'Stoneleigh Abbey and its Furniture', *Connoisseur*, clxix, 1947. For Watergall House, see G. Tyack, *Warwickshire Country Houses*, Chichester 1994, 267; Norma Hampson, 'Watergall: a Shadow of its Former Self', *Warwickshire History*, x, no. 5, 1998, 177-84.

8. SBTRO, DR 18/56-7; DR 823/3.

9. H.M. Colvin, *Biographical Dictionary of British Architects, 1600-1840*, New Haven and London 1995, 881-2.

10. SBTRO, DR 18/17/16/25; DR 823/3; DR 823/19.

11. For a full account of his career, see below, Chapter 6.

12. H.K. Causton, *The Leigh Peerage*, London 1832.

13. SBTRO, DR 823/3.

14. Lightoler had proposed creating a Music Room here for the fifth Lord Leigh: above, p. 97.

15. SBTRO, DR 18/17/55, 10 January 1837, 29 July 1838.

16. SBTRO, DR 18/17/17/27. There are also payments in the accounts to the Warwick decorator and stained-glass manufacturer, William Holland.

17. SBTRO, DR 671/33; DR 823/3.

18. Repton had proposed making the closet into a Book Room and the bedchamber into a 'Cabinet'.

19. SBTRO, DR 18/17/55, 8 April 1837.

20. SBTRO, DR 823/3. He wrote in 1836 about 'new building on the other side of the court', meaning either the south range or the kitchen area.

21. SBTRO, DR 18/17/55, 7 September 1836.

22. *Complete Peerage*, vii, 570.

23. Colvin, *Dictionary of Architects*, 190.

24. SBTRO, DR 671/269.

25. SBTRO, DR 671/381. The visit lasted from 14-16 June.

26. J. Bateman, *The Great Landowners of Great Britain and Ireland*, London 1876, 264.

PART TWO: PEOPLE

CHAPTER FIVE

1. Figures from J. Bateman, *Great Landowners of England and Wales*, London 1883, reproduced in tabular form in Geoffrey Tyack, *The Country Houses of Warwickshire 1800-1939*, Warwickshire Local History Society, Occasional Paper no. 7, 1989, 60-61.

2. *The Visitation of the County of Warwick in the Year 1619*, ed. John Fetherston, Harleian Society, xii, 1877, 80-1. For the Cheshire pedigrees see *The Visitation of Cheshire in the Year 1580*, ed. J.P. Rylands, Harleian Society, xviii, 1882, 152-4.

3. Index cards in the archives office of the Mercers' Company at Mercers' Hall, London.

4. For the mercer career of Sir Thomas Leigh see: Mercers' Hall, London, Act Book of the Mercers' Company, 1527-1560, ff. 86r, 108r, 168r, 172v, 177r, 209r, 218r, 234v-244r, 250v, 265v, 267r, 298v, 302r, 305v; Act Book … , 1560-1595, f. 206r. His civic career is outlined in A.B. Beaven, *The Aldermen of London*, 2 vols, London 1908-13, *passim*.

5. Corporation of London, Letter Book S, f. 190b; Public Record Office (PRO), PROB 11/4 (will of Sir Rowland Hill, proved at London, 7 November 1561).

6. Shakespeare Birthplace Trust Records Office (SBTRO), DR 18/13/9/1 (original and office copy will).

7. SBTRO, DR 18/1/1405.

8. SBTRO, DR 18/1/85; DR 18/1/750; DR 18/3/47/35. Rowland Hill's heirs were Thomas and Alice.

9. In his will, Thomas left five marks each to his kinsman Edward Leigh of Shawell (a village in Northamptonshire near Churchover) and Edward's brothers Thomas and another unidentified.

10. SBTRO, DR 18/3/47/1a.

11. According to the pre-nuptial settlement of Thomas Leigh and Katherine Spencer, 11 September 1572, Alice was the wife of Thomas Cony, citizen and mercer; Katherine of Edward Baber, Lincoln's Inn, esquire, Winifred of George Bonde, citizen and haberdasher, and Mary of Michael Cobbe, gentleman: SBTRO, DR 18/13/1.

12. Richard may have died unmarried for by 1595 Alice conveyed her estate in Kilburn to Thomas her son and John, his son. In 1598 all three joined in a conveyance of the Islington property: SBTRO, DR 18/1/1795-1799.

13. SBTRO, DR 18/13/9/1 (original and copy will); DR 18/1/1568a (Inquisition *Post Mortem*). The inscription in the Mercers' Chapel, replaced after the Great Fire, reads:

> Sir Thomas Leigh bi civil life
> All offices did beare
> Which in this city worshipfull
> Or honorable were
> Whom as God blessed with great wealth
> So losses did he feele;
> Yet never changed his constant minde
> Tho' fortune turned her wheele.
> Learning he lov'd and helpt the poore
> To them that knew him deere;
> For whom his lady and loving wife
> This tomb hath builded here

14. There seems to have been a feeling among the children of Sir Thomas that the settlements made for them by their father needed to be reinforced by personal acts. Thus, during the 1570s-1590s a series of transactions confirmed the rights of Thomas (II) to Stoneleigh and Rowland to Adlestrop and Longborough: SBTRO, DR 18/1/761-2, 767, 777-9. In 1576 Alice agreed that she would only take the profits of Stoneleigh when resident there. In her absence they were to the use of Katherine Leigh, wife of Thomas the younger. Similarly the terms of the marriage settlement of Thomas Leigh and Katherine Spencer in 1572, were altered in 1595, making void the earlier provision for her jointure if she were permitted to occupy Stoneleigh Abbey for her life during widowhood: DR 18/13/1/1; DR 18/1/782.

15. A deed poll of 1 March 1579 states that the almshouses had been erected according to the interest and will of Sir Thomas and Alice and that the queen had issued letters patent, 21 June 1577, granting corporate status to the inhabitants of the almshouses and their two wardens: *Victoria County History, Warwickickshire*, vi, 239.

16. SBTRO, DR 18/13/1/1; DR 18/13/1/3; DR 18/3/55/17.

17. SBTRO, DR 18/31/2. This volume contains a late sixteenth-century translation of the Stoneleigh Leger Book. Four blank pages at the end were used by Thomas (II) and Thomas (III) to record family births, marriages and deaths: 'John Leigh my eldest son was married to Orseley Hodesdone … 3 Jan 1590 by one Mr Martine personne of Ashoe … in my dining chamber at Stoneleigh'.

18. SBTRO, DR 18/13/1/3a-4. These Bedfordshire estates were largely leasehold, held for lives from variously the Prebendary of Leighton and the Dean and Chapter of Windsor. During the upheavals of

the Civil War, the first Lord Leigh sold his lease 'very disadvantageously' to Colonel John Okey, and was forced to appeal to the Crown for a regrant when the regicide's estates were granted to the duke of York at the Restoration: *Calendar of State Papers, Domestic (CSPD), 1660-1661*, 248-9.

19. SBTRO, DR 18/31/2: 'I Thomas Legh was knighted by Que: Elizabeth on the whisson sonndaye in Ao 1589'.

20. None of the printed pedigrees record this marriage, for which the settlement survives at SBTRO, DR 18/13/1/9. Nor is it recorded on the manuscript pedigree compiled for the visitation of 1682: DR 18/26/8. The Leighs retained an interest in these estates long after the death of Robert, the son of the marriage, on whose behalf Sir Thomas was involved in a long Chancery case: DR 18/18/18/8. Eleanor Lady Leigh left money for the apprenticing of a poor boy from Ashby in her will, 1705: DR 18/13/1/11.

21. SBTRO, DR 18/1/2032-3 (Quietus Roll, 1580-1); DR 18/1/2039 (Quietus Roll, 1594-5); DR 18/1/2047-50, 2052-3 and DR 18/3/73/2-4 (collector's receipts for 1609 and 1612). Dugdale wrote of him that he lived 'to a great age in much reputation, being "Custos Rotulorum" for the county, and in all publique employments of the time one of the superior rank.'

22. SBTRO, DR 18/13/4/13-4.

23. SBTRO, DR 18/1/1877-1844. The licence of 1629 (DR 18/1/1910a) specifies twenty messuages, ten cottages, two mills, twenty gardens, twenty orchards, five hundred acres of land, two hundred acres of meadow, one thousand acres of pasture, two hundred acres of wood, two hundred acres of heath, twenty acres of marsh, two parks and the advowson.

24. SBTRO, DR 18/31/2: 'My sonne Sir John Leigh Knight departed this life at my house at Ridewayre in the county of Stafforde on a Thorseday being the 29 of december in the yeare of ower Lo: 1609 ... To whome if god had lente him longer life the 4 day of maye next he had byne xxxijth yeare of age.' The following entry records: 'His wife was delivered of a son the 27 of July followinge [1609] whose name is John christened by my selfe, Mr Chamberlayne and the old Lady Cope ...'. In his son's marriage settlement, dated 30 October 1610, he was described as Sir John Leigh, knight, deceased: DR 18/13/1/9.

25. SBTRO, DR 18/3/45/1-6.

26. SBTRO, DR 18/10/101/7; and see above, p. 227.

27. Alice, the second daughter of Sir Thomas Leigh (II) and his wife Katherine, married, before September 1597, as his second wife, Sir Robert Dudley, the son of Robert, earl of Leicester by Douglas, widow of John, Lord Sheffield. In 1605 the Star Chamber gave judgement against him in his claim to legitimacy and he left England for Italy where, claiming his previous marriages were invalid, he contracted another. Alice Lady Dudley remained in England with her daughters, Katherine and Anne, being created by Charles I in 1644, Duchess Dudley for her life, in reference to her husband's creation in 1620 as a Duke of the Holy Roman Empire. She spent most of her life in charitable works (details of which are inscribed on her monument), dying in January 1669, aged 90. She was buried at Stoneleigh. For fuller details see *The Complete Peerage*, iv, 486-7; vii, 550-1; William Dugdale, *The Antiquities of Warwickshire*, 2 vols, London 1730, i, 261.

28. Thomas was bequeathed two of the best horses, except those best suited for the testator's wife's coach, and the heirloom bowl given to the testator's mother, Alice Barker, by Sir John Spencer, his father-in-law. Alice Lady Dudley received the best basin and ewer 'in token of my love' and John Leigh, son of Sir John by his second wife Ann, was left £100 at the age of 21.

29. SBTRO, DR 18/4/1; DR 18/10/101/9.

30. SBTRO, DR 18/13/1/9; DR 18/1/2057-60; DR 18/3/55/9; DR 18/22/18/1.

31. SBTRO, DR 18/3/47/23.

32. *CSPD, 1645-7*, 384; SBTRO, DR 18/17/24/17.

33. Historical Manuscripts Commission (HMC), 5th Report, 1876, 47, 108; *CSPD, 1644-1645*, 34, 42, 80, 234; HMC, 8th Report, 1881, 3a, 5b (Marlborough papers). An order of 4 June 1644 allowed John Leigh, esq., brother of Sir Thomas Leigh, knight, a delinquent, to receive his rents and estate as formerly, he having taken the covenant and not being a delinquent or a papist.

34. .During the 1640s and 1650s identities can become confused for, even after his elevation in 1643, Sir Thomas Leigh (III) is often referred to by his former title, as is his son, another Sir Thomas and

active supporter of the royalist cause. During the Commonwealth, Lord Leigh is only ever referred to in deeds as Sir Thomas Leigh, baronet: SBTRO, DR 18/17/24/18; HMC, 6th Report, 1877, 215a.

35. SBTRO, DR 18/31/2: 'The first sonne of my grandechilde Tho. Leigh was borne at Stonley the 15 of July being Seynt Swithence daye in the morning … his name is Thomas.'

36. The assumption as to his University education is based on a letter from Samuel Hinton to Sir Richard Leveson, dated 16 May 1649. In it Hinton writes: '... Sir Tho: Leigh has Clutterbooke to read to him in Camb[ridge] under his tutor ...'. HMC, 5th Report, 182. The marriage settlement is dated 9 July 1642 and provides for successive remainders to Charles, Christopher and Ferdinando Leigh, the other sons of Sir Thomas: SBTRO, DR 18/12/7/2.

37. Delinquents were deemed to be those who had failed actively to support Parliament against the King. Leigh's biographical entry in B. D. Henning, *The House of Commons 1660-1690*, 3 vols, London 1983, ii, 730, asserts that he was only a passive royalist, his delinquency being incurred by his leaving Hamstall Ridware to join the garrison at Lichfield.

38. Geoffrey Tyack, *Warwickshire Country Houses*, Chichester 1994, 178-9.

39. HMC, 5th Report, 182, 186, 206. He was back in London in the following April with his wife and daughter, Lady Tracy for the coronation but '... Lord Lee continues weak and ill': HMC, 5th Report, 170, 146.

40. The parish register of Hamstall Ridware records the baptism on 13 April 1665 of 'Mr Fitzmorris Gifford, son of Richard Gifford, esq. and of lady Jane his wife'. They seem to have been living there in 1666 when the Hearth Tax returns credit thirty chargeable hearths in the home of Richard Gifford, esquire. Jane was possibly dead by 1672 when her three daughters were granted the precedence of the daughters of a baron: *CSPD, 1672*, 285. On 3 March 1666 the Privy Council ordered the earl of Orrery, President of Munster, to send Lord Leigh's grandchild immediately over to England. It seems that he had been privately carried over into Ireland by 'Mr Giffard and Dame Jane Leigh his wife', in contempt of the directions of the Privy Council. Lord Leigh presumably disapproved of his daughter-in-law's remarriage.

41. HMC, 5th Report, 150b. The estates were mortgaged to family trustees, including Sir William Egerton, husband of Lord Leigh's granddaughter Honora. They lived in the house until 1680: SBTRO, DR 18/1/1919-1920. Honora married twice, firstly Sir William Egerton, then Lord Willoughby of Parham. Of her sisters, Mary married Arden Bagot of Pipe Hall, and Jane, her first cousin, William Lord Tracey.

42. SBTRO, DR 18/13/9/5. The will was proved at Doctors' Commons, 6 May 1672.

43. Buried as Thomas Leigh of London, gentleman, on 22 December 1698. A grant of the administration of his goods, as Thomas Leigh of St James, Clerkenwell, was made to William Taylor on 29 December 1698 who declared that the deceased had died a bachelor leaving no parents, brother, sisters nephews or nieces: SBTRO, DR 18/13/9/45. Nevertheless, it was later to be alleged that Thomas had, in fact, married and produced sons, the ancestors of the peerage claimants in the nineteenth century (above, pp. 157, 181-2).

44. Papers concerning the dispute and separation are at SBTRO, DR 671/10; DR 18/1/2073-78. See also *The Diary of Thomas Isham of Lamport (1658-81) kept by him in Latin…at his Father's command*, trans. Norman Marlow; with introduction and notes by Sir Gyles Isham, Bart., Farnborough 1971, 196.

45. Thomas Isham of Lamport, Lord Leigh's nephew, kept a diary 'at his Father's command' during the years 1671-3. Among various entries which refer to the Leigh family, that for 6 March 1673 records: 'Lady Leigh had a miscarriage': *The Diary of Thomas Isham*, 195.

46. The original marriage settlement is not among the Leigh manuscripts, being only briefly recited in the articles relating to the marriage of Edward, the third Lord, and Mary Holbech. This does not mention any marriage portion: SBTRO, DR 18/13/1/14. For Charles Leigh's will, dated 5 June 1704, proved 2 January 1705, see SBTRO, DR 18/13/9/9.

47. 'Princess Anne of Denmark' was Anne, younger daughter of James II by his first wife, Anne Hyde. In 1683, she married George, Prince of Denmark and, involved in the deposition of her father in 1688, had the crown settled on her, after the death of her sister Mary. She acceded to the throne in 1702. As an acknowledged upholder of the Protestant tradition it is interesting to speculate what service the high Tory Lord Leigh might have been engaged upon.

48. SBTRO, DR 18/13/1/11.

49. SBTRO, DR 18/5/707, 791-2, 823, 833, 1710.

50. SBTRO, DR 18/13/1/12-14.

51. Thomas Verney was the eldest son of the Reverend George Verney who became Lord Willoughby de Broke on the death of his father in 1711. Thomas died of smallpox in May 1710, leaving Eleanor pregnant with a daughter, also Eleanor, who married George Bowes and died without issue: *Collins's Peerage of England*, 9 vols, London 1812, vi, 702.

52. SBTRO, DR 18/13/7/2. Mary Biddulph was the widow of Arden Bagot of Pipe Hall, who had remarried after his death. The date of this marriage and christian name of her spouse have not yet been ascertained. In addition to increasing the legacy to his sister, Leigh's codicil was mainly concerned with personal gifts to his sons and grandson. Edward, the heir was left 'my large carved sword'. His grandson, another Edward, inherited 'my Gold cupp' and son Charles received 'the loose barrell Gun & Lock that he brought me from beyond sea, One pair of double barrell pistolls either the horse or pad pistolls which he likes best, my long Leighton Gun and my silver sighted Gun, my best carved hunting hanger with the gold handle and the Green Silk belt and my young Gray stone horse'.

53. She was buried there, though, in 1713. A daughter Eleanor was also buried at Stoneleigh, 22 November 1709, wrongly identified in the register as the daughter of Thomas Lord Leigh. Mary's date of birth is given as 19 June 1711 on the pedigree compiled in 1799 by Isaac Heard, Garter King at Arms: SBTRO, DR 671/344.

54. J. Foster, *Alumni Oxonienses 1500-1714*, 4 vols, Oxford 1891, iii, 897. Land for the school was not, in fact, conveyed to trustees until 1740, by Edward's son. In the interim Anne Leigh, daughter of the second lord, had also made provision for the education of the poor. In her will, dated 1730, she left £1,000 for the education of 'both Boys and Girls Sons and Daughters of the inhabitants of the Town and Parish of Stoneleigh': SBTRO, DR 18/13/7/3.

55. SBTRO, DR 18/3/53/1-5; DR 671/77. Lady Willoughby was Honora, daughter of the first lord who had married, firstly, Sir William Egerton and, secondly, Hugh, Lord Willoughby of Parham, who died in 1712. She died in 1730 aged 81: *Complete Peerage*, xii, 713. Charles wrote to his brother '... her son in law Mr Bagott has removed her La[dy]shipp. None of her Relations knows where, as Mr Bagott I'm told used his wife my Cozen ill ...'. Lord Leigh was one of her grandchildren's' trustees and his brother later wrote '... as she's Aunt to us both I think humanity obliges us to ask after her ...'. Thomas Arden Bagot had married Honora, one of her four daughters by Sir William Egerton.

56. SBTRO, DR 18/3/53/1. For fuller details of the work carried out at Stoneleigh, see above, pp. 83-89.

57. *Complete Peerage*, vii, 568 n.(a); bills at SBTRO, DR 18/5/811, 814, 971; DR 671/16 (summons to Parliament); DR 17/25/12-14 (correspondence); John Britton, J.N. Brewer et al, *The Beauties of England and Wales ... Warwickshire*, London 1814, 44.

58. His matriculation allegedly took place on 9 August although not recorded in Foster; but Best writes from Balliol.

59. SBTRO, DR 18/17/25/8, 10-11, 15-16, 19, 21.

60. Hassall had received a legacy of £50 under the will of Thomas, the second lord, who died in 1710. He was vicar of Weston-under Wetherley from 1711.

61. SBTRO, DR 18/13/7/6-7 (Chancery petition and papers); Public Record Office (PRO), C 11/147/2 (Chancery case, Leigh v. Meadows); SBTRO, DR 18/13/7/12 (will of Thomas, Lord Leigh); DR 18/5/4244, DR 18/31/461, DR 18/17/30/73 (payments).

62. SBTRO, DR 18/13/7/6-7, 10. These fortunate ladies were, in fact, Edward's cousins by marriage, his uncle Charles being married to Lady Barbara Lumley, sister of the earl of Scarborough, another sister, Lady Mary, being Lady Halifax.

63. He may have been ill for the preceding year. Surviving bills from May 1736 are almost entirely presented to Hon. Thomas Leigh rather than his father. This suggests either that he had handed over affairs to his son or that he was travelling/staying elsewhere for his health: SBTRO, DR 18/5, DR 18/13/9/19.

64. The death of Fulwar, fourth Lord Craven, in 1764 without issue, saw the title pass to the eldest son of John Craven. It was William, fifth lord, who was to be one of the Trustees and Committees of his

nephew, Edward, fifth Lord Leigh. He was brother-in-law twice over to Thomas Leigh, the latter's second wife, Catherine Berkeley, being sister to his own wife Jane. The marriage with Maria Rebecca took place at Corley on 9 August 1735 by licence: SBTRO, DR 18/17/27/183.

65. SBTRO, DR 18/3/62/1.

66. SBTRO, DR 18/13/1/15 (marriage articles dated 16 January 1748); DR 18/13/7/12 (will and codicil, proved 7 April 1750).

67. SBTRO, DR 18/4/27 (inventory); DR 671/22 (account of personal estate); DR 18/6/18/1 (rental of estates of Charles Leigh).

68. SBTRO, DR 18/4/80; DR 671/26; DR 18/17/4/9.

69. SBTRO, DR 18/17/27/52.

70. SBTRO, DR 18/5/4036, 4040, 4051, 4056 *et seq*. In a letter to his sister Mary, dated 15 March 1764, he expressed his hopes for the future '... tho it may not be my fortune to do much good, yet I hope that keeping the happy medium I shall ever avoid doing much harm; For it is & allways will be the greatest of my wishes & aims to serve my God, my country, & my relations & friends uprightly and honestly to the best of my abilities, such as they are, but with which I am contented': DR 18/17/27/71.

71. SBTRO, DR 18/17/27/75, 96, 97 107. Most of the references to the work at Stoneleigh are to be found in Andor Gomme, 'Stoneleigh after the Grand Tour', *The Antiquaries Journal*, lxviii, 265-286, and see above, pp. 95 ff.

72. A portfolio of plans for work at Stoneleigh, some of which, attributed to the new baron, are of a fanciful nature, have been used as evidence of Edward's incipient mental illness: SBTRO, DR 671/33. However, these are watermarked 1809 and must therefore be ascribed to a later member of the family. The plans attributed to Edward are bound with plans by Lightoler and Smith which were listed by Edward. In a letter dated 24 May 1766, Samuel Butler writing to John Franklin, the gardener at Leighton Buzzard about plants and seeds sent to Stoneleigh, thanks him for his trouble, adding 'yet I am certain it will appear as little so to you as myself as we work for so good a master': SBTRO, DR 18/17/27/145.

73. In April of that year his election as High Steward of Oxford University had been confirmed by Convocation: SBTRO, DR 18/1/2097-8.

74. Surviving accounts do not make it clear whether or not the intended foreign trip took place. There are no receipts or vouchers tendered by foreign tradesmen, although an abstract from Joseph Hill's accounts includes the entry: 'Paid Mr Graaff your Lordship's draft from Bezier' which might indicate that some time was spent in France: SBTRO, DR 18/29/6, Box 1.

75. SBTRO, DR 18/13/9/24 (will);, DR 18/29/6, Box 1 (abstract of payments); DR 18/5/4959, 5029, 5096, 5107, 5115, 5126 (bills and receipts).

76. SBTRO, DR 18/23/15 (lease); DR 18/17/27/200-205 (correspondence).

77. A bill of costs presented in January 1774 includes a payment for a search at the Petty Bag for former commissions against peers and drawing and ingrossing affidavits of Dr Willis and Mr Spicer of the lunacy: SBTRO, DR 671/36. These affidavits have not, as yet, been located.

78. PRO, C 211/15/54 (original writ and commission). I am grateful to Gervase Hood for locating these documents for me; SBTRO, DR 18/4/42-3 (inventories).

79. Four mutes led the procession, followed by the principal artificers, fifty principal tenants, twelve underbearers, pages and attendants. The hearse, drawn by six horses, was followed by three coaches containing mourners and his own, empty. The procession ended with the rest of the domestic two and two: SBTRO, DR 18/29/6, Box 1.

80. SBTRO, DR 18/17/27/171.

81. For this library, see Mark Purcell, '"A lunatick of unsound mind":Edward, Lord Leigh (1742-1786) and the refounding of Oriel College Library', *The Bodleian Record*, 2001, 246-260.

82. SBTRO, DR 18/13/7/13; DR 18/17/32/147.

83. In 1790 it was described as situated near the One Mile stone between Kensington and Knightsbridge: SBTRO, DR 18/23/15.

84. Letters inserted in SBTRO, DR 671/77; DR 671/56 (note of keepsakes).

85. SBTRO, DR 18/5/6069.

86. Reverend Thomas Leigh was the third, but eldest surviving son of William Leigh of Adlestrop and his wife, Mary Lord. His eldest brother James had died in 1774 leaving, by his wife Lady Caroline Brydges, a son, James Henry Leigh. James Leigh Perrott, of Scarlets, the second life tenant under Mary Leigh's will, was first cousin to the Reverend Thomas, being the son of another Reverend Thomas Leigh, a younger brother of William of Adlestrop. James Leigh had added the surname Perrott on succeeding to the Oxfordshire estates of his great-uncle in 1751 (see family tree on p. 164).

87. SBTRO, DR 18/13/7/16. The dates of her various wills and codicils, not all of which relate to estates, are 2 August 1786, 23 December 1786, 20 June 1788, 23 November 1791, 12 October 1794 and 20 December 1803. The last codicil makes detailed provision for her funeral and clearly recognises Thomas Leigh as the head of the family, asking him to ensure that the black plumes on the horses and velvet pall 'look fresh'.

88. The obituary was copied by Agnes Leigh into an earlier history, SBTRO, DR 671/77; DR 18/31/7, 35, 37, 44 (rentals).

89. G.H. Tucker, *A Goodly Heritage, a History of Jane Austen's Family*, Manchester 1983, 82 ff. The negotiations for the settlement are detailed in SBTRO, DR 18/17/33-34; and see below, Chapter 6.

90. SBTRO, DR 671/77; DR 18/31/44-45. Estate correspondence for the years 1806-1813 is to be found at DR 18/17/32-39.

91. The manuscript family history by Mary Leigh, wife of Reverend Thomas, describes the *coup de foudre* which occurred when James Henry met his fourteen-year-old cousin then visiting with her parents at the Parsonage. '... On entering - he was instantaneously shot! - shot in a vital part by the mischievous wicked eyes of his fair Cousin ... the Sorceress was not quite fiveteen': SBTRO, DR 671/77, p.75.

92. SBTRO, DR 18/17/39/15. Repton's Red Book survives at DR 671/76; and see above, Chapter 10.

93. Between 1802 and 1823 James Henry Leigh served continuously as a Member of Parliament, which may account for the prominent part played by Julia Judith in the running of the estate. From 1802 to 1818 he represented successively Marlborough and Great Bedwyn, two constituencies in the interest of his kinsman, the earl of Ailesbury. From 1818 until his death he served for Winchester in the interest of the marquess of Buckingham. A letter from Buckingham in 1818 refers to him as 'Bunny Leigh'. It was originally intended that Chandos should take over when he came of age, but after James Henry's death the seat eventually passed to Charles Lennox Grenville Berkeley, his son-in-law: R. G. Thorne, *The House of Commons 1790-1820*, 5 vols, London 1986, iv, 408.

94. SBTRO, DR 18/5/6986-7236 *passim* (bills); DR 18/31/52 (rental).

95. SBTRO, DR 18/3/32/17a. Mary and Augusta both married in 1817, to Frederick Colvile and Charles Lennox Berkeley respectively. Caroline Eliza married James Buller East in 1822.

96. SBTRO, DR 762/121, f.101.

97. Sir Edward Chandos Leigh, *Bar, Bat & Bit*, London 1913, 9-10

98. SBTRO, DR 18/5/7129. He was abroad in 1818, writing from Paris to ask for money to be forwarded to Geneva as he has bought a carriage and spent most of his allowance. £300 was sent to him: DR 18/17/44/16, 20.

99. SBTRO, DR 671/111 (abstract of marriage settlement).

100. Two of the accused were safely dead and Griffin tried to soften his charge against Chandos: 'I never thoroughly believed he was [guilty]. I am still unwilling to believe he is. The literary tastes, the domestic virtues, the general mildness and benignity of character forbid me to conclude him guilty of the crime recently laid to his charge, without the most cogent and indubitable evidence.' For further details concerning these claims, see pp. 181-2, above.

101. SBTRO, DR 18/17/55/38, 79.

102. SBTRO, DR 671/221 (death certificate).

103. Lady Louisa Stuart wrote of her in 1830: 'A very pretty pleasing woman, so perfectly natural and unaffected, that put her where you will she would seem in her proper place: never shy and never forward or vulgar ...': *Complete Peerage*,vii, 570, note f. Her son, Edward Chandos Leigh was more partisan: 'She was a most beautiful woman. She was kind and hospitable as a hostess, a perfect Lady Bountiful to her poorer neighbours; she was a good artist. She will long be remembered by all who knew her': Leigh, *Bar, Bat & Bit*, 16-17.

104. For a fuller account of William Henry, see Chapter 7.

105. SBTRO, DR 671/222 (marriage settlement). The children were Julia Ann Eliza, born 1820; Emma Margarette, 1822; William Henry, 1824; twins Augusta and Caroline, 1825; Mary, 1827; Louisa Georgiana, 1829; Edward Chandos, 1832; twins James Wentworth and Sophia, 1838.

106. The bulk of the surviving family correspondence and papers dates from the accession of the Adlestrop Leighs, the majority for the period 1840-1910.

107. The total acreage for all county estates was 20,965 with a rental value of £32,013 p.a.; *Complete Peerage*, vii, 571; SBTRO, DR 18/17/59b (report).

108. A. Venn, *Alumni Cantabrigenses...* Part II, 6 vols, Cambridge 1951, iv, 146.

109. Complete Peerage, vii, 571.

110. SBTRO, DR 18/7/17/17-25; DR 18/31/786b; DR 18/31/786b (volume of obituaries).

111. SBTRO, DR 18/31/786b.

Chapter 6

1. Shakespeare Birthplace Trust Records Office (SBTRO), DR 18/17/29; and see above, pp. 155-156.

2. George Holbert Tucker, *A Goodly Heritage*, Manchester 1983, 63.

3. Deirdre Le Faye, ed., *Jane Austen's Letters*, new edition, Oxford 1995, 37 (L18).

4. SBTRO, DR 671/77.

5. Lichfield Record Office, B/A/3 1792.

6. Le Faye, *Letters*, 37 (L18).

7. R.A. Austen-Leigh, ed., *Austen Papers 1704-1856*, London 1942, 237.

8. *Austen Papers*, 239-241.

9. Le Faye, *Letters*, 227 (L89).

10. SBTRO, DR 18/17/32/38.

11. *Austen Papers*, 243.

12. SBTRO, DR 18/17/32/52.

13. SBTRO, DR 18/17/32/52.

14. SBTRO, DR 18/17/32/49.

15. Le Faye, *Letters*, 154 (L61).

16. Le Faye, *Letters*, 216 (L86).

17. SBTRO, DR 18/17/32/53.

18. *Austen Papers*, 244-247.

19. Quoted from the Lefroy Manuscript in Park Honan, *Jane Austen Her Life*, London 1987, 225-6.

20. V. Blain, P. Clements, I. Grundy, *The Feminist Companion to Literature in English*, London 1990, 500.

21. Le Faye, *Letters*, 103 (L44).

22. SBTRO, DR 671/77.

23. SBTRO, DR 671/77.

24. Tom Ferber, 'Robert Holt Leigh (Landed gent, politician, benefactor and new industrialist)', March 1983, unpublished dissertation, The Local History Shop, Wigan.

25. Letter in possession of Joan Austen-Leigh.

26. Wigan Records Office, D/D Lei C.

27. Le Faye, *Letters*, 85 (L36).

28. SBTRO, DR 18/17/32/97.

29. SBTRO, DR 18/17/32/137.

30. SBTRO, DR 671/77.

CHAPTER 7

1. *The Diary of a Cotswold Parson: Reverend. F.E. Witts*, ed. David Verey, Gloucester 1979, 30.

2. Shakespeare Birthplace Trust Records Office (SBTRO), DR 18/5/7129.

3. SBTRO, DR 762/121, f.101 (Agnes Leigh's ms. history).

4. SBTRO, DR 18/5/7097-8.

5. SBTRO, DR18/ 17/57(I).

6. Elizabeth Longford, *Wellington: the Years of the Sword*, London 1979, 164.

7. SBTRO, DR 18/17/57(I).

8. SBTRO, DR 18/17/45/11.

9. Folger Shakespeare Library, Z.e.16 (Drury Lane Account Books).

10. SBTRO, DR 18/26/1a(II).

11. SBTRO, DR 18/17/57(I).

12. SBTRO, DR 18/17/57(I).

13. Longford, *Wellington*, 166.

14. SBTRO, DR 18/17/44/16.

15. SBTRO, DR 18/17/44/20.

16. SBTRO, DR 18/17/57(I).

17. SBTRO, DR 18/17/45/16a.

18. SBTRO, DR 18/17/45/16b.

19. SBTRO, DR 671/77 (marriage certificate).

20. *Diary of a Cotswold Parson*, 30.

21. SBTRO, DR 18/17/49/25-6.

22. SBTRO, DR 18/17/50/19.

23. *The Complete Peerage*, vii, 569.

24. SBTRO, DR 18/17/56.

25. SBTRO, DR 671/221 (death certificate, 27 September 1850).

26. SBTRO, DR 18/23/17.

27. SBTRO, DR 18/17/55/79.

28. SBTRO, PR 231/12, 16.

29. Edward Chandos Leigh, *Bar,Bat &Bit*, London 1913, 10.

30. SBTRO, DR 671/112.

31. Leigh, *Bar, Bat and Bit*, 14.

32. Leigh, *Bar, Bat and Bit*, 15.

33. SBTRO, DR 18/17/55/38.

34. SBTRO, DR 18/17/55/114.

35. Leigh, *Bar, Bat and Bit*, 10.

36. SBTRO, DR /62/10/.

37. SBTRO, DR 18/17/56.

38. SBTRO, DR 18/23/17.

39. Lord Leycester Hospital, Warwick, Visitors' Book, 1862.

40. *Warwick Advertiser*, 10 July 1869.

41. SBTRO, DR 18/17/55/114.

42. SBTRO, DR 18/17/55/114.

43. Ann Blainey, *Immortal Boy: a Portrait of Leigh Hunt*, Beckenham 1985, 174.

44. Lady Violet Hardy, *As It Was*, London 1958, 22.

45. British Library, 11644eee52(2).

46. SBTRO, DR 18/17/55/114.

47. SBTRO, DR 18/26/1c (obituary, *Leamington Courier*).

48. SBTRO, DR 18/26/1a.

49. SBTRO, DR 18/31/878.

50. Geoffrey Tyack, *The Country Houses of Warwickshire 1800-1939*, Warwickshire Local History Society Occasional Paper, vii, 1989, 59.

51. SBTRO, DR 18/31/650.

52. Howard Newby, *The Deferential Worker*, London 1977, 51.

53. SBTRO, DR 18/26/1c.

54. SBTRO, DR 18/31/739-746; DR 671/231-241; DR 18/31/944.

55. SBTRO, DR 18/26/1c.

56. Janet Saunders, 'Warwickshire Magistrates and Prison reform 1840-75', *Midland History*, xi, 1986, 89-95.

57. SBTRO, DR 18/26/2.

58. SBTRO, DR 671/362.

59. SBTRO, DR 18/26/1c.

60. SBTRO, DR 18/26/1c.

61. SBTRO, DR 18/17/58/192, 198-9.

62. Hardy, *As It Was*, 24.

63. SBTRO, DR 962/15.

64. SBTRO, DR 762/96.

65. SBTRO, DR 962/28, 3.

66. SBTRO, DR 671/269, 381.

67. David Roberts, *Paternalism in Early Victorian England*, London 1979, 3.

68. Howard Newby, *Green and Pleasant Land*, London 1979, 48.

69. Oscar Wilde, *The Importance of being Earnest*.

70. Hardy, *As It Was*, 25.

71. SBTRO, DR 18/26/1c.

PART THREE: LANDS

CHAPTER 8

1. *The Stoneleigh Leger Book,* ed. R.H. Hilton, Dugdale Society, xxiv, 1960. Other medieval material is to be found in the Leigh Collection at the Shakespeare Birthplace Trust Records Office (SBTRO).

2. The story of the abbey's origins and foundation comes from *Leger Book*, 12-16. This is analysed in D. Knowles and R.N. Hadcock, *Medieval Religious Houses in England and Wales*, London 1971, 125-6.

3. This section on the Cistercians is based upon D. Knowles, *The Religious Orders in England*, i, 2nd edition, Cambridge 1962, 64-77; D. Knowles, *The Religious Orders in England*, ii, Cambridge 1957, 125-9; G. Coppack, *The White Monks*, Stroud 1998, 15-22; C. Platt, *The Monastic Grange in Medieval England*, London 1969, 12-14; R.A. Donkin, *The Cistercians: Studies in the Geography of Medieval England and Wales,* London 1978, 51-6. For other Arden Cistercian houses see Knowles and Hadcock, *Medieval Religious Houses*, 112-26 and A.D. Watkins, 'Merevale Abbey in the Late 1490s', *Warwickshire History*, ix, 1994, 87.

4. *Leger Book*, 5, 7, 23-4; P. Vinogradoff, *English Society in the Eleventh Century*, London 1908, 130, 328-9.

5. *Leger Book*, 15-17, 21-26.

6. *Victoria County History (VCH), Warwickshire*, ii, 79.

7. *Leger Book*, 17-8.

8. SBTRO, DR 18/1/45, 49, 54, 55, 839; *Catalogue of Ancient Deeds Preserved in the Public Record Office*, ii, B1918, B1920, B1951, B3621; iii, D91.

9. *VCH, Warws.* v, 142, 145; J.E.B. Gower, A. Mawer, and F.M. Stenton, *The Place-Names of Warwickshire*, English Place-Name Society, xiii, 1936, 272-3; *Catalogue of Ancient Deeds*, ii, B2981; iii, A4667; P.R. Coss, *Lordship, Knighthood and Locality*, Cambridge 1991, 202.

10. SBTRO, DR 18/1/705.

11. For example see *Leger Book*, 1; Gower etc., *Place-Names of Warwickshire*, 180. For the background to the Arden at this time see: G.T. Warwick, 'Relief and Physiographic Regions' in, The British Association for the Advancement of Science, *Birmingham and its Regional Setting*, Birmingham, 1950, 11-14; R.H. Hilton, *Social Structure of Rural Warwickshire in the Middle Ages*, Dugdale Society Occasional Paper, ix, 1950, reprinted in R.H. Hilton, *The English Peasantry in the Later Middle Ages*, Oxford 1973, 123-33; B.K. Roberts, 'A Study of the Medieval Colonisation of the Forest of Arden, Warwickshire', *Agricultural History Review*, xvi, 1968, 103-13; J.B. Harley, 'Population Trends and Agricultural Developments from the Warwickshire Hundred Rolls of 1279', *Economic History Review*, 2nd series, xi, 1958-9, 8-18; J.B. Harley, 'The Settlement Geography of Early Medieval Warwickshire', *Transactions of the Institute of British Geographers*, xxxiv, 1964, 115-31.

12. *Leger Book*, 18.

13. This topographical description is based on R.H. Hilton's introduction to *Leger Book*, xliv-lviii.

14. *Leger Book*, 50-4; 'Lay Subsidy Roll, Warwickshire, 1327', ed. W.W. Wilson, *Transactions of the Midland Record Society*, v, 1901, 6; SBTRO, DR, 18/30/24/11, 24, 38.

15. *The Warwickshire Hundred Rolls of 1279-80*, ed. T. John, British Academy Records of Social and Economic History, xix, 1992, 58-76; *Leger Book*, 50-4; *Lay Subsidy Roll of 1327*, 6.

16. Hilton, 'Introduction', in *Leger Book*, xliv-xlvii. For a recent discussion of Stoneleigh's woodland see S. Wager, *Woods, Wolds, and Groves: the Woodland of Medieval Warwickshire*, BAR British Series, 269, 1998, 37-42.

17. Hilton, 'Introduction', in *Leger Book*, xlviii-l; *Leger Book*, 15-6, 23, 24-6, 60-3; R.H. Hilton, *A Medieval Society*, Cambridge 1983, 20-1; SBTRO, DR 18/1/696, 1121-5, 1127, 1129-32.

18. Hilton, 'Introduction', in *Leger Book*, xlviii-l; Wager, *Woods, Wolds, and Groves*, 37-42.

19. A. Watkins, 'The Woodland Economy of the Forest of Arden in the Later Middle Ages', *Midland History*, xviii, 1993, 19-32; A. Watkins, 'Peasants in Arden' in R.H. Britnell, ed., *Daily Life in the Late Middle Ages*, Stroud 1998, 95; Hilton, 'Introduction', in *Leger Book*, xlv; Wager, *Woods, Wolds, and Groves*, 39-40; *The Warwickshire Hundred Rolls*, 59.

20. J.R. Birrell, 'Common Rights in the Medieval Forest: Disputes and Conflicts in the Thirteenth Century', *Past and Present*, cxvii, 1987, 48-9. For an earlier dispute see Hilton, *Medieval Society*, 120.

21. *Calendar of the Charter Rolls Preserved in the Public Record Office*, ii, 273; *Placita de Quo Warranto temp. Edward I, II, and III*, Record Commission 1818, 778; W.A. Baker, 'Warwickshire Markets', *Warwickshire History*, vi, 1986, 161-85; A.D. Watkins, *Small Towns in the Forest of Arden in the Fifteenth Century*, Dugdale Society Occasional Paper, xxxviii, 1998, 5-6.

22. Knowles, *Religious Orders in England*, 64-77; Platt, *Monastic Grange*, 12-14; Donkin, *Cistercians*, 51-6; Watkins, 'Merevale Abbey in the late 1490s', 90-1, 95-97.

23. *Leger Book*, 16; Watkins, 'Merevale Abbey in the late 1490s', 90; M.W. Beresford, 'The Deserted Villages of Warwickshire', *Transactions of the Birmingham Archaeological Society*, lxvi, 1945-6, 83.

24. Hilton, 'Introduction', in *Leger Book*, xlvi; *VCH, Warws.*, v, 142, 145; *Taxatio Ecclesiastica Anglia et Walliae auctoritate P. Nicholai IV circa A.D. 1291*, Record Commission 1802, 255.

25. R.A. Donkin, 'Cistercian Sheep Farming and Wool Sales in the Thirteenth Century', *Agricultural History Review*, vi, 1958, 2; E. Power, *The English Wool Trade*, London 1944, 22; Hilton, *Medieval*

Society, 81-3; W. Cunningham, *The Growth of English Industry and Commerce in the Middle Ages*, London 1905, 633; *Calendar of Close Rolls, 1323-27*, 180.

26. Hilton, *English Peasantry in the Later Middle Ages*, 125-33.

27. *Warwickshire Hundred Rolls*, 59; *Leger Book*, 100-05.

28. *Leger Book*, 103. For later rolls of the court of bedripe see, for example, SBTRO, DR 18/30/24/16, 26, 36, 43.

29. C.C. Dyer, *Warwickshire Farming 1349-1520*, Dugdale Society Occasional Paper, xxvii, 1981, 6; Hilton, 'Introduction', in *Leger Book*, xxxix, 185-6; P. Ziegler, *The Black Death*, London 1969, 228; Lichfield Joint Record Office, B/A/1/2, fols 50-55v; B/A/1/2, fol. 52.

30. J.M. Bean, 'Plague, Population and the Economic Decline in the Later Middle Ages', *Economic History Review*, 2nd series, xv, 1962-3, 428-31.

31. For the general background to the later medieval economy see R.H. Britnell, 'The Economic Context', in A.J. Pollard, ed., *The Wars of the Roses*, London 1995, 41-64; J. Hatcher, 'The Great Slump of the Mid-Fifteenth Century', in R.H. Britnell and J. Hatcher, eds, *Problems and Progress in Medieval England: Essays in Honour of Edward Miller*, Cambridge 1996, 237-72; E. Miller, 'Introduction: Land and People' in E. Miller, ed., *The Agrarian History of England and Wales, iii, 1348-1500*, Cambridge 1991, 1-33.

32. For the Arden in particular see Dyer, *Warwickshire Farming, passim*; C. Dyer, 'A Small Landowner in the Fifteenth Century', *Midland History*, i, 1972, 1-14; C. Dyer, 'The West Midlands', in T*he Agrarian History of England and Wales*, iii, 77-91, 222-37, 636-47; A.D. Watkins, 'Cattle Grazing in the Forest of Arden in the Later Middle Ages', *Agricultural History Review*, xxxvii, 1989, 17-23; Watkins, 'The Woodland Economy of the Forest of Arden', 19-32. For Merevale Abbey see Watkins, 'Merevale Abbey in the late 1490s', 87-104. For Maxstoke Priory see A.D. Watkins, 'Landowners and their Estates in the Forest of Arden in the Fifteenth Century', *Agricultural History Review*, xlv, 1997, 18-33; A.D. Watkins, 'Maxstoke Priory in the Fifteenth Century: the Development of an Estate Economy in the Forest of Arden', *Warwickshire History*, x, 1996, 3-18. For Nuneaton Priory see British Library, Additional Rolls 49767, 49768. For Coventry Cathedral Priory see *The Coventry Leet Book*, ed. M.D. Harris, Early English Text Society, Original Series, cxxxiv, 1907-8, 438-9; C. Phythian-Adams, *The Desolation of a City*, Cambridge 1979, 22.

33. Various leases of demesne assets by successive abbots in the later fifteenth and early sixteenth centuries are to be found in SBTRO, DR 18/1/60, 66, 17, 21, 22, 25. DR 18/30/24/38 is a rental which reveals much of the demesne assets of the abbey at lease in 1497. Surveys made after the Dissolution in the late 1530s and early 1540s show the whole estate at farm. See SBTRO, DR 18/1/733 and *Abstract of the Bailiffs' Accounts of Monastic and Other Estates in the County of Warwick for the Year 1547*, ed. W.B. Bickley, Dugdale Society, ii, 1923, 3-9.

34. SBTRO, DR 18/30/24/11.

35. SBTRO, DR 18/1/723. For Maxstoke Priory's involvement in horse breeding see Watkins, 'Maxstoke Priory in the Fifteenth Century', 2-13. For the numbers at Stoneleigh Abbey on surrender, see *VCH, Warws.*, ii, 81.

36. SBTRO, DR 18/1/733.

37. W. Dugdale, *Monasticon Anglicanum*, ed. J. Caley and others, 6 vols in 8, London 1817-30, v, 448-9.

38. For a general background to peasant life in the Arden see Dyer, *Warwickshire Farming, passim*; Dyer, 'The West Midlands', 77-91, 222-37, 636-47; Watkins, 'Cattle Grazing in the Forest of Arden', 17-23; Watkins, 'The Woodland Economy of the Forest of Arden', 19-32; Watkins, 'Peasants in Arden', 83-101.

39. SBTRO, DR 18/30/24/7, 18, 28, 30, 44, 45.

40. Hilton, 'Introduction', in *Leger Book*, xxxvi; SBTRO, DR 18/30/24/8, 14, 17, 18, 21, 38, 44, 45.

41. Hilton, 'Introduction', in *Leger Book*, xl-xliv; Dyer, *Warwickshire Farming*, 5-8; Dyer, 'The West Midlands', 636-47; Watkins, 'Peasants in Arden', 85-7; SBTRO, DR 18/1/60, 722, 725; DR18/30/24/3.

42. Examples of peasant families building up large holdings can be seen at SBTRO, DR 18/1/880, 1031; DR18/30/24/5, 8. For Oliver Burdet, see *Leger Book*, 226-9, 234. For Bacon, see Hilton, 'Introduction', in *Leger Book*, lv, and SBTRO, DR 18/30/24/5.

43. Hilton, 'Introduction', in *Leger Book*, li-lvii; Hilton, *English Peasantry*, 134-8; Watkins, 'Peasants in Arden', 88; B.K. Roberts, 'Field Systems of the West Midlands', in A.R.H. Baker and R.A. Butlin, eds, *Field Systems in the British Isles*, Cambridge 1973, 188-231; V.H.T. Skipp, 'The Evolution of Settlement and Open Field Topography in the North Arden down to 1300', in T. Rowley, ed., *The Origins of Open Field Agriculture*, Oxford 1981, 162-83.

44. Hilton, 'Introduction', in *Leger Book*, lii; SBTRO, DR 18/30/24/38, 45.

45. For Arden enclosure in general, see Dyer, *Warwickshire Farming*, 25-8; Watkins, 'Peasants in Arden', 88-90. For Stoneleigh, see SBTRO, DR 18/30/24/45. For later enclosure in the parish, see N.W. Alcock, *People at Home*, Chichester 1993, 7.

46. *The Domesday of Inclosures*, ed. L.S. Leadam, Royal Historical Society, London 1897, 449-50; *Bailiffs' Accounts of Monastic Estates*, 3-10.

47. SBTRO, DR 18/30/24/38; *Domesday of Inclosures*, 440-2; *VCH, Warws.*, vi, 230.

48. *VCH, Warws.*, vi, 230; Beresford, 'The Deserted Villages of Warwickshire', 96-7.

49. Watkins, 'Peasants in Arden', 85; SBTRO, DR 18/30/24/45.

50. Alcock, *People at Home*, 187-89; Dyer, *Warwickshire Farming*, 23-4, 29-30; Watkins, 'Peasants in Arden', 91-2, 94.

51. Dyer, *Warwickshire Farming*, 9-12, 18-21; Watkins, 'Peasants in Arden', 92-4; *Coventry Leet Book*, 438-9; M.D. Harris, 'Laurence Saunders, Citizen of Coventry', *English Historical Review*, ix, 1894, 633-51.

52. SBTRO, DR 18/30/24/3-45 *passim*; Alcock, *People at Home*, 190-1.

53. SBTRO, DR 18/30/24/13, 7, 32.

54. For general background to the peasant exploitation of woodland resources see Watkins, 'The Woodland Economy of the Forest of Arden', 25-8. For Stoneleigh see SBTRO, DR 18/30/24/8, 40, 45.

55. SBTRO, DR 18/30/24/7, 8, 28, 38; DR 18/1/60; DR 18/30/24/73, 721, 733; *Bailiffs' Accounts of Monastic Estates*, 3-10; Alcock, *People at Home*, 179-82.

56. SBTRO, DR 18/30/24/12.

57. SBTRO, DR 18/1/716, DR 18/1/718.

58. *Leger Book*, 252-4.

59. For Pype's role in writing the Leger Book, his likely origins, and a full discussion of his career at the abbey, see Hilton in *Leger Book*, xvii-xxi. For Dugdale's view, see W. Dugdale, *The Antiquities of Warwickshire*, 2 vols, London 1730, i, 257.

60. *Valor Ecclesiasticus*, The Record Commission, iii, 1817, 7-8; *VCH, Warws.* ii, 81.

CHAPTER 9

1. *The Stoneleigh Leger Book*, ed. R.H. Hilton, Dugdale Society, xxiv, 1960; map of Cross Grange, Bericote and Ashow (including Stareton) by John Goodwine, 1597 (Shakespeare Birthplace Trust Records Office (SBTRO), DR 671/2); map of Stoneleigh by John Goodwine, 1597 (SBTRO, DR 671/3); map of Hurst, Fletchampstead and Canley by John Goodwine, 1597 (SBTRO, DR 18/25/69a); survey accompanying maps (SBTRO, DR 18/30/24/279a).

2. Christopher Dyer,'Rural Settlements in Medieval Warwickshire', *Transactions of the Birmingham and Warwickshire Archaeological Society*, c, 1996, 117-132.

3. *Leger Book*, ix-lvii.

4. SBTRO, DR 671/2.

5. *Leger Book*, xlvi.

6. *Victoria County History (VCH), Warws.*, vi, 24-5.

7. *Leger Book*, xvvii, 24-5.

8. *Leger Book*, xvvii, 24-5

9. SBTRO, DR 18/1/722.

10. DR 671/3; DR 18/30/24/279a.

11. Oliver Rackham, *The History of the Countryside*, London 1987, 47-9, 292-3.

12. *Leger Book*, 240.

13. *Leger Book*, 8, 240,

14. *Leger Book*, 8, 240.

15. British Library (BL), Harl. ms. 3650, fols xviii-xix (microfilm copy, Warwickshire County Record Office M392/1); BL, Add. ms. 47677 (microfilm copy, WCRO, M392/2); 'A Book of Divers Compositions between the Abbot of Stoneley and the Prior of Kenilworth,' SBTRO, DR18/31/4. There is a useful Ph.D. thesis by C. Watson, 'Edition of the Kenilworth Cartulary', Birkbeck College London, *c.* 1968 (microfilm copy, WCRO, M238): Watson transcribed many of the charters of the Harleian cartulary and his numbering for this document will be used. He appears to have been the first to have noticed some discrepancy between the Leger Book account and Kenilworth cartulary charters relating to Cloud hermitage (Watson, 223).

16. The early spelling, 'Cluda', is good evidence that the word is derived from the Old English *clud* meaning 'land with rocky outcrops' (John Field, *English Field Names: a Dictionary*, London 1972, 47) and one of the early charters mentioned a quarry, 'quarrea de...Cluda.': BL, Add. ms. 47677, fol. cxxxviii. The outcrops of rock were a feature of the underlying Bromsgrove (Keuper) sandstone of the Triassic period, which run as a narrow band from south-west to north-east.

17. BL, Harl. ms. 3650, fol. xviii; BL, Add. ms. 47677, fol. cxxxvii; SBTRO, DR 18/31/4.

18. BL, Harl. ms. 3650, fol. xviii (*c.* 1175-1224); SBTRO, DR 18/31/4.

19. BL, Harl. ms. 3650, fol. xix; BL, Add. ms. 47677, fol. cxxxix; SBTRO, DR 18/31/4.

20. *Leger Book*, 141: the phrase, 'iuxta Sprotforde versus le Cloudebridge' appears elsewhere in the Leger Book.

21. BL, Add. ms. 47677, fol. cxxxvii; SBTRO, DR 18/31/4.

22. *The Warwickshire Hundred Rolls of 1279-80, Stoneleigh and Kineton Hundreds*, ed. Trevor John, 1992, 77-8.

23. See note 17.

24. BL, Add. ms. 47677, fols cxxxviii, cxl; SBTRO, DR 18/31/4.

25. *Warwickshire Hundred Rolls*, 77.

26. BL, Add. ms. 47677, fol. cxxxix.

27. BL, Add. ms. 47677, fol. cxxxviii.

28. *Leger Book*, 197-202, 210-11.

29. *Leger Book*, 129, 198, 210.

30. *Leger Book*, 123, 200. Richard de la Cloud's sons, Thomas and William, died before their sisters, Juliana and Isabella.

31. BL, Add. ms. 47677, fols cxl, cxli.

32. *Leger Book*, 118-21.

33. *Leger Book*, 120.

34. SBTRO, DR 18/30/24/161.

35. SBTRO, DR 18/1/720a; DR 18/1/728.

36. *Leger Book*, 120.

37. SBTRO, DR 18/30/24/127; DR 18/1/725.

38. SBTRO, DR 18/1/726.

39. *Calendar of Patent Rolls, Elizabeth I, 1560-63*, 320-21; SBTRO, DR 18/3/64/3.

40. SBTRO, DR 18/10/101/2 (1551); DR 18/30/24/105 (1549-50); DR 18/30/24/107 (1550-51).

41. SBTRO, DR 18/31/5a; DR 18/30/24/161.

42. SBTRO, DR 18/30/24/279a.

43. SBTRO, DR 18/30/24/116,161; DR 18/1/742.

44. SBTRO, DR 18/30/24/161; DR 18/31/5a.

45. SBTRO, DR 18/30/24/116, 306, 340.

46. *Leger Book*, 255; Colin Platt, *The Monastic Grange in Medieval England: a Reassessment*, London

1969, 57; G. Constable, *Monastic Tithes from their Origin to the Twelfth Century*, London 1964, 220-306. Before the Lateran Council of 1215 land already acquired by the Cistercians tended to be tithe free.

47. *Leger Book*, 119.

48. SBTRO, DR 18/1/722.

49. *The Domesday of Inclosures*, 1517-18, ed. J.S. Leadham, 2 vols, London 1897, ii, 450.

50. C. J. Bond, 'Deserted medieval villages in Warwickshire and Worcestershire,' in T.R. Slater and P. J. Jarvis, eds, *Field and Forest: an Historical Geography of Warwickshire and Worcestershire*, Norwich 1982, 147-171; *VCH, Warws.*, vi, 230.

51. N.W. Alcock, *People at Home: Living in a Warwickshire Village*, 1500-1800, Chichester 1993, 172-75; *Leger Book*, xxxix-xlii.

52. *Leger Book*, 245.

53. N.W. Alcock, 'Report on Stareton Park', unpublished report, 12,14; SBTRO, DR 836/8/5.

54. SBTRO, DR 18/30/23/3.

55. 'A Survey of the Demesne Lands and the Park ... at Stoneleigh Abbey ... April 1749 By Thos Wilks', SBTRO, DR 671/24; 'A Map of Part of the Manor and Parish of Stoneley containing the Demains etc 1766 [Matthias Baker]', SBTRO, DR 671/31, 34; field drawings, DR 18/25/77.

56. The Parklands Consortium, *Stoneleigh Deer Park, Stareton, Warwickshire: Survey Grounds Development Plan*, Stoneleigh 1997, Fig. 2.4.

57. *VCH, Warws.*, vi, 234; SBTRO, DR 18/10/1021/7; Geoffrey Tyack, *Warwickshire Country Houses*, Chichester 1994, 245.

58. SBTRO, DR 18/10/101/9.

59. SBTRO, DR 18/1/722; *Leger Book*, 160.

60. SBTRO, DR 18/17/13/1.

61. Survey by Thomas Banks, January 1639: SBTRO, DR 18/18/30/23/4.

62. 'A Plott of the Towne of Stareton ... 1683'; SBTRO, DR 671/12.

63. SBTRO, DR 18/30/24/340.

64. SBTRO, DR 18/30/24/345, 348.

65. SBTRO, DR 18/30/24/340.

66. SBTRO, DR 671/12.

67. Alcock, 'Stareton', 12.

68. *Leger Book*, 243-5; Alcock, 'Stareton', 9.

69. Alcock, 'Stareton', 15.

70. Alcock, *People at Home*, 189.

71. SBTRO, DR 671/12.

72. SBTRO, DR 671/24.

73. R.W. Brunskill, *Illustrated Handbook of Vernacular Architecture*, London 1987, 106-7.

74. SBTRO, DR 823/19/22; DR 671/381.

75. SBTRO, DR 18/3/47/48/2 (copy, 23 September 1839, from an original dated 1776).

76. SBTRO, DR 18/3/53/2/2.

77. See note 75.

78. SBTRO, DR 671/31, 34.

Chapter 10

1. Shakespeare Birthplace Trust Record Office (SBTRO), DR 671/769, p.9.

2. *Victoria County History (VCH), Warwickshire*, vi, 226.

3. D.T.N. Booth, *Warwickshire Watermills*, Smethwick 1979, 37.

4. See above, Chapter 9.

5. SBTRO, DR 671/24.

6. See above, Chapter 3.
7. SBTRO, DR 18/17/16/4.
8. SBTRO, DR 18/17/16/1.
9. SBTRO, DR 671/31.
10. G. Tyack, *Warwickshire Country Houses*, Chichester 1994, 182; and see above, p. 97.
11. SBTRO, DR 671/77.
12. Samuel Ireland, *Picturesque Views of the Avon*, London 1795, 98.
13. Caroline Austen, *The Reminiscences of Caroline Austen*, Jane Austen Society 1986, 21.
14. SBTRO, DR 671/77.
15. M. Batey and D. Lambert, *The English Garden Tour*, London 1990, 248.
16. Mary C. Hill, *Jane Austen Her Home Her Friends*, London 1902, 163-66.
17. SBTRO, DR 671/769 (Stoneleigh Red Book, letter).
18. SBTRO, DR 671/769, Introduction.
19. SBTRO, DR 671/769, p.2.
20. SBTRO, DR 671/769, p.6.
21. SBTRO, DR 671/769, p.11.
22. SBTRO, DR 671/769, p.9.
23. SBTRO, DR 671/769, p.18.
24. SBTRO, DR 671/769, p.19.
25. SBTRO, DR 671/769, p.24.
26. SBTRO, DR 671/769, p.25.
27. SBTRO, DR 671/769, plan.
28. SBTRO, DR 18/17/35/5.
29. SBTRO, DR 662/129/32.
30. SBTRO, DR 18/17/1712.
31. Warwickshire County Record Office, QS 47/59 (Ashow and Stoneleigh, 1814).
32. SBTRO, DR 18/18/17/17/4.
33. SBTRO, DR 18/17/39/29.
34. SBTRO, DR 18/31/467-9.
35. SBTRO, DR 18/17/17/38.
36. SBTRO, DR 671/769, p.28.
37. SBTRO, DR 18/17/17/28.
38. SBTRO, DR 18/17/17/5.
39. SBTRO, DR 671/769, p.4.
40. SBTRO, DR 18/3/63/11.
41. SBTRO, DR 823/19.
42. SBTRO, DR 18/31/467-9.
43. SBTRO, DR 18/17/17/12.
44. SBTRO, DR 18/17/55/89.
45. SBTRO, Scrapbook letter 3/1/1848.
46. *Midland Florist*, Jan 1858, 21-27.
47. SBTRO, DR 671/381.
48. SBTRO, DR 671/381.
49. *Country Life*, 28 Oct 1899, 528.
50. *Country Life*, 27 July 1901, 104-105.
51. R. Webber, *Percy Cane Garden Designer*, Edinburgh 1975, 186.